Thomas Ingoldsby

Life and Letters

With a Selection From His Miscellaneous Poems. Vol. 1

Thomas Ingoldsby

Life and Letters
With a Selection From His Miscellaneous Poems. Vol. 1

ISBN/EAN: 9783744687676

Printed in Europe, USA, Canada, Australia, Japan

Cover: Foto ©Thomas Meinert / pixelio.de

More available books at **www.hansebooks.com**

THE LIFE AND LETTERS

OF THE

REV. RICHARD HARRIS BARHAM,

AUTHOR OF

The Ingoldsby Legends:

WITH A

SELECTION FROM HIS MISCELLANEOUS POEMS.

BY HIS SON.

IN TWO VOLUMES.

VOL. I.

LONDON:

RICHARD BENTLEY, NEW BURLINGTON STREET,

Publisher in Ordinary to Her Majesty.

1870.

LONDON: PRINTED BY
SPOTTISWOODE AND CO., NEW-STREET SQUARE
AND PARLIAMENT STREET

PREFACE.

———◆◇◆———

Prefixed to the first edition of the Third Series of the *Ingoldsby Legends* was a memoir of the author. It was hastily put together, occupied about a hundred and eighty pages, and has long been out of print. This memoir forms the groundwork of the present volumes. It has been re-written, and enlarged by the addition of numerous letters and several unpublished poems, to which a selection from others contributed by Mr. Barham to various journals with which he was connected has been appended; and I have endeavoured generally to render it more complete by the introduction of details, and more copious extracts from the diaries, as well as by a more exact observance of chronological order. But; regarded as a biography, it must still appear very imperfect; there is still need to remind the reader, that it is only in a literary point of view—only as a writer whose wit and humour have attracted more than common notice—only, in short, as Thomas Ingoldsby, that Mr. Barham is brought before the public at all. Of the new materials employed in the present work, the

most interesting have been kindly furnished by Mr.
THOMAS HUGHES, M.P. They consist of letters addressed
to his grandmother, one of my father's best friends, at
whose suggestion—I may almost say at whose desire—
the original memoir was compiled. As will be seen,
lapse of time has enabled me in most cases to dispense
with the awkward veil afforded by the use of initials, and
to admit anecdotes which could hardly with propriety
have been presented before. If some of the stories here
retained have grown at all threadbare, it is to be observed that the first edition of the book appeared not
less than four-and-twenty years ago, and that large
portions of it have been from time to time transferred
to the pages of subsequent publications, frequently without acknowledgment, by the literary collectors of un-
considered trifles.

With respect to the Poems placed at the end of the
second volume, and which have not hitherto been acknowledged, they have been included by the wish of Mr.
BENTLEY, to whose judgment in such matters I feel bound
to defer. They are all of earlier date than the *Legends*,
and will serve, at all events, to show the gradual development of the author's style.

R. H. D. BARHAM.

DAWLISH: *October.*

CONTENTS

OF

THE FIRST VOLUME.

————◆◆————

/.

CHAPTER V.

[1831-1835.]

CHAPTER VI.

[1835-1836.]

LIFE

OF THE

REV. RICHARD HARRIS BARHAM.

———◦◦◦———

CHAPTER I.

[1788—1821.]

Family History—Reginald Fitzurse and Thomas à Becket—Sir Nicholas
Barham—Birth of Richard Harris Barham—Tappington—St. Paul's
School—Serious Accident—Dr. and Mrs. Roberts—School Compositions—
Poetical Criticism—School Intimacies—The Quakers' Meeting—Brasenose
College—Gaming—The Cornish Mine Speculation—Regular Habits—
The Wig Club—Mr. Harley the Comedian at Canterbury—Epilogue to
'Rule a Wife and have a Wife'—Determination to enter Holy Orders—
Melancholy Death of an Undergraduate—Bishop Copleston — Mr. Barham
obtains successively the Curacies of Ashford and Westwell—Anecdote of
a Parishioner—The Westwell Witch—His Marriage—Presented to the
Living of Snargate—Moves to Warehorn—Smugglers—Romney Marsh
and the Clergy—Ghost Story—Country Life—Invitation to Dr. Wilmot—
'Benevolence'—Accident—'Baldwin'—Commencement of 'My Cousin
Nicholas'—Journey to London—The intercepted Letter—'An Adieu to
the Country'—Elected Minor Canon of St. Paul's.

It is hardly to be denied that, though sought after with
considerable avidity, memoirs of literary men may be
ranked among the least satisfactory portions of biography.
Their lives, indeed, are best written in their works.
When given in the form of narrative, by the hand of

VOI

another, they too commonly betray a woful deficiency of
incident, or serve to excite a painful interest by disclosures
of a melancholy and humiliating cast. We shall here
find no exception to the general rule. If the subject of
the present imperfect sketch was, on the one hand, removed from the daily struggles and temptations of those
unfortunate or improvident sons of genius whose necessities compel them to 'forestall the blighted produce of
the brain,' on the other, his career was wholly unmarked
by events of a striking and romantic turn. His course
indeed, uniformly prosperous and tranquil, resembled one
of those unnumbered, nameless streams which pass from
the spring-head into ocean without a 'rapid' and without
a check. To this easy flow of life, his sacred calling
naturally conduced. Not that he was other than a man
of action and energy; the management of even a comparatively small London parish, to say nothing of other
duties, is not to be carried on without an incessant expenditure of labour, and pretty frequent trials, too, both
of temper and discretion. But the real secret of his success lay in that enviable combination of tact, benevolence,
and good humour, supported by unflagging spirit, which,
while it carried him through a vast amount of work, enabled him invariably to avoid giving needless offence, and
generally to soften if not disarm opposition. One who
knew him well, one moreover who possessed every qualification for forming an opinion, thus speaks of him in a
letter addressed to a common friend :

'I am perfectly convinced that the same social influence would
have followed Mr. Barham into any other line of life that he

might have adopted; that the profits of agitating pettifoggers would have materially lessened in a district where he acted as a magistrate; and that duels would have been nipped in the bud at his regimental mess. It is not always an easy task to do as you would be done by; but to think as you would be thought of and thought for, and to feel as you would be felt for, is perhaps still more difficult, as superior powers of tact and intellect are here required in order to second good intentions. These faculties, backed by an uncompromising love of truth and fair dealing, indefatigable good nature, and a nice sense of what was due to every one in the several relations of life, both gentle and simple, rendered our late friend invaluable, either as an adviser or a peacemaker, in matters of delicate and difficult handling. How he managed to get through his more important duties is a marvel. Certain it is that they were well and punctually performed in every point relating to cathedral matters, as well as his engagements as a parochial incumbent and priest of the Household, which I believe was the nature of his office at the Chapel Royal.' [1]

He used to say of himself that he was naturally an idle but not an indolent man. However this may have been, very certain it is that he was rarely, if ever, to be seen unoccupied. If Fox thought lying under a tree with a book a luxury only to be surpassed by lying under a tree without one, Mr. Barham would hardly have sympathised with the statesman. His very amusements and hobbies, such as manfully struggling through the stiffest of Kentish coverts, in the old style, after pheasants which, to say the

---

[1] 'Sketch of the late Rev. R. H. Barham, with a few lines to his memory in a letter to the editor of the *New Monthly Magazine* (W. Harrison Ainsworth), from John Hughes, Esq.' Colburn's *New Monthly Magazine*, August, 1845.

truth, he very seldom bagged, or pursuing, half smothered by dust, genealogical and antiquarian researches in the libraries of St. Paul's and Sion College, or sitting up till three and four o'clock in the morning, after a hard day's work, scribbling articles for *Blackwood* or *Bentley*—all this, which was really his play and recreation, would be thought to tax rather severely the powers of the majority of men.

With the details of his experience as a clergyman, rarely suitable for publication as such particulars are, I do not propose to deal. Of course an outline will be given of his professional progress, but the reader must once for all be requested to bear in mind, that it is intended in the following pages simply to throw together some slight records of his leisure hours and recreative pursuits. Making no attempt to furnish a complete and regular biography of my father there will be the less necessity for me to obtrude remarks of my own. I shall do so as little as possible; and shall content myself with repeating such particulars as I remember to have heard from his own lips, and with so arranging his correspondence and the miscellaneous entries in his diaries or common-place books—they partook of the nature of both—as to allow these passages of his social life to be told pretty much in his own words.

Hasted, in his *History of Kent* (vol. iii. p. 755) gives the following account of the establishment of the family of Barham[1] in the neighbourhood of Canterbury, where,

---

[1] 'The word *Barham* probably signifies *extentionis domus*—a large or strong home or fortress. It appears to be etymologically derived from the Hebrew *bar* or *ber*, to extend, or enlarge, or open. This ideal signification of develop-

from the time of the Conquest till almost the present day, its representatives have resided and held land :

'Barham Court is a manor or seat in the parish of Barham situated close to the Church. It was probably the court lodge of the manor of Barham in very early times, before it became united to that of Bishopsbourne. And in King Henry the Second's time it was held of the Archbishop of Canterbury as half a knight's fee by Sir Randal Fitzurse, who was one of those four knights belonging to the King's household who murdered the Archbishop, Thomas à Becket, in the cathedral of Canterbury, 1170.'

This Sir Randal or Reginald was the grandson of one Ursus, who came over with the Conqueror to England. After aiding William de Tracy, Richard Brito, and Hugh de Moreville, in the murder of Becket, who appears, by the way, to have been not only the Sovereign's opponent, but— a curious coincidence, to say the least of it—the knight's landlord also, Sir Reginald not unnaturally retired to Ireland, where he assumed the name of McMahon (son of a bear). Subsequently, he proceeded to Rome and obtained absolution from the Pope on condition of making a pilgrimage to the Holy Land, for which country he departed about the close of the same year (1171), having previously made over his lands, the manors of Willeton in

ment or expansion runs through all its derivative terms. Hence *bar* sometimes implies creation or genesis, a son; a bar or extended barrier, strength, a bear, a boar; baron, a strong man; to bear or carry; bare or naked; bier, a litter; beer, a drink, &c., &c. Again the word *ham* is derived from the Hebrew name, to protect or cover, and signifies a home, house, dwelling, village, a skin, muscle, &c., &c.'—*The Foster Barham Genealogy.* Privately printed.

To the modern philologist the foregoing derivation will appear obsolete, but the meaning of the word is given with sufficient accuracy.

Somersetshire and Berham in Kent among the number, to his brother Robert. In Palestine he is said to have ended his days as became a gallant warrior and respectable son of the Church, and to have been buried at a place called the Black Mountain.[1] Robert on succeeding to the estates again changed the family name to De Berham, which, modestly clipped and modernised, has been retained to the present time by the descendants of his younger sons. To their elder brother John, who adhered to the old patronymic and who inherited the lands in the west of England, the families of Fischer and Furse are said to owe their origin. Hasted goes on to observe, with reference to the Kentish property, that—

' From him (Robert) it descended in an uninterrupted line down to Barth. Barham, who did homage for it to Archbishop

---

[1] In the first instance the knights fled to Knaresboro' Castle, belonging to De Moreville ; and according to the commonly accepted tradition they one and all died in the odour of sanctity in the Holy Land. But a tomb is shown at the curious little church of Morte, in North Devon, as that of Tracy, who is said after a temporary concealment in a cavern at Ilfracombe to have been admitted into holy orders by his relative, the Bishop of Exeter, and to have founded the church in question. The slab undoubtedly bears the effigies of a certain Sire de Tracy, an ecclesiastic, but this has been pronounced by experts to be too late by nearly a century for that of the murderer of Becket. Again there appears some reason for believing that Fitzurse himself, notwithstanding the denunciation,

> ' Highest thou Urse,
> Have thou God's curse ! '

may have come safely back from Palestine, retired to Urswick in Richmondshire, and there founded the church which was not in existence in the time of Domesday, but was given to Furness Abbey within half a century after. Such at least is the suggestion of Mr. Barham, expressed in his genealogical notes, from which I have drawn more freely than otherwise I should have done in consequence of their compilation having been one of his favourite occupations.

Wareham, *anno* ix. *Hen.* VIII.; and in his possession it continued till Thomas Barham, Esq., in the beginning of James the First's reign, alienated it.' [1]

It is unnecessary to trace the history of the Barhams through the subsequent reigns. Many individuals of this name of some note are mentioned in the county histories of Hasted and Horsfield [2]—for instance, Sir Nicholas Barham, a celebrated lawyer, whose duty it was, as sergeant-at-law to Queen Elizabeth, to arrange and apply the evidence on all state prosecutions. And this duty he is reported to have performed on the occasion of the important trial of Thomas Howard, Duke of Norfolk, in 1571, with, I regret to say, 'rather more zeal for the interests of the. court than justice in compiling what in our times would be considered a fair and impartial epitome of the depositions.' He died during the black assizes at Oxford, in 1577, of the extraordinary gaol fever described by Camden and other historians. Another worthy may be mentioned—Dr. Henry Barham, the learned author of *Hortus Americanus*, a scarce and valuable work published at Kingston in Jamaica, 1794.

Meanwhile, about the end of the seventeenth century, some small portion of the alienated lands once held by the notorious Sir Reginald were recovered on the marriage of Thomas Barham with the only daughter and heir of Thomas Harris, of Canterbury, who brought to her husband as her dower the manors of Parmstead (in the old

---

[1] More recently it came into the possession of Charles Noel Noel, Baron of Barham Court and of Teston, afterwards Earl of Gainsborough.

[2] See Horsfield's *History of Sussex*, vol. i. p. 415.

deeds Barhamstead) and Tappington Everard.   Fourth in
descent from Thomas was born, December 6, 1788, in
Canterbury, the subject of this memoir, Richard Harris,
only son of Richard Harris Barham, by Elizabeth, daughter
of Mathew Fox, Esq., of Manston.   Mr. Barham's father,
who was certainly not to be ranked among the purblind
class *qui propter patrimonia vivunt*, and was even
something of a *bon-vivant*, possessed much of that kindliness of heart and genial humour which were afterwards
so fully developed in his son.   Judging from the marginal
notes in his handwriting by which his copies of the classics
are freely illustrated, we may conclude he was not wanting
in literary taste, and that he must have brought away with
him from Christchurch enough, and more than enough, of
scholarship to set up any two or three country gentlemen
of the period.   In point of activity, both of mind and
body, he was unquestionably deficient, as perhaps may
be inferred from the fact of his having attained to the
enormous weight of seven-and-twenty stone before he
completed his forty-eighth year.

Dying in 1795, he bequeathed a moderate estate, somewhat encumbered indeed, and shorn of its fair proportions,
to his only son, then about five or six years of age.   A
portion of this property consisted, as I have said, of the
farm known as Tappington, or Tapton Wood, so often
alluded to in the *Ingoldsby Legends*; and, albeit the
description of the mansion therein given is rather of what
it might, could, would, or should be, than of what it
actually and truly is, many of the particulars are, nevertheless, perfectly correct.   Dismissing, then, the 'shaded

avenue, terminating in a lodge, whose gates support the Ingoldsby device,' together with Mrs. Botherby and the secret passage, as pardonable myths, a very comfortable and picturesque manor-house, haunted or not haunted, still remains, boasting its 'gable ends, stone stanchions, and tortuous chimneys,' and, above all, its blood-stained stair, the scene of the remarkable fratricide, which is a genuine tradition, and the sanguinary evidence of which is pointed out with enviable faith by the present tenants.

The house, as I remember it at first, possessed another unpleasant peculiarity. The windows of two or three of the best rooms approached by the principal staircase were bricked up, and although this had doubtless been done with the simple design of escaping Mr. Pitt's tax, it tended materially to enhance the mysterious awe which oppressed me as I passed by the gloomy portraits of the brothers on my way to bed. In after years it was a favourite amusement of my father's to plan the restoration of the old place, which he always regarded with a particular affection. The disused rooms were to be made available; possibly the wing which had been pulled down might be rebuilt; timber was to be cut from the wood, and carving procured from Wardour Street; the whole thing was to cost a mere trifle. But as mere trifles in brick and mortar are apt to weigh heavily on the resources of men of moderate means, it is as well perhaps that the scheme, though not finally abandoned, fell through. Nevertheless the beauty and tranquillity of the spot, situated at the junction of two

---

[1] The history of the true 'Spectre of Tappington' will be found in the annotated edition of the *Ingoldsby Legends*, vol. i. p. 34.

narrow valleys which, parti-coloured with patches of hop-garden and pasture and cornland, sweep round the sides of a long sloping and well-wooded hill, and there form a level plateau whereupon stand the house and farm-buildings—the whole embraced and sheltered by a semi-circle of yet higher ground, rich with the remains of the old Kentish forest—invited and might have warranted some judicious outlay.

In consequence of the feeble health of his mother the boy, himself weakly enough, was left under the threefold guardianship of Mr. Morris Robinson, afterwards Lord Rokeby, Mr. Abbot, and a certain attorney who, for reasons which will appear, shall be nameless. After fit preparation at the hands of two kindhearted maiden ladies named Dix, one of whom I believe survived her pupil, the latter was sent off at the age of nine years to St. Paul's School, and placed in the house of Dr. Roberts, the high-master. Here he made rapid progress in the classics ; for mathematics he had no taste. No knowledge of the science was at that day required in public schools, and to no knowledge of it did he ever attain.

An accident, however, occurred about the year 1802 which not only interrupted his studies for a time, but well-nigh led to the transfer of Tappington and all thereunto appertaining to the possession of strangers, and which exercised a lasting influence over the future life of its proprietor. This was no other than the mutilation of his right arm, occasioned by the upsetting of the Dover mail, in which he was travelling on his way to town. Bewildered by the terrific pace of the horses, which had taken fright, he thrust his hand from the window for the purpose of opening the door ; at that moment the vehicle turned over upon its side, pinning the exposed limb to the ground, and dragging it a considerable distance along a recently repaired road.[1] On being released from his situation, his shattered arm was hastily bound up, and he was despatched *alone* in a hackney-coach—for the accident occurred at the Bricklayers' Arms—to his destination, and was naturally found when he arrived lying in a pool of blood and perfectly insensible.

As may be supposed, the effects of so dreadful a laceration, aggravated by neglect in the first instance, and acting upon a frame which at that time gave no promise of the vigour which it afterwards exhibited, soon brought the sufferer to the very verge of the grave. So certain did his speedy death appear in the eyes of those whose wish, may be, was 'father to that thought,' that, to obviate any disagreeable delay in the disposal of the expected property, they sent their surveyor (somewhat prematurely), with instructions to report on the state of the farm-buildings, look to the repair of fences, mark out timber for felling, and enquire as to the term of unexpired leases.

It was, under God's blessing, mainly owing to the unwearied care of Mrs. Roberts, the wife of the worthy high-master, that these gentlemen were gratified in respect of little but their curiosity, for, contrary to the

---

[1] Both coachman and guard had left the vehicle, the horses bolted, and were stopped at last by the courage and presence of mind of a cripple who, unable to get out of the way, supported himself on one crutch and with the other struck one of the leaders below the knee, and brought him to the ground.

expectations of all, more especially of the surgeons who
refrained from amputation only from a fear of hastening
the catastrophe, not only did the patient begin to mend,
but the appearance of the wounded limb induced a hope
that it might eventually be restored in some measure to
the exercise of its proper functions.   An ingenious piece
of mechanism was invented and applied to the hand, consisting of lengths of catgut fastened to the extremity of
each finger, and passing through silver rings to a sort of
bracelet which was attached to the wrist.   By this means
the contracted fingers were to be assisted to open, and
action was to be restored to the joints.   It was a pretty
toy, cost twenty guineas, and proved of little or no use.
Mrs. Roberts, meanwhile, was far from confining her
kindness to the sick-bed.   As ' we plant a twig, and water
it because we have planted it,' so a similar feeling seems
to have taken possession of the lady in question ; certain
it is, she began to regard her young charge with an
unusual degree of interest, and, on becoming convalescent,
he was frequently permitted to be present at certain
réunions of a literary character which were held at her
house.   Here, as most of the *habitués* were of the softer
sex, his first attempts at composition met with every
encouragement, and he stood in some peril of being prematurely forced under their fostering care into a kind of
poetical phenomenon.   Among these ladies was Miss
Smith, afterwards Mrs. Bartley, a tragic actress of some
note, who gave him instructions in the art of delivering
what he had composed, and in whose society his early taste
for the drama was encouraged and developed.   Even the
irrefragable doctor contributed in no small degree to fan

the flame, by employing him to write speeches, not only for himself, but for the younger boys.

A selection from these school-boy compositions was printed in 1807, and obtained the favourable notice of *Mr. Sylvanus Urban*, to whom the author was indebted for his first introduction to the public. The performance is thus spoken of in the *Gentleman's Magazine*, November 1808 :—

'These verses, considering them the offspring of early years, we do not hesitate to say, display much promise of future excellence. They contain many passages which are striking, picturesque, and glowing; while the whole attest a native poetical vein and an harmonious ear.'

A few lines, part of a speech spoken by a precocious young gentleman aged ten years, will afford a taste of the poet's quality :—

But hold! methinks I hear some critic cry,
'The boy's too late; the time has long gone by;
Young Roscii now have lost the power to charm,
And infant orators no longer swarm :
At length aroused, our strange delirium o'er,
Their puny efforts please our ears no more.'

'Tis true I'm young : perhaps, too, somewhat small;
But that has been the common lot of all :
Grave rev'rend sages, heroes six feet high—
Nestor himself—were once as young as I :
The sturdiest oak that ploughs the boist'rous main,
The guardian bulwark of Britannia's reign,
A sapling once, within its native vale,
Shrank from the blast and bow'd at every gale.

Ladies, to you I turn ; my cause befriend,
Blame not a fault each day will help to mend.
In these sage times of wisdom so profuse,
This reign of reason, sense, and Mother Goose,
Consult your hearts, and blame us if you can,
If boys, when men turn children, ape the man.

One of these poems, which had for its subject the
battle of Trafalgar, bears remarkable testimony to the
taste of the worthy high-master himself. Towards the
conclusion occurred the following stanza :—

' Presumptuous thought ! ' Britannia's genius cries ;
' Rise, my loved sons, my brave defenders, rise ;
Tell them, while each with emulation strives—
Though Nelson falls, *a* Collingwood survives ! '

This, however, was not only found wanting in emphasis,
but was also pronounced to be an unpardonably familiar
mode of introducing a nobleman, and one not even
demanded by the exigence of metre. An order was
accordingly given that the last line should be both printed
and spoken,

' Though Nelson falls, *Lord* Collingwood survives ! '

A stroke of criticism not unworthy of a Greek commenta-
tor, and only to be surpassed by that of a gallant captain
of militia, who returned a volume of Campbell's poems
with the happy emendation—

Wave, Munich, all thy banners wave,
And charge—with all thy *cavalry !*

At St. Paul's School Mr. Barham formed friendships with many of his fellows, Dr. Roberts (no relation of the high-master), Mr. Bentley, Sir Charles Clark, the Pollocks, Frederick and David, and Charles Diggle (afterwards governor of the military college at Sandhurst), among the number, which, outlasting the common run of boyish intimacies, closed only with his life. From the first of these early companions he received, in seasons of sickness and bereavement, such constant counsel and assistance, as could scarcely have been required at the hands of the nearest relative ; and whose professional advice, had it been strictly and promptly carried out, would, in all human probability, have brought his last illness to a very different result ; while his connection with Mr. Bentley, composed of far stronger ties' than serve to unite author and publisher, the existence of which it preceded and outlived, led to the production of those remarkable articles upon which his literary reputation chiefly rests.

Of Diggle Mr. Barham used to tell many absurd stories : how, for instance, he used to steal the shoe-strings of Isaac Hill, the second master, and avowed his intention of continuing the robbery till he got enough to form a line that would reach from one end of the school to the other (seventy feet), but was unluckily removed from school before he had half accomplished his task. The most amusing, however much to be condemned, of his practical jokes was one in which his friend Barham also had a share. The two boys having, in the course of one of their walks, discovered a Quakers' meeting-house, forthwith procured a penny tart of a neighbouring pastrycook; furnished with this, Diggle marched boldly into the building, and holding up the delicacy in the midst of the grave assembly said with perfect solemnity,

'Whoever speaks first shall have this pie.'

'Friend, go thy way,' commenced a drab-coloured gentleman, rising; 'go thy way and——'

'The pie's yours, sir!' exclaimed Master Diggle politely, and placing it before the astounded speaker hastily effected his escape.

Having continued, in consequence of his youth, for two years 'captain' of St. Paul's School, Mr. Barham entered as a gentleman commoner at Brasenose College, and was speedily elected a member of the well-known Phœnix Common Room, at that time one of the 'crack' University clubs. Here he found a kindred spirit in the gay and eccentric Lord George Grenville (afterwards Lord Nugent). Here, too, he was again thrown into contact with one whom he had known in earlier days, Cecil Tattersall, the friend of Shelley and Lord Byron, and like most of that misguided party, but too well known by his abused talents and melancholy end. And here also his intimacy with Theodore Hook took rise, whose residence, however, did not extend beyond a couple of terms, and who, at first, was well nigh refused matriculation by Dr. Parsons for professing an accommodating readiness to subscribe not only to thirty-nine, but forty articles, if required.[1]

---

[1] Though I believe the anecdote to be perfectly true, it is almost needless to say that the joke, such as it is, is not original. Foote puts it into the mouth of *Mrs. Simony.*

College life, more especially at that day, was likely to present numerous and sore temptations to one who was overflowing with good nature and high spirits, and whose early loss had not only placed a perilous abundance of funds at his disposal, but had left him, as it happened, utterly unchecked by parental counsel and authority, for his mother, a confirmed invalid, had for some time been incapable of exercising any control over his conduct. Of his guardians, on the other hand, but one busied himself at all in his affairs; and of him, the attorney before alluded to, the youth had come to conceive a strong dislike, a feeling not unmixed with suspicion, which proved but too well founded, of the man's honesty. It was scarcely to be expected that such an ordeal should be passed through without scathe. Brasenose, too, was an expensive college: it was commonly reported that the Principal 'hated a college of paupers,' and the young men were ready enough in this respect to follow the cue which they believed had been given. Mr. Barham, like many others, spent there a great deal of money to very little purpose. Among other extravagances gaming was the fashion there as elsewhere. Whether, indeed, college 'hells' were in existence at that time, as they certainly were a generation later, I am not able to say, but a good deal of high play went on, and although this was certainly a vice to which my father had no natural inclination, he was on one occasion induced to join a party at ' unlimited loo,' or something of the sort, and with the happiest result —he lost heavily;—a great deal more, that is to say, than he was in a condition to pay. Direct communication

on such a subject with the lawyer at Canterbury was on
many accounts extremely distasteful. A lecture from him
would have proved particularly galling ; there was nothing
for it, therefore, but to apply to Lord Rokeby, and this
Mr. Barham did, earnestly begging him to authorise the
advance of a sum, from the property in trust, sufficient to
discharge the obligation. Lord Rokeby very decidedly,
and it need hardly be said very properly, declined to
accede to the request. As a guardian, he said, he could
not for a moment entertain the question, but he very
good-naturedly added, that as a friend he would give the
money. The present showed tact as well as kindness, and
clearly rendered any second application of the sort impossible. And it is a fact that, from that day to his last,
Mr. Barham held entirely aloof not only from gambling
in the ordinary sense of the word, but from speculation of
every kind and degree. A railway investment he looked
upon as a certain step towards utter ruin ; and when one
of the most accomplished of projectors, a gentleman who
had succeeded in getting some very pretty sport, especially
among the clergy, called on him with the prospectus of a
certain Cornish mining company, and tried hard to persuade him to join with many of his brethren in the adventure, his habitual distrust was not to be overcome : ' Tell
me candidly,' asked he, ' all exaggeration apart, what
dividend do you really calculate will be paid?'

' Not one farthing short of twenty per cent. !'

' You are in earnest?'

' Absolutely in earnest, on my honour.'

' Thank you,—that is rather too good a thing for me to

meddle with. I wish you all possible success, and—a very
good morning!' and he buttoned up his pocket, bowed
out his friend, and could never be persuaded to resume
the negotiation. Those who persisted in the scheme—
two of his intimate friends among the number—were
ruined, or nearly ruined, by its collapse. But excessive
as perhaps his caution may be considered in some particulars, he was careless enough in money matters generally, and notwithstanding the suspicion with which he
had for some time viewed the proceedings of the attorney
to whose management his property had been committed,
he neglected, on attaining his majority, to place his
affairs in other hands. Whether, had he acted in the
matter with all possible promptitude, the result would
have been very different, may be doubtful; as it was, his
connection with that gentleman terminated in a loss of
not less, I believe, than eight thousand pounds. This
was a blow, a severe one, and one which crippled him for
a time, inducing him to grant leases at low rents on payment of fines, and so on, but it fell early in life and he
bore it lightly.

Meanwhile, it is not to be supposed that he was passing
his time at Oxford in idleness—of that he was incapable;
he yielded, however, more to the seductions of an agreeable
society than was prudent, deferring his reading mostly to
midnight, and frequently continuing it till break of day.

His reply to Mr. Hodson, his tutor, afterwards Principal
of Brasenose, will convey some notion of the hours he was
wont to keep. This gentleman, who, doubtless discerning
spite of an apparent levity much that was amiable and

high-minded in his pupil, treated him with marked indulgence, sent for him on one occasion to demand an explanation of his continued absence from morning chapel.

'The fact is, sir,' urged his pupil, 'you are too *late* for me.'

'Too late?' repeated the tutor, in astonishment.

'Yes, sir—too late. I cannot sit up till seven o'clock in the morning: I am a man of regular habits; and unless I get to bed by four or five at latest, I am really fit for nothing next day.'

An impertinence better rebuked by the look of dignified displeasure which it called up, than by any amount of punishment that could have been inflicted. All affectation was cast aside on the instant—an apology sincerely offered, and silently accepted.

Whatever amendment in point of attention to college discipline may have resulted from this conversation, the habit which gave rise to it was one for 'time to strengthen, not efface.' No one might have quoted the old Scotch ballad with greater feeling and sincerity than my father :—

> ' Up in the morning's nae for me,
>   Up in the morning airly :
> I'd rather watch a winter's night
>   Than up in the morning airly.'

Most men have their seasons of late hours, and among undergraduates especially there are not wanting those who, after an evening's dissipation, esteem it passing 'fast' to sit up half the night nodding over their books with wet towels tied about their heads : such feats at least, if not reduced to common practice, are considered by a certain class, as those fearful and mysterious ceremonies, yclept 'Little Go,' 'Mods,' and 'The Great,' draw nigh, to be mere matters of course and indications of spirit. It was far otherwise with Mr. Barham. With him a strong natural bent supplied the place of caprice or love of singularity, and he sat up because he found that as the morning advanced his ideas flowed more freely, and his mental energies became in every way more active than at any other period of the twenty-four hours. It could hardly fail of exciting a considerable degree of astonishment, to mark how, after a day spent without one moment's rest or relaxation in the intricacies of business, often of a harassing and momentous nature, his eye would light up and his spirits overflow as the chimes of midnight were approaching; an entirely fresh set of faculties seemed to come into play, and if there was no one at hand to benefit by his conversation—to listen to his inexhaustible fund of anecdote and observation, he would devote himself to the investigation of some obscure genealogical point, or the perusal of some treasured volume in black letter, with a keenness and vigour not to be surpassed by the most orderly of mortals. At these times, too, his powers of conposition reached their culminating point, and he wrote with a facility which not only surprised himself, but which he actually viewed with distrust; and he would not unfrequently lay down his pen, from an apprehension that what was so fluent must of necessity be feeble also. Indeed, he was no adept in the art of cudgelling the brain, and, at all events in respec of poetry, he wrote easily or not at all. The slightest check would often delay the completion of an article of this kind for months, and there are numbers of his manuscripts, now in my possession, whose unfinished state is to be attributed to some trifling stumbling-block which a little labour might have levelled or avoided.

Of his life during the period which elapsed from his entrance at the University to his ordination there is little to be recorded. But among the freaks of those youthful days may be mentioned the establishment of a sort of burlesque debating society, of which he was, I believe, the founder and president, and which, under the title of the Wig Club, held its meetings in a large summer-house attached to his residence at Canterbury. The members used to assemble in a masquerade dress, of which the wig, clerical, forensic, full-bottom, scratch, or brown George—the more ridiculous the better—was the principal feature. During the assize week the barristers on circuit were usually invited, and took part in the whimsicalities of the evening; in the course of which personalities, no matter how severe, were considered allowable, and were, with rare exceptions, endured with great good humour. On one occasion, however, the raillery running higher than common, the temper of one of the party gave way, and as it unluckily happened that swords as well as wigs formed part of the club costume, the angry disputant drew his weapon. A grand mêlée ensued, some awkward thrusts were given and taken, and the president narrowly escaped being run through the body in his own garden.

Of course the Wig Club patronised the drama, which was then represented at Canterbury by a travelling company under the management of a certain Mrs. Baker. The principal light comedian was a youth as yet 'to fortune and to fame unknown,' but destined ere long to win the smiles of both—no other than the late popular favourite, Mr. Harley. He often used to tell how he was extricated from one of his early professional difficulties by the aid, good naturedly offered, of my father. Harley had been cast for the part of *Goldfinch* in *The Road to Ruin*, but the resources of the establishment were limited, and the wardrobe afforded no dress better suited to the character than an old tarnished laced frock of *Macheath's*, with a pair of jack-boots to match—the whole much too large for the figure of the young actor. There was no time—to say nothing of money—to provide a more appropriate costume, and in his embarrassment he consulted Mr. Barham, who was a constant visitor both before and behind the curtain. The latter settled the matter at once by presenting him with a complete suit of his own. It consisted of a green single-breasted coat with gilt buttons, a crimson waistcoat, edges and pockets trimmed with fur, buff buckskin breeches, top-boots, and silver spurs ! Harley was delighted, so it is to be hoped was the audience ; assuredly a more complete buck of the period was never before presented to their notice.

Although of later date by a few years than the anecdote just narrated, an epilogue may here be conveniently introduced, which was written for an amateur performance, got up with a charitable object by the officers quartered at Canterbury.

*Occasional Epilogue, to ' Rule a Wife and have a Wife,'
spoken by Major Hart, in the character of Michael
Peres, at the Canterbury Theatre, May* 1821, *the performance being for the benefit of Mr. G. Questead and
family.*

(*Behind.*) Speak the address ? Who, me? I can't indeed!
Prompter. Why, sir, your name 's announced, so pray
    proceed !
They'll grow impatient.
Major H.   Well, upon my word,
Was ever anything half so absurd !
You can't be serious?
Prompter.   Sir, 'tis very true.
Major H. O ! mighty pretty. (*Enters with a paper.*)
        Ladies, pray what say you?
My name 's announced, he says, and I not know it !
And then what's here !   The deuce is in the poet—
'Tis arrant tragedy ! all rant and whine !
Upon my life I couldn't speak a line ;
Observe these lineaments—peruse each feature—
Ladies, is this a face for doleful metre ?
Say, am I fit to cry ' alack for pity,'
Or quaver out some lamentable ditty,
Recite a dismal tale of woe on woes,
While sad complainings murmur through my nose ?
But hold ! I may be wrong—methinks you smile,
Perhaps ' I do mistake me all this while.'
By Jupiter, it may be worth the trying—
How I should like to set you all a-crying !

But then I'm shy—too diffident by half,—
Faith, I will venture it, but pray don't laugh.
Thus, then, the bard.

(*Reads.*)   No common claims to-night
Thalia's vot'rys to her fane invite ;
The sympathising Muse, to Pity true,
Appeals to mild Benevolence—and you—
Warmly implores your gen'rous aid to raise
The hopes of him who once knew better days :
Nor vain the call, for when did Beauty's ear
Affliction's suppliant voice disdain to hear,
Or when did Beauty's bounty fail to flow
To soothe Misfortune's child, and heal his woe ?
Ye who have viewed on this eventful night
The manly Leon guard a husband's right,
Or sat and gaily smiled with genuine glee
At cozen'd Peres, (that's a hit at me !)
By his own arts and vanity betray'd,
And Estifania's wiles, (confound the jade !)
Our task perform'd, reflect with cheerful heart,
Ye too have play'd, and play'd a noble part !
And O ! may still such parts your minds engage,
Through Life's great drama, on the world's wide stage !
And when, with many a well-play'd act between,
Ye reach at length the last, the closing scene,
Then shall the good and wise your efforts cheer,
And mark your exit with th' approving tear ;
No snarling critic vex with envious brawls,
But Heaven applaud you, when the curtain falls.

It was during the course of a short, but severe illness, not inopportunely sent, that Mr. Barham first entertained the notion of becoming a candidate for holy orders; and though he so far prosecuted his original design of preparing for the practice of the law, as to become a pupil of an eminent conveyancer,[1] he soon relinquished that profession in favour of one for which a disposition abounding in goodwill towards men, and imbued with a spirit of active though unostentatious piety, assuredly qualified him. It would be too much, perhaps, to assume that he was in any degree influenced in his determination of entering the Church, by an occurrence which took place during the latter part of his residence at Brasenose,—no other than the death, under most distressing circumstances, of a young man with whom he was more than slightly acquainted— but he was beyond question most seriously if not permanently affected by it.

A death at the University, at least among the junior members, always seems to produce an effect more solemn and appalling than elsewhere. Much of this may be attributed to the youth and parity of age in the circle that is broken; much to the course of folly—to say the least of it—in which too often the victim is arrested; but most of all, perhaps, to the comparative rarity of the event, and to its being in general of a sudden if not violent nature. A gloom, however, unusually heavy hung round the fate of the individual in question. He was the only son of a gentleman of respectable standing, but straitened

---

[1] In point of fact he paid but three visits to the office of Mr. Chitty, to whom he paid a hundred guineas for the privilege.

means. Regardless, and probably not altogether aware, of the difficulty his parent experienced in supplying him with the means of qualifying for a liberal profession, he launched into the expensive gaieties of college life. His demands upon his father's purse becoming larger and more frequent, the latter at length, on inclosing a considerable sum which he could ill spare, positively refused to make any further sacrifices on his behalf.

It is, however, by no means an easy matter for a young man to stop short in a career of extravagance, without possessing the means of discharging the debts he has already incurred. At the Universities, in particular, his resources are gauged with the nicest accuracy, and the unhappy victim is allowed no peace till all are exhausted. It may be a hazardous matter to lay the hand of legislation upon so delicate a fabric as that of credit; but some restriction is urgently demanded with regard to the disastrous system pursued at Oxford, and, though to a less extent, at Cambridge also. To many, the accumulated debts incurred in that residence of a year and a half (for in point of fact it amounts to no more), if not of weight to crush them at once, form the nucleus of an incumbrance which presses upon and impedes them through life.

To return to ———. Having availed himself to the utmost of the usual expedients, such as increasing his orders, borrowing of his companions, and raising money upon accommodation bills, in a fit of utter desperation he again applied to his father, laid his case fully and fairly before him,—pledged himself to a thorough change of life in the event of being released from his embarrassments, and concluded by stating that his very existence depended upon the reply, which he should look for by return of post.

There was no mistaking the intimation conveyed in the latter portion of the letter; and the fond parent, in an agony of alarm at the bare possibility of losing his child, hastily penned an answer, forgiving all, and undertaking that the sums necessary to set him once more in an independent position should be forthwith placed at his disposal. Fearful of trusting so important a missive to the chances of the post-office, he unfortunately gave it into the custody of the mail-guard, feeing the man with a sovereign on his engaging to deliver it with his own hands as soon as the College gates should be opened. Eagerly on the following morning did poor —— rush towards the porter who was going his usual round with the letters—fruitlessly he searched the packet again and again—there was not one for him. He returned to his rooms, whither the guard, reeling drunk, made his way late in the afternoon, only to find a coroner's inquest being held over the body of their former occupant, whose head was shattered to atoms by a pistol-ball.

Having passed his examination, Mr. Barham took his Bachelor's degree; to that of Master he never proceeded —an omission which once brought him under the animadversion of Bishop Copleston. On the occasion of some University contest, I forget what, the Bishop enquired how he was going to vote.

'I am not going to vote at all, my lord.'

'Not vote?' repeated his lordship. 'I have no respect,

sir, for indolence or indifference. It is a question upon which every man must have formed an opinion, and it is his duty to record it by giving a vote on one side or the other.'

'But there may be a third course open to him,' suggested Mr. Barham.

'I can't imagine one.'

'Not, my lord, where a man has no vote to give?'

The fact was, putting aside fees and the inconvenience of having to qualify for a Master's degree by keeping an additional term of residence, a vote for the University, sixty years ago, conferred rather an unenviable privilege than otherwise. It was the custom, at least it was the custom at Brasenose, to decide in the common room which candidate should be supported, and for him the members were expected to vote in a body; so that a man might be called upon to take a troublesome and expensive journey for the mere gratification of having the alternative presented to him of offending his college or voting against his principles.

In March 1813, Mr. Barham was admitted to the curacy of Ashford, in Kent. Thence in the year following he proceeded to Westwell, a small parish some few miles distant, adjoining Eastwell Park, at that time the property of Mr. Hatton, grandfather of the present Earl of Winchelsea, in whom he found a pleasant and hospitable squire.

In this cure he was succeeded by the Rev. G. R. Gleig, the well-known author of *The Subaltern*, *The Country Curate*, &c., who drew many of his sketches in the latter work, among which may be numbered the Poacher and the Smuggler, from living originals in that neighbourhood. One of the desperate characters with which the neighbourhood was infested, having been shot through the body in an affray with the Custom-House officers, sent for my father, and actually confessed, while lying on what he believed to be his death-bed, that there was not a crime in all the dark catalogue of human guilt that he had not committed.

'Murder is not to be reckoned among them, I hope?'

'Too many of *them*, sir,' was the reply.

The man recovered for the time, only to afford another testimony to the truth of the old saw respecting the effect sickness is supposed to have upon a certain individual and his followers, but fell dead upon his face, after the lapse of a few years, while in the act of planting vegetables in his garden.

Among my father's memoranda I find an account, abridged from Scott's curious work, of a case of witchcraft which occurred at this village of Westwell in the reign of Elizabeth, and which was professionally treated with marked success by the minister of the parish:—

'I will begin with a true story of a witch practising her diabolical witchcraft and ventriloquie anno 1574, at Westwell, in Kent, within six miles of where I dwell, taken and noted down by two ministers of God's Word, four substantial yeomen, and three women of good fame and reputation, whose names are after-written.—October 13. Mildred, the base daughter of Alice Norrington, and now servant to Will. Spooner, of Westwell, co. Kent, being of the age of seventeen years, was possessed with Satan in the day and night aforesaid. About two o'clock in the afternoon of the same day there came to the said Spooner's house Roger Newman, minister of Westwell, John Brainford, minister of Kinington, with others whose names are under-written, who made their prayer to God to assist them in that needful case, and then commanded Satan in the name of the Holy Trinity to speak with such a voice as they might understand, and to declare from whence he came.'

At first the devil proved refractory, but the exorcisers insisting, he confessed that he had been sent to the girl by 'old Alice,' who, among other things, had moved him to kill three persons, Edward Agar, a gentleman of forty pounds by the year, his child, and Wolton's wife; and that finally he was commissioned by the said 'old Alice' to kill the possessed. The devil being exorcised and driven out, an account was drawn up, signed, and testified as aforesaid. Eventually the girl was arrested as an impostor, confessed her crime and received 'condigne punishment.'

According to Scott the trick was managed by means of ventriloquism. The Holy Maid of Kent is also said by him to have practised the same art.

A second extract from the same volume (p. 61 of the edition of 1654) runs as follows:—

'I remember another story written in " Malleus Maleficarum," repeated by Bodmin, that one soldier called Punker daily throughout witchcraft killed with his bowe and arrows three of the enemies as they stood peeping over the walls of a castle besieged, so as in the end he killed them all quite, saving one. The triall of the archer's sinister dealing and a proof thereof ex-pressed is for that he never lightly failed when he shot, and for that he killed them by three a day, and had shot three arrows into a rod. *This was he that shot at a peny on his sonnes head and made ready another arrow to have slaine the Duke that commanded it.*'[1]

'Query, origin of William Tell?'

In 1814, Mr. Barham married Caroline, third daughter of Captain Smart of the Royal Engineers ; the founder of whose family was one John Smert, a Norman by birth who was created Garter King-at-Arms in 1449, succeeding his father-in-law William de Burges, the first 'Garter' on record.   Of this union were born at Westwell two boys, the younger of whom died an infant.   Shortly after the death of his second child in 1817, Mr. Barham was collated by the Archbishop of Canterbury to the rectory of Snargate ; and he gladly exchanged his former un-healthy and dilapidated parsonage for that of Warehorn, the curacy of which parish was at the same time offered to him.   The villages which formed his new cure were about two miles apart and situated, the former in, the latter on the verge of, Romney Marsh ; and, as may be supposed, they abounded even more than the spot he had just quitted in desperadoes engaged in what, by a technical euphemism, was termed ' The Free Trade.'

But, notwithstanding the reckless character of these men, the rector met with nothing of outrage or incivility at their hands.   Many a time indeed, on returning home-wards late at night, has he been challenged by a half-seen horseman who looked in the heavy gloom like some misty condensation a little more substantial than or-

---

[1] Scott's *Discovery of Witchcraft*, book vii.

dinary fog, but on making known his name and office, he was invariably allowed to pass on with a 'Good night, it's only parson !' while a long and shadowy line of mounted smugglers, each with his led horse laden with tubs, filed silently by. Nay, they even extended their familiarity so far as to make the church itself a depôt for contraband goods ; and on one occasion a large seizure of tobacco had been made in the Snargate belfry—calumny contended for the discovery of a keg of hollands under the vestry-table. When it is added, that the nightly wages, paid whether a cargo was run or not, were at the rate of seven and sixpence to an unarmed man, and fifteen shillings to one who carried his cutlass and pistols, little surprise can be felt if nearly the whole population pursued more or less so profitable an avocation.

The district, moreover, appears up to a late period to have been utterly neglected in point of religious instruction and superintendence. It seems to have been one of the last strongholds of the Trullibers. Will it be credited that in the nineteenth century one of the reverend gentlemen in question has been known on a Sabbath-day to cart a load of bricks, in *propriâ personâ*, to the church-yard, for the purpose of repairing the chancel ? Such was the fact.

Indeed, it was this gentleman's ordinary custom, living as he did at some distance from his cure, to drive over on a Sunday at any hour which might happen to be most convenient, and, having put up his horse and gig, to enter the public-house parlour and there sit down to discuss the state of the markets over a glass of toddy and a pipe with the landlord, who was parish clerk as well, together with any neighbours who might happen to drop in. Meanwhile a lad was despatched to ring the bell, and by the time the rest of the congregation had assembled, the rector and his company were usually ready to repair to the church, where after a fashion divine service was performed. But one blunder Mr. —— unfortunately committed—he outlived his age. Old friends died off, new parishioners intruded, a stricter discipline was on all sides growing up; and one day before the cheering— would that we could say not inebriating—glass was emptied, or the fragrant ' screw' half consumed, the bell suddenly and unexpectedly stopped! What could it mean? off started clerk and clergyman, indignant at the interruption, to ascertain its cause, and discovered to their consternation a stranger in the reading desk. It was the Rural Dean! What steps were subsequently taken I do not remember to have heard, but they were such as to relieve Mr. —— of the necessity of hurrying over his Sunday morning's refreshment for the future.

It is recorded of the same individual that even during divine service it was not unfrequent for him to mingle secular matters with divine, in a manner no less ludicrous than indecorous—leaning, for example, over his churchwarden's pew as he passed from the reading desk to the pulpit, and observing, as the result of long and recently concluded deliberation, ' Well, Smithers, I'll have that pig.'

I may here introduce a somewhat singular occurrence which took place at the residence of another clergyman in this neighbourhood; one, however, it is to be observed, in every respect the opposite of the gentleman just mentioned. He had lost a beloved daughter, under circumstances peculiarly affecting. She was playing in the garden in high spirits and apparent health, when suddenly approaching her father she looked up in his face, and saying, 'Father, take care of my fowls!' without another word laid her head upon his knees and died. The blow was stunning, and Mr. —— never entirely recovered from its effects. For some months his reason was despaired of, and though afterwards restored to cope in full vigour with ordinary subjects, it sank into monomania on the mention of one—his daughter!

A belief took full possession of his mind that he was constantly subject to the visits of his lost child; he intimated, moreover, that the spirit spoke of poison having been administered, and urgently pressed upon him the avenging of the murder. In the earlier stages of the disease, his friends entertained hopes of reasoning or rallying him out of so distressing a delusion. Mr. Barham, among the rest, being present at his table, took an opportunity of addressing to him some sceptical remarks on the theory of apparitions.

' I sincerely hope, sir,' replied his host, ' you may never have occasion to change your opinion ; but, unless I greatly err, your unbelief will meet with a manifest check in the course of this very night.'

The words had scarcely passed his lips, when the party was startled by a loud noise, as of a falling body, proceeding from the hall. Mr. —— looked round with an air of calm triumph, while his guest, not altogether convinced that the interruption was necessarily to be attributed to spiritual agency, opened the door to ascertain its cause. He returned with his own hat which had been dislodged, probably by the wind which happened to be unusually high, from the wall.

'You see, gentlemen, I am no false prophet,' said the host, quietly.

'Well,' urged Mr. Barham, half annoyed at the aptitude of the accident, 'if that be the handiwork of your familiar, I should take it as a favour if you would represent to him or her, as the case may be, that, as the hat happens to be my best——'. 'Oh!' interrupted the seer, 'if you are still disposed to treat the matter with levity, we will drop it at once.' Dropped accordingly it was, leaving the unfortunate gentleman more confirmed than ever in his visionary creed.

To those who knew Mr. Barham only in the latter part of his life, his position in a parish desolate, remote from all educated society, placed indeed almost beyond the borders of civilisation, for such the Marsh—or, as the natives called it, the Mesh—really was, must appear about as ill-suited to his character as any that can be well imagined. And yet this was not altogether the case. He possessed a disposition which readily accommodated itself to circumstances; he went to work at his duties with the same earnestness which he always exhibited, and manifested the same attractive qualities which, it is not too much to say, won him friends wherever he went. A writer in *Bentley's Miscellany* speaks of him as 'essentially a peacemaker,' and

one of the earliest incidents I can remember is his being
called out one winter's night to interpose his good offices
in a slight domestic difference between man and wife, in
the course of which the former was enforcing his argu-
ments, by the aid of a broomstick, with rather more
action than the neighbours thought necessary or safe.
Then there were the ordinary amusements of a country
life for which he had a natural relish, although the
crippled condition of his right arm precluded his pursuing them with very great success. It was indeed
scarcely to be expected that the cultivation of literature should flourish in so uncongenial an atmosphere,
however favourable it might prove for the development
of that 'holy vegetation' of which *Mr. Peter Plymley*
so pleasantly discourses; still my father, even at this
time, was by no means idle with his pen. Of the many
amusing trifles which he was in the habit of addressing
to his friends, one of the best perhaps is an invitation to
Dr. Wilmot of Ashford, conveyed under the form of a
parody on 'O Nanny, wilt thou gang with me?'

O Doctor! wilt thou dine with me,
    And drive on Tuesday morning down?
Can ribs of beef have charms for thee—
    The fat, the lean, the luscious brown?
No longer dressed in silken sheen,
    Nor deck'd with rings and brooches rare,
Say, wilt thou come in velveteen,
    Or corduroys that never tear?

O Doctor! when thou com'st away,
    Wilt thou not bid John ride behind,
On pony, clad in livery gay,
    To mark the birds our pointers find?
Let him a flask of darkest green
    Replete with cherry brandy bear,
That we may still, our toils between,
    That fascinating fluid share!

O Doctor! canst thou aim so true,
    As we through briars and brambles go,
To reach the partridge brown of hue,
    And lay the mounting pheasant low?
Or should, by chance, it so befall
    Thy path be cross'd by timid hare,
Say, wilt thou for the gamebag call
    And place the fur-clad victim there?

And when at last the dark'ning sky
    Proclaims the hour of dinner near,
Wilt thou repress each struggling sigh,
    And quit thy sport for homely cheer?
The cloth withdrawn, removed the tray—
    Say, wilt thou, snug in elbow-chair,
The bottle's progress scorn to stay,
    But fill, the fairest of the fair?

Some similar lines were despatched to the great man
of the neighbourhood, 'Squire' Hodges, who hunted the
Marsh country with a scratch pack of beagles, and had

happened to lose his hare in the Rector's cabbage-garden :—

BENEVOLENCE.

The lark sings loud, 'tis early morn,
    These woodland scenes among,
The deep-toned pack and echoing horn
    Their jovial notes prolong.

And see poor puss, with shorten'd breath,
    Splash'd sides, and weary feet,
In terror views approaching death,
    And crouches at my feet !

Her strength is gone, her spirits fail,
    Nor farther can she fly ;
The hounds snuff up the tainted gale,
    And nearer sounds the cry.

Poor helpless wretch ! methinks I view
    Thee sink beneath their power !
Methinks I see the ruffian crew
    Thy tender limbs devour !

Yet O ! in vain thy foes shall come :
    So cheer thee, trembling elf !
These guardian arms shall bear thee home—
    I'll eat thee up myself !

Under the date of May 13, 1819, the following con-cise entry appears in an old-fashioned pocket-book, in

which a few particulars of this least interesting period of
my father's life are recorded :—

'Drove William and Dick into Ashford—overturned
the gig—broke my right leg and sprained my left ancle.
Mary Anne came back in the chaise with me.'

The injuries were serious, more particularly the sprain,
and confined him to the house for several weeks, a
tedious seclusion which served to bring fairly into play
a taste which might otherwise have died out for lack of
exercise.

A novel, entitled *Baldwin*, rapidly thrown off in a
few weeks, was the result; a work faulty perhaps in
style, but by no means destitute of merit as regards plot
and delineation of character, but which fell still-born
from the Minerva press, under the management of the
matrons of that establishment. The price he received
for the book was twenty pounds, with additional advantages dependent on certain publishing 'contingencies,'
which Theodore Hook used to describe as *things that
never happen*. The definition was not violated in the
present instance.

Baldwin disposed of, and his inability to move about
continuing in consequence of a rheumatic affection which
followed hard upon the accident, he proceeded to sketch
the plan and write the opening chapters of *My Cousin
Nicholas*, which eventually appearing in the pages of
Blackwood met with considerable success. The character,
however, of his attack gradually became more acute, and
he was compelled to lay aside his new story and for a
while to relinquish writing altogether. Scarcely was

his restoration to health complete, when, for the third
time, illness, though on this occasion exhibited in the
person of one of his children, proved indirectly the cause
of a complete diversion of the current of his life. It led
him

> To fresh woods and pastures new,

and was the means of ushering him into a field of action
which afforded full scope for his talents and industry—a
field wherein, upon the whole, the day went prosperously
with him, and from which he retired at last with cheerfulness and resignation, as one who had not proved
altogether barren and unprofitable in his generation.

He had undertaken a journey to London for the purpose of consulting Sir Astley Cooper in the case alluded
to, when he chanced to encounter an old friend who was
walking along the Strand swinging a letter in his hand.
He had carelessly passed the post-office, and taking Mr.
Barham's arm turned back with the intention of dropping
into the box what he had just been writing. It was, he
said, an invitation to a young clergyman to come up
from the country and stand for a minor canonry then
vacant in the cathedral of St. Paul's. Simultaneously the
question occurred to both—why should not Mr. Barham
himself become the candidate? His friend had been
commissioned to find one sufficiently eligible, but had
never thought of addressing himself to his former schoolfellow, being under the impression that the latter was
well content with his position in Kent. The whole
thing was what is commonly called the merest matter of
chance. Be that as it may, the intercepted letter was

forthwith scattered to the winds, and it was arranged that Mr. Barham should return by that night's mail to Warehorn, talk the business over with his wife, and forward his decision within eight-and-forty hours. This he did characteristically enough in a poetical epistle containing

THE RESOLUTION;

OR,

AN ADIEU TO THE COUNTRY.

O, I'll be off! I will by Jove!
　　No more by purling streams I'll ramble,
Through dirty lanes no longer rove,
　　Bemired and scratch'd by briar and bramble.

I'll fly the pigstye for the parks,
　　And Jack and Tom and Ned and Billy
I'll quit for more enlighten'd sparks,
　　And Romney Marsh for Piccadilly.

Adieu, ye woods! adieu, ye groves!
　　Ye waggon-horses, ploughs and harrows!
Ye capering lambs! ye cooing doves!
　　Adieu, ye nightingales and sparrows!

Adieu, ye nasty little boys,
　　So sweetly in the puddles playing!
Adieu, adieu, the cheerful noise
　　Of grunting pigs and asses braying!

O, I'll begone ! at once farewell
    To gooseberry wine and pear and codling !
Farewell the sheep's harmonious bell !
    Farewell the gander's graceful waddling !

Farewell the compost's sweet perfume !
    Farewell rum-punch, nectareous liquor !
Farewell the pimples that illume
    The noses of the squire and vicar !

Adieu my pipe ! not that of old
    By swains Arcadian tuned so gaily,
But that of modern frame and mould,
    Invented by Sir Walter Raleigh.

And I'll renounce my dog and gun,
    And ' bob ' no more for eels in ditches ;
The huntsman, horn, and hounds I'll shun
    And I'll cashier my leather breeches !

For me the fox may prowl secure,
    The partridge unmolested fly,
Whist, loo, and cribbage I abjure,
    And e'en backgammon's lures defy.

At country ' hops,' at country balls,
    At christening treats no more I'll be !
No more I'll pay my morning calls,
    Nor with old ladies take my tea !

Adieu the vestry and the bench,
    The rate and justice's approval,
The overseer, refract'ry wench,
    Appeal, and order of removal !

The fair, its gingerbread and toys,
    Rough roads, deep ruts, and boist'rous weather,
Ye scenes of bliss, ye rural joys,
    Adieu ! and, Bless ye, altogether !

A few weeks afterwards, having determined to relinquish his curacy and given the required notice—the
rectory of Snargate was resigned some months later—
he followed his letter to London, and commenced canvassing under the auspices of his friend the Rev. Christopher Packe, the only one in the body to whom he was
personally known. His friends, according to the diversity
of their gifts, ridiculed, blamed, or condoled with him on
the step he had taken. To all, failure appeared certain.
It befell otherwise ; and in spite of knowledge, in spite
of prophecy, in spite of the *utter impossibility of the
thing* (an objection, by the bye, which throughout life
never daunted him, providing, as he observed, it *stood
alone*), he was returned together with a fellow candidate,
by majorities respectively of eight and six, for nomination,
to the Dean and Chapter. On the following day the election fell on him, and on April 6, 1821, he received his
first piece of metropolitan preferment.

CHAPTER II.

[1821–1825.]

Arrival in London—Birth of a second Daughter—Literary Employment—St.
Paul's—Anecdotes of Dr. Blomberg, Mr. Baber, Lord Eldon, and George IV.
—The Blomberg Ghost Story—The Doctor's Fiddles—The Cato Street
Conspiracy—Murder of Mrs. Donatty—'The Predominance of Ideas'
—Major Hart and the Mesmerist—Appointment as Priest in Ordinary
—Presentation to the Living of St. Mary Magdalene and St. Gregory
—Parish Politics—The Rev. E. Cannon—Anecdote of him—Offence
given to the Prince Regent—Reconciliation—Anecdotes of Lord Thurlow,
George III., and George IV.—Curran—Liberality of George IV.—An-
ecdotes of Cannon—His disinterested Conduct—Curious Will Case—His
Death—Mr. Barham's removal to St. Paul's Churchyard—Death of his
eldest Daughter—Lines.

TOWARDS the close of the summer of 1821, Mr. Barham
quitted Kent, and took up his abode permanently in
London, arriving, it would seem, just in time to witness
from St. Paul's the procession of the Queen's funeral
(August 14). The first thing to be done was, of course,
to secure a suitable home, and one of his great objects in
selecting a situation was to get as far westward as was
compatible with his regular attendance at the Cathedral.
Accordingly, after one or two temporary arrangements, he
settled in a comfortable house in Great Queen Street,
Lincoln's Inn Fields, where a second daughter was added
to the two boys and a girl whom he had brought with
him from the country. Now it has been quaintly said

that literature is an excellent walking-stick, although a bad crutch; and doubtless at this period of his life it proved a serviceable auxiliary to Mr. Barham, who found his income diminished at the very time when an increasing family and a residence in town would admit of no curtailment of expenditure. He set to work with his accustomed vigour, and while articles of the lighter sort, mostly bearing on the topics of the day, were struck off in rapid succession as occasion called them forth, he undertook the more laborious and responsible task of editing the *London Chronicle* (a journal originally conducted by Dr. Johnson), till that paper became merged in the *St. James's Chronicle*, when Mr. Barham's connection with it ceased.[1] But his professional duties, which were gradually extending, soon precluded his continuing any regular literary engagement, or engaging in any work of importance. Poetical trifles, indeed, fell as usual from his pen, and, together with an occasional review, made their appearance in the *John Bull*, the *Globe and Traveller*, the *Literary Gazette*, *Blackwood*, and other periodicals. In his note-book is the following entry, made evidently about this time:—

'My wife goes to bed at ten, to rise at eight, and look after the children and other matrimonial duties. I sit up till three in the morning, working at rubbish for *Blackwood*. She is the slave of the ring, and I of the lamp.'

Subsequently, he found time to join Mr. Gordon

---

[1] The *London Chronicle* was sold by the proprietor, Colonel Torrens, who was also one of the largest shareholders of the *Globe and Traveller*, to Mr. Charles Baldwin, for 3co*l.*

in the production of a Biographical Dictionary, which appeared in 1828. Of the articles contained in these volumes, about one-third were contributed by Mr. Barham. In the course of these literary occupations, he seems to have made the acquaintance of his first critic, *Mr. Sylvanus Urban,* from whom he received a piece of information, which in the narrator's own words may be described as ' curious, if true : '—

' 1820. In the churchyard of Warminster, a person lies buried, who directed the following inscription to be put upon his tombstone :—

Here lies the author of Junius.

Mr. Nicholls (Sylvanus Urban) mentioned this to me, and added that he believed him to have been at one time secretary to Lord Shelbourne. Mr. Nicholls expressed at the same time his conviction that Sir Philip Francis was not *Junius,* and said Mr. Woodfall agreed with him. Of course, the expression, " author of Junius," is conclusive as regards the claim of the Warminster gentleman.'

Meanwhile, at St. Paul's, to quote again the *Letter from John Hughes, Esq.,*[1]—

' In proportion as his standing and influence increased in that section of the cathedral church to which he more immediately belonged, their effects were in several unequivocal ways visible for good. It may be well supposed that no corporate body, save the hierarchy of angels, is exempt from occasional differences and discussions. Not that I have any reason to believe that the worthy conclave of which I speak, whose blood is mostly

[1] See p. 2. The writer was son of Dr. Hughes, canon residentiary of St. Paul's.

sweetened by the domestic charities of life, deserve that wicked
wag Colman's gibe at popish *célibataires* :—

> ' 'Twould seem, since tenanted by holy friars,
>   That harmony and peace reign'd here eternally :
> The folks that cramm'd you with that tale were liars ;
>   The holy friars quarrell'd most infernally.'

But whatever their temporary variances may have been, it is
certain that no member of the body was more influential than
Mr. Barham in promoting, by a happy union of humour and
reason, a tone of harmony and gentlemanlike feeling in their
relations to the chapter, and to each other. I can confidently
say that, as his character and merits became better known, he
was trusted and consulted by the best and most talented men
among the residentiaries as one of themselves.'

With Dr. Blomberg and others, he entered and continued upon terms of friendship, and with Dr. Hughes
and his family, and at a later period with Bishop Copleston, the Dean, he contracted close and lasting intimacies.
But of his life during the first five or six years of his
residence in London, he has left but a very scanty and
imperfect record. Some few notes there are which shall
be submitted to the reader :—

'1822. *May* 12.—Dined with Dr. Blomberg, residentiary
of St. Paul's, and foster-brother to the King.[1] He mentioned that, having purchased a bronze bust of George IV.,
and sent it to his house in Yorkshire, the workman who
was putting it up, enquired if it was really like his Majesty. On being assured by the Doctor that the resem-

---

[1] This, as will appear, is an error. Dr. Blomberg was brought up with
the Prince of Wales, but was not his foster-brother.

blance was a striking one, the man exclaimed, ' Well, sir, I had no idea before that the King is a black man! '

To many a similar story will occur of Judge Taunton, who, coming out of Westminster Hall with Thessiger, was criticising Canning's statue, and found fault with the likeness. ' Besides,' said he, ' Canning was not so tall! ' ' No, nor so *green*,' said Thessiger.

An equally genuine and yet more touching instance of simplicity is noted down by my father as having been told to him by Mr. Baber of the British Museum.

' A short time after Mr. Baber, who succeeded Mr. Beloe at the British Museum, had entered upon his office as one of the keepers, he attended a party from the west of England over the building, and explained, in his official capacity, many of the curiosities which it contains. In one of the rooms he pointed out to their observation a collection of beautiful antique vases, all of which, he informed them, had been dug up at Herculaneum. One of the party echoed his words with the greatest astonishment.

' " Dug up, sir ? "

' " Yes, sir."

' " What, out of the ground ? "

' " Undoubtedly."

' " What, just as they now are ? "

' " Perhaps some little pains may have been taken in cleaning them, but in all other respects they were found just as you see them." The Somersetshire sage turning to one of his companions with a most incredulous shake of the head assured him in an audible whisper,

' " He may say what he likes, but he shall never persuade me that they ever dug up ready-made pots out of the ground ! " '

Diary—June 1.—Anecdote of Lord Chancellor Eldon narrated to me by Dr. Blomberg.

' The Chancellor is very fond of shooting, and usually retires into the country for six weeks towards the end of the season, where he is in the habit of riding a little Welsh pony, for which he gave fifty shillings. One morning last year his lordship intending to enjoy a few hours' sport after a rainy night, ordered " Bob," the pony, to be saddled. Lady Eldon told him he could not have it, but company being in the room gave no reason. In a few minutes, however, the servant opened the door and announced that " Bob " was ready.

' " Why, bless me ! " cried her ladyship, " you can't ride him, Lord Eldon, he has got no shoes on."

' " Oh yes ! my lady," said the servant, " he was shod last week."

' " Shameful ! " exclaimed her ladyship, " how dared you, sir, or anybody, have that pony shod without orders?" " John," continued she, addressing her husband, " you know you only rode him out shooting four times last year, so I had his shoes taken off, and have kept them ever since in my bureau. They are as good as new, and these people have shod him again ; we shall be ruined at this rate ! " '

' Repeated a story which I had from Dubois, that a friend of his walking one day in Hyde Park with Lord Eldon, was stopped by the latter, who pointed to a house and said :—

'In that house the present Lady Eldon formerly dwelt, and from that house, in consequence of my addresses being thought presumptuous, I was banished. During my exile I was informed that her father was going to give a masked ball, and I resolved to make my way in disguised. I mingled with the company, and when I came to my present lady, I said, " Don't be alarmed, my love, it is I— John Scott !" She, however, could not command herself, and screamed. I was detected and kicked out of the house.'

' George the Third scolded Lord North for never going to the concert of antient music : " Your brother, the bishop," said the King, " never misses them, my lord." " Sir," answered the premier, " if I were as deaf as my brother, the bishop, I would never miss them either !" Told me by Doctor Blomberg who was present.'

The name of Dr. Blomberg is well known in connection with the celebrated ghost-story so frequently narrated by George IV. As several versions of this strange occurrence are in existence, it may be worth while to give the one which Mr. Barham heard at the Doctor's own table, either on the occasion when the foregoing anecdotes were told, or a few days later.

' During the American War, two officers of rank were seated in their tent, and delayed taking their supper till a brother officer, then absent upon a foraging party, should return. Their patience was well-nigh exhausted, and they were about to commence their meal, concluding something had occurred to detain the party, when suddenly his well-known footstep was heard approaching.

Contrary to their expectation, however, he paused at the
entrance of the tent, and without coming in called on one
of them by name, requesting him with much earnestness,
as soon as he should return to England, to proceed to a
house in a particular street in Westminster, in a room of
which (describing it) he would find certain papers of
great consequence to a young lad with whom the speaker
was nearly connected. The speaker then apparently
turned away, and his footsteps were distinctly heard
retiring till their sound was lost in distance. Struck
with the singularity of his behaviour, they both rose,
and proceeded in search of him. A neighbouring sen-
tinel on being questioned denied that he had either
seen or heard anyone, although, as they believed, their
friend must have passed close by his post. In a few
minutes their bewilderment was changed into a more
painful feeling by the approach of the visiting officer of
the night, who informed them that the party which went
out in the morning had been surprised, and that the
dead body of poor Major Blomberg (their friend) had
been brought into the camp about ten minutes before.
The two friends retired in silence, and sought the corpse
of the person who, as both were fully persuaded, had just
addressed them. They found him pierced by three
bullets, one of which had passed through his temples and
must have occasioned instant death. He was quite cold,
and appeared to have been dead some hours. It may easily
be conceived that a memorandum was immediately made
of the request they had both so distinctly heard, and of
the circumstances attending it, and that on the return of

the regiment to Europe, no time was lost in searching for the papers. The house was found without difficulty, and in an upper room, agreeably with the information they had received in such an extraordinary manner, an old box was discovered, which had remained there many years, containing the title-deeds of some property now in the possession of the Rev. Dr. Blomberg, who was the " lad " mentioned by name by the voice at the tent door.

' This story,' adds Mr. Barham, ' was repeated to me by Mr. Atwood, the King's organist, at Dr. Blomberg's own table in his temporary absence. Mr. Atwood declared that he had heard the story related by George IV. (whose foster-brother Dr. Blomberg was) more than once, and on one occasion when the doctor himself was present. He further stated that the King had mentioned the names of all the parties concerned, but that, with the exception of Major Blomberg's, they had escaped his memory.'

Since the foregoing pages were prepared for the press a very different version of the story has reached me, furnished by a member of the family to the head of which the Yorkshire property has descended. The account given by my informant contains the substance of a narrative of the circumstances under which the alleged supernatural communication was made, drawn up by the officer to whom it was more particularly addressed. It runs as follows :—

Captain (? Major) Edward Blomberg was left a widower, with one little boy, two years old, who was heir to a fair estate in Yorkshire then in the possession of Baron Blomberg. The captain's regiment being stationed in the island of Martinique, he was, in the course of duty, sent off with despatches to a place at a considerable distance from head-quarters.   One night, shortly after his departure, an officer who, in consequence of the crowded condition of the barracks, was sharing his chamber with a comrade, was aroused, just as he was dropping off to sleep, by the opening of the door.   Captain Blomberg entered, walked slowly to his friend's bed, and drew back the mosquito curtains.

'Why, Blomberg,' exclaimed the latter in astonishment, 'what on earth has brought you back ?'

The intruder answered: 'This night I died at ——, and I have come hither to beg you to take charge of my little orphan boy.'   He then gave the address of the child's grandmother and aunt, who were residing in London, and requested that his son might be sent to them immediately ; adding directions as to the searching for certain papers necessary to establish the boy's title to the property of which he was heir.   This done, without waiting for a reply, the figure departed.   Perplexed, not to say alarmed, and thinking it just possible that his imagination might have played him false, the officer called to the occupant of the other bed :

'Did you,' he asked, 'see anyone come into the room ?'

'Yes,' was the answer ; 'it was Blomberg, was it not? What did he want ?'

'Didn't you hear what he said ?'

'No,' returned the other ; 'I could hear that he was talking to you, but what he said I was unable to make out.'

The first speaker then related the extraordinary communication he had just received. Both officers were much affected by the strangeness of the affair, and were not a little ridiculed on the following morning when they narrated the occurrence at breakfast in the mess-room. In the evening, however, a message was forwarded to the general in command to the effect that Captain Blomberg's death had taken place on the preceding night, just at the time of his appearance in the bed-room. It came out that he had died of fever, evidently brought on by depression of spirits occasioned by the loss of his wife. No time was lost in seeking out the child, who was found and despatched to England, where he appears to have been somewhat coldly received by the grandmother. His story, however, happened to reach the ears of Lady Caroline Finch, the Queen's governess, who repeated it to her Majesty. The Queen, struck by the interest attaching to the boy, declared that little Blomberg should never want a home; and immediately sending for him ordered that he should be brought up in the Royal nursery. She afterwards provided for his education, and saw to the settlement of his property. In addition to this, when the lad reached the age of nine years, the Queen employed Gainsborough to paint his portrait, and subsequently presented the picture to the original. This lad, brought up at the palace, became in due time chaplain to George IV. and residentiary of St. Paul's. He married Miss Floyer, a Dorsetshire lady, but, continuing childless, adopted her niece; and narrative and portrait, papers and estate—to say nothing of the ghost's plates and spoons—

are, I am told, at the present time in the possession of this lady's representative.

Dr. Blomberg was an amiable man, that he was a sound divine may be taken for granted, and assuredly he was a very excellent musician. Fiddling was his strong point and his unfailing amusement; there were people who believed that he kept a greased bow for silent play on Sundays. Three fiddles he possessed—three fiddles that he loved, I had almost said, like children. And no wonder; they were mellow marvellous instruments—one a genuine Straduarius of incalculable value. It is curious how players become attached to their fiddles! I speak in ignorance, but I never heard of anyone conceiving a strong affection for a trombone, or a big drum, or a key bugle, but there appears to be something exceptionally fascinating about a fiddle—something which commends that simple parent of sweet sounds to its master's heart in a degree not attained by organs more powerful or more elaborate. There are some fiddles too, I believe, which love their owners—at least they speak as if they do. But this by the way. One morning Dr. Blomberg came to my father in dire distress. The tears, without figure of speech, were in his eyes as he told his pitiful story. He had been robbed—robbed of his fiddles—robbed of all three—all three were gone! A former servant who had been detected in some petty dishonesty and discharged was, it was pretty clear, 'the gentleman concerned in the abstraction.' But what was to be done? How get at the offender—or rather at the fiddles, one of which, the solace of the Doctor's life, his incomparable Straduarius, was, as

had been intimated by the culprit's wife, lying in pledge
at a pawnbroker's shop in the neighbourhood of Smithfield? It was impossible for Dr. Blomberg himself, a
dignified clergyman in shorts and shovel hat, to penetrate
the recesses of Cock Lane and Barbican. Would Mr.
Barham help him at his need? This, it is needless to
say, my father very readily promised to do, and as he happened to number among his acquaintances not only the
chief magistrate at Bow Street, Sir Richard Birnie, but
both Townshend and Ruthven, the celebrated 'runners,'
he obtained from one or other of these experts some
practical hints, acting upon which he paid a visit that very
evening to the Smithfield establishment.

After an animated discussion with the proprietor, and an
offer, hastily declined, to refer the matter to the arbitra-
tion of Sir Richard, the missing violin was produced,
and, in consideration of the repayment of five pounds
which had been advanced upon it, handed over to the
applicant. Wrapping his prize up in a silk pockethand-
kerchief, my father hurried off, late as it was, to the
Doctor's house in Amen Corner, and restored the recovered
Cremona to his arms. The old gentleman's delight was
touching to witness. He jumped up, seized his bow and
ran it over the strings; the tone was unimpaired; he
tapped and sounded the lungs of his favourite—they were
sound as ever. His gratitude was overwhelming; and my
father always maintained that had the living of Totten-
ham been vacant at that moment, and at the Doctor's
option, he would to a certainty have at once bestowed
upon his benefactor the best piece of preferment in the

gift of the Dean and Chapter.   Eventually the other two
fiddles were restored by his exertions.

Mr. Barham's acquaintance with Sir Richard Birnie
has been mentioned.   It was of old standing and of sufficient weight to procure an entrance into the police office
and a seat on the bench, during the examination of the
Cato-street conspirators on the night of the 29th of
February, 1820; and I have often heard him (my father)
speak of the thrill of horror which ran through the court
on the production of the bag which the butcher, Ings,
had destined for the reception of Lord Castlereagh's
head.   Happily the villains were betrayed.   But about
the time of which I am writing, viz. 1822, a murder
was actually committed which produced a sensation in
the town unequalled in intensity by any similar event
since the massacre of the Marrs and Williamsons in
Ratcliffe Highway, and which in point of dramatic interest would vie with any of later days.   The spot was
a house in a narrow street, at the northern end of
Gray's Inn, running parallel with Bedford Row, and
called Robert Street.   The victim was one Mrs. Donatty,
the widow of a sheriff's officer, who, in the exercise of
his vocation, had amassed a considerable sum of money,
a large proportion of which had been obtained by the
sale of pictures painted by Morland, whose custodian he
had happened frequently to be.   One evening this poor
woman was found lying dead in the passage of her home
with her throat cut from ear to ear and a handkerchief
stuffed by way of a gag into her mouth.   After the
removal of the body, Sir Richard Birnie and Ruthven,

accompanied by Mr. Barham, went to examine the premises, and nothing in the history, genuine or fictitious, of modern detectives can surpass the description which the latter used to give of the sagacity exhibited by the trained intelligence of the police officer—one of the most acute as well as resolute that Bow Street could boast.[1] He corrected without any affectation, or failure of respect, the hasty and occasionally erroneous guesses of the magistrate; gave his reasons simply for believing that the assassin had been admitted in the usual way at the front door, and had effected his purpose as the woman was preceding him to the sitting-room—inferring that he was either an habitual visitor or that he had been expected on this particular occasion; commented on the height of the man who had inflicted the wound from its position,—a calculation curiously confirmed by a subsequent discovery; and then remarking that an inner door had been forced—

'Ay, with this chisel,' interrupted the magistrate, picking up a heavy tool.

'Pardon me, Sir Richard, not with that; it is too large to produce the marks you see about the lock. It was done with a narrower instrument, one with which he also broke open this small box.' 'Why, it is merely an old tea-caddy!' objected the other. 'Yes, Sir Richard, an old tea-caddy, but it has been forcibly opened, as you may see.'

The party then proceeded to a small yard at the back of the house, a grimy, damp, well-like looking place, shut

---

[1] He headed the officers in the attack upon the loft in Cato Street, without waiting for the arrival of the Coldstream Guards.

in by high walls, in one angle of which stood a half-rotten water-butt.   After a careful examination of this spot the officer observed :—

'The man was disturbed before he had time to ransack the house, probably by a knock at the front door, which prevented his leaving by the way he entered, so he had to make his escape over that wall, and so got into Great Ormond Street.   Here you see, sir,' pointing out a small space on the stand of the water-butt, from which the dark green mould had lately been detached, 'here he placed his left foot ; there his left hand—he is a tall man, as I supposed ; here came his right foot—you can see the brick scraped by the toe of his boot ; there his right hand grasped the top of the wall.   With a spring he raised himself up, knocking out the mortar, as you observe, in the scramble ; and he then dropped easily down on the other side.'

Certain slightly suspicious circumstances led to the arrest of a young man, the nephew of the deceased, indeed, the only relative she had.   He was of a dissolute character and, though as a boy a great favourite of the old lady's, had of late been known more than once to have exchanged angry words· with her.   In person he was *tall.* This was pretty much all that could be alleged against him at the time.   On the other hand, his horror and grief at the bloody deed appeared genuine, and the magistrate, notwithstanding the opinion of the police, saw no sufficient cause for detaining him.   The next day he disappeared, but many years afterwards the man, then being on his death-bed in America, confessed that he was indeed the murderer; that the murder had been effected as Ruthven had surmised; that he had broken open the tea-caddy, which he knew to contain his aunt's will, by the provisions of which, as she had informed him, he was left penniless in consequence of his repeated misconduct; that he had secured the document and destroyed it, in the expectation of coming in as heir for the whole of the property, not being at the time aware that as an illegitimate child, which he was, he was debarred by law from inheriting a farthing. He added that he had been disturbed by a knock at the door, and compelled to secure his retreat by the route so cleverly tracked by the Bow-street officer. Mr. Townshend's remarks, made in the hearing of my father, on the simplicity of Sir Richard Birnie in letting the fellow slip through his fingers after the police had fairly secured him, were in that worthy's usually forcible and figurative style.

It was in the spring either of this year, 1822, or of the year following, that Mr. Barham became a witness of one of those extraordinary exhibitions of the influence of the imagination or faith upon the bodily organs which forms, we are told by the orthodox physicians, the basis of the ephemeral systems, whether of the school of Mesmer or others, that are continually springing up around us. With instances indeed of the injurious effects which mental impressions are capable of producing upon the body medical works abound. Dr. Hughes Bennett, in his *Lectures on Clinical Medicine*, No. iv. p. 174, gives

one especially marvellous case of what he terms ' the predominance of ideas':—

'A butcher,' he says, 'was brought into a druggist's shop (at
Edinburgh) from the market-place opposite, labouring under a
terrible accident.   The man, on trying to hook up a heavy piece
of meat above his head, slipped, and the sharp hook penetrated
his arm, so that he himself was suspended.   On being examined,
he was pale, almost pulseless, and expressed himself as suffering
acute agony.   The arm could not be moved without causing
excessive pain, and in cutting off the sleeve he frequently cried
out; yet when the arm was exposed it was found to be quite
uninjured, the hook having only traversed the sleeve of his coat.'

The same author allows that, in like manner, so far
from its being improbable that real cures are occasionally
effected through the medium of the imagination, 'all that
we know of the effects of confident promises on the one
hand, and belief on the other, render it very likely that
such have occurred.'

The case that fell under Mr. Barham's observation
was that of an old friend, the Major Hart mentioned
before as the speaker of an epilogue at the Canterbury
Theatre. I can remember him (for he was fond of
children—fond, that is to say, of teasing them,—and
children were of course fond of him), a slight, short man
with a pale face, white hair, and glittering eyes, and
the possessor of a certain bright shilling which was the
object of my thoughts by day and my dreams by night.
As an officer in the Rifle Brigade, he had seen a good deal
of service; had been frequently and severely wounded ;
and was now sinking under a complication of disorders, of

which partial paralysis was one. He had become utterly prostrate. The country doctors—he was living, I believe, at Maidstone—shook their heads, and admitted they could do no more. Then it was that some one whispered—' Try mesmerism!' Hart caught at the suggestion at once. There was in London, at this time, a professor of animal magnetism, whose fame had reached even unto Maidstone. His success was wonderful. Every human ill, old age scarcely excepted, was to be cured by some new and occult process, of which he was the fortunate discoverer. If men persisted in dying of disease, it was simply through their own wilfulness, obstinacy, and incredulity. To this man the Major was determined to apply, and although he had been for several weeks considered incapable of quitting his bed-room, he insisted upon being placed in a carriage and con-veyed to my father's house in town. With the assistance of a servant, the coachman, and Mr. Barham, he was re-moved from the vehicle to the apartment prepared for him. After resting a couple of days, during which he scarcely spoke, he was, in like manner, lifted into a hack-ney coach and driven off to the residence of the celebrated practitioner. The same care was necessary and was ob-served in carrying the patient into the consulting room, so completely unable was he to take a step, or even to stand, without the support of others. Placed gasping into a chair he was submitted to the keen, and for some time silent, examination of the doctor. At length the latter turned to my father and spoke to this effect :—

' You must be quite aware, sir, that exaggerated notions of my invention, as of everything displaying great and incomprehensible power, have got abroad. I am not, however, the charlatan that people would make me out. Sufferers are constantly brought here to whom I can hold out no hope of relief, and with whom I would rather have nothing to do. I am nevertheless perhaps obliged to operate, and little or no good follows. Now, sir, the case of your friend, on the contrary, I undertake with the utmost satisfaction. It is in every particular, both as regards his temperament and the character of his disorder, precisely the case adapted to the influence I shall bring to bear upon it. I have never met a subject whom I have approached with more perfect confidence. I stake my reputation upon a cure.'

' *Credat Judæus!* ' thought my father, and the gentleman continued :—

' A great effect will doubtless be produced this very morning, but it will be the work of some time, during which I require to be left alone with my patient. Call again in an hour and you shall judge for yourself.'

My father was inclined to object to the dismissal. ' Better go, Barham,' said the Major in a tone distinct and clear, very different from that he had hitherto employed, and Barham went. He took the opportunity of transacting some business in the neighbourhood, by which he was detained a few minutes beyond the time specified. Finding he was late, he took a coach and drove back, with the intention of carrying away his friend in it.

' Is Major Hart ready ? ' he enquired of the servant who opened the door.

' The Major, sir, was tired of waiting, so he has walked

on; he said you would be sure to overtake him before he got home, he shouldn't hurry.'

'Hurry!' exclaimed my father, 'why he can't move—I am speaking of the gentleman you helped to carry in.'

'Yes, sir; that is the gentleman—he has walked on.'

At this moment out came the doctor himself, 'It is quite true,' he said; 'Major Hart has left the house, and insisted upon walking.'

'Impossible!'

'It is nevertheless so. His sensibility is even greater than I expected to find it; his cure will be proportionably rapid; meanwhile you had better perhaps overtake him as soon as you can, and persuade him to ride the remainder of the distance.'

Half pleased, half alarmed, and wholly bewildered, Mr. Barham hurried away, and ere long caught sight of his friend looking contentedly into the window of a print shop. The change worked in him was certainly to all seeming nothing short of miraculous. He could walk, use his limbs freely, was free from pain, and in the highest possible spirits, overflowing with gratitude to his benefactor and respect for science. He admitted he was a little tired, so got into a coach and returned to Queen Street. Towards evening his new strength gradually died away. By next morning it was clean gone; and on the third day he was again all but speechless. A second visit to the doctor was paid, and a repetition of the treatment attempted, but faith had in the interval expired, and no further effect could be produced. He said he would go back to Kent and die comfortably at home. Happily he was enabled to reach his home alive; and the next news we heard of him was that one sunny afternoon, as he sat by the window in his easy chair with his bible before him, he closed the book, lay back and fell asleep, passing out of life so imperceptibly that his niece, who was sitting opposite, was for some time unaware that he was dead.

In 1824 Mr. Barham received the appointment of priest in ordinary of his Majesty's Chapels Royal, and was shortly afterwards presented—by another of those chances with which every man's life abounds, and which serve to show how slight and seemingly insignificant are the pivots on which the wheels of human fortune turn—to the incumbency of St. Mary Magdalene and St. Gregory by St. Paul.[1]

At the time of his application there happened to be two livings vacant, both in the gift of the Dean and Chapter of St. Paul's: as the junior minor canon, Mr. Barham had naturally asked for that which was the less eligible in point of emolument and position, and which, situated in the marshes of Essex, rejoiced in the euphonious and characteristic name of Mucking. His application was favourably received, and the presentation papers of both benefices were, I believe, actually signed, sealed and all but delivered, when the sudden and inexplicable commission of a grave offence led to the removal of his fellow-candidate from the body, and the forfeited preferment was offered to my father.

On admission he found the 'united parishes' in a state of most admired disorder. Two hostile parties, one led

---

[1] His fortuitous meeting with Mr. Packe, which led to the appointment to a minor canonry, will not have been forgotten.

by a revolutionary oilman, and both altogether opposed
to the discipline and interests of the church, held possession of the vestry-room, and rendered it the scene of
ceaseless and indecent squabbling. Shortly after Mr.
Barham's induction, a meeting was held for the despatch
of parish business, at which he, as a matter of course,
proceeded to take the chair. This led immediately to a
violent outbreak on the part of the assembled ratepayers.
Another chairman was proposed and seconded, and a vote
demanded. Mr. Barham declined to put the question :
'he sat there by right, and not in virtue of the will of a
majority.' . A perfect uproar ensued. At one time there
appeared a disposition to remove him by force from the
position he had taken. His opponent thought better of
that. Then an adjournment to the body of the building
was suggested. But some suspicion was entertained of
the legality of the step. Next, amid loud acclamations,
a second chair was ordered to be brought in and placed
by the rector's side.

'Now sir,' said he, addressing the leader of the riot,
'you have brought in that chair and placed it here—let
me see you dare seat yourself in it, and within four and
twenty hours you shall find yourself in the ecclesiastical
courts.'

I presume the chairman had some more distinct idea
of what would happen in such a case than Speaker
Onslow when he threatened to 'name' a refractory
member; at all events the man was cowed, a vague
apprehension of ex-communication, or of some worse
thing, if worse there be, prevailed, the chair remained

empty and the business of the evening was at length allowed to proceed.

As the more quietly disposed of the inhabitants had for sometime withdrawn themselves from these displays of party feeling, few were found prepared to support the new rector; and it is to be taken as no slight evidence of his peculiar tact and conciliatory art, that, in the course of a few months, he not only succeeded in restoring peace and propriety to these meetings, but carried such measures as were essential to the interests committed to his care, and effected much towards promoting a cordial and lasting unanimity among his parishioners.

With regard to himself, as he became more generally known, but one feeling seems to have prevailed, that of affectionate esteem.

In the pulpit he was not remarkable, less perhaps from the want of power, than from a rooted disapproval of anything like oratorical display in such a place—anything, in short, that might seem calculated to convert the house of prayer into a mere theatre for intellectual recreation.

His sermons were carefully prepared and even polished compositions, with something of the smack of the older essayists about them, but they were perhaps, with a few exceptions, deficient in vigour; and he never permitted himself to arouse attention by the slightest approach to eccentricity. In doctrine he was what used to be termed ' High Church '—' high and dry ' is the phrase now—but he would tolerate no leaven of Popery. By ' Church and King ' he would stand while able to stand; and by

'Church' he understood Episcopacy and Protestantism, and by 'King' loyalty to the throne and strict Tory principles.

It was not, then, as a popular preacher, 'pleasant to sit under,' that he was beloved, still less as a party one; he published no pamphlets, presented no petitions, nor was his voice lifted up in Exeter Hall; but he was ever watchful over the welfare of his people, temporal and eternal : to the poorer portion of his brethren more especially did he commend himself by the kindness and assiduity with which he relieved their necessities and furthered their views. He would bestow as much time and attention in conducting the cause of one of the meanest of these as though the interests of those nearest and dearest to him were involved in the result. Most fortunate, too, was he in the companionship of one who, as a Christian clergyman's wife, fulfilled with exemplary zeal those numerous and nameless officers of charity which fall more peculiarly within the scope of woman's superintendence.

But his exertions on the behalf of others were by no means confined to the limits of his own parish. From various quarters, and from various ranks of society, came applications for assistance and advice; piles of letters, consisting of alternations of request and acknowledgment, bear ample testimony to the wide circle through which his influence extended. And herein he found his pleasure —this was his delight; never was he so completely at home, never so happy as when engaged in promoting the happiness of others. Verily he had his reward, for it has probably fallen to the lot of few in his station of life to have enjoyed so many and ample opportunities of tasting ' the luxury of doing good.'

His appointment in the Chapel Royal [1] led to an acquaintance, which quickly ripened into a warm friendship, with the Rev. Edward Cannon, also one of the priests of the household, and who for many years previously had been on intimate terms with the family of Mrs. Barham. This singular being, introduced to the world under the name of Godfrey Moss, in Theodore Hook's celebrated novel *Maxwell*, claims some notice, the more so as he has scarcely met with justice at the hands of his facetious friend.

For a general idea of his mannerism, I can but refer to the striking portrait referred to, one of the most perfect ever committed to paper. As he is there de-

[1] Among his undated memoranda is an entry referring to the plate belonging to the Chapel Royal, at St. James's Palace, to which he was now attached.

' The splendid sacramental paten always used on Easter Sunday is the most beautiful piece of plate of that description I ever saw. It is said to be the work of Benvenuto Cellini. It bears the arms of France and England (the former with the three lilies) in the first and fourth quarter, Ireland in the dexter base, Scotland in the sinister chief. In different compartments and in very bold relief, are the descent of the Holy Ghost; our Saviour and the disciples at Emmaus ; our Lord washing Simon's feet; our Lord breathing on his disciples ; and the Last Supper, in which are introduced a boy with an ewer, a dog with a bone in his mouth, &c. There was also a remarkable knife at the Chapel Royal belonging to the yeoman of the vestry, which has been lost since Mr. Howse's death. It was used for cutting the sacramental bread, and had inscribed round the pummel— "Thomas Haynes, Sergeant of His Majestyes Vestry," and just above the blade was " E. L., January 1664." On the pummel was a coat of arms ; *Argt.* Three annulets, *gules*, divided by a fess of the second, charged with three coronets. For crest, on an esquire's helmet a coronet like those in the coat.'

picted, so precisely did he live and move in daily life
—not an eccentricity is exaggerated, not an absurdity
heightened! It is, however, to be regretted that the
great master restricted himself to the delineating the
less worthy features of the outward and visible man, and
touched but lightly those high and noble traits of character which had gone far to relieve the mass of cynicism
and selfishness but too correctly drawn.

Mr. Cannon, was, in fact, both a spoiled and a disappointed man. Brought up under the immediate care
of Lord Thurlow, his brilliant wit, his manifold accom-
plishments, and, as may be hardly credited by those who
knew him only in his decline, his fascinating manners,
procured him a host of distinguished admirers and proved
an introduction to the table of royalty itself. A welcome
guest at Carlton House, Stow, and other mansions of the
nobility, patronised by the Lord Chancellor, courted and
caressed by men—to say nothing of women—of the highest
rank and influence, he might possibly have become too
extravagant or too impatient in his expectations; while
more reasonable views would scarcely have been met by
a chaplaincy to the Prince of Wales, and a lectureship
at St. George's, Hanover Square—the only preferment
he ever obtained. This neglect, as he esteemed it, was
especially calculated to work evil on a disposition naturally independent to a fault, and associated, as it was,
with a humour tinctured overmuch with bitterness. His
caprices indulged and fostered, and his hope delayed, he
fell gradually into utter disregard of all the amenities
and conventional laws of society. The extreme liberties

he began to take, and the bursts of sarcasm, which he took the less heed to restrain as he advanced in years, deprived him betimes of all his powerful patrons, and at the last alienated most of his more attached friends.

At one of the annual dinners of the members of the Chapel Royal, a gentleman had been plaguing Mr. Barham with a somewhat dry disquisition on the noble art of fencing. Wishing to relieve himself of his tormentor, the latter observed that his crippled hand had precluded him from indulging in that amusement; but pointing to Cannon who sat opposite, he added, 'That gentleman will better appreciate you; he was an enthusiastic admirer of fencing in his youth.'

After a few minutes the disciple of Angelo contrived to slip round the table, and commenced a similar attack upon Cannon. For some time he endured it with patience, till at length, on his friend's remarking that Sir George D—— was a great fencer, Cannon, who disliked the man, replied, 'I don't know whether Sir George D—— is a great fencer, but Sir George D—— is a great fool.'

A little startled, the other rejoined, 'Well possibly he is; but then a man may be both.'

'So I see, sir!' said Cannon, turning away.

As regards the circumstances which led immediately to his dismissal from the palace, his conduct was certainly not chargeable with blame, but was the natural working of an unbending spirit which scorned to flatter even princes.

Possessing, in addition to the attractions of his conversation, the charm of a voice so unusually sweet as to have gained him the name of Silver-tongue Cannon, he was admitted to the more select parties of the Prince of Wales, where his great musical taste and talent not unfrequently procured him the honour of accompanying his royal master on the pianoforte. On one occasion, at the termination of the piece, the Prince enquired, 'Well, Cannon, how did I sing that?'

Cannon continued to run over the keys, but without making any reply.

'I asked you, Mr. Cannon, how I sang that last song, and I wish for an honest answer,' repeated the Prince. Thus pointedly appealed to, Cannon, of course, could no longer remain silent.

'I think, sir,' said he, in his quiet and peculiar tone, 'I have heard your Royal Highness succeed better.'

'Sale and Attwood,' observed the latter sharply, 'tell me I sing that as well as any man in England.'

'They, sir, may be better judges than I pretend to be,' replied Cannon.

George the Fourth was too well bred as well as too wise a man to manifest open displeasure at the candour of his guest, but in the course of the evening, being solicited by the latter for a pinch of snuff, a favour which had been unhesitatingly accorded a hundred times before, he closed the box, placed it in Mr. Cannon's hand, and turned abruptly away.[1] A gentleman in waiting quickly

[1] Cannon had previously succeeded in affronting Mrs. Fitzherbert. On being asked by the lady what he thought of a new upright pianoforte which she had just purchased, he replied, scarcely deigning to examine it,—'I think, Madam, it would make a very good cupboard to keep your bread and cheese in.'

made his appearance, for the purpose of demanding back the article in question, and of intimating at the same time that it would be more satisfactory if its possessor forthwith withdrew from the apartment.

Cannon at first refused to restore what he chose to consider no other than a present.

'The *creetur* gave it me with his own hand,' he urged, 'if he wants it back let him come and say so himself.'

It was represented, however, that the Prince regarded its detention in a serious light, and was deeply offended at the want of respect which had led to it. The box was returned without further hesitation, and Mr. Cannon retired for the last time from the precincts of Carlton House.

He was, however, not a man to permit a single affront to obliterate from his memory all traces of former kindness, and accordingly, when the trial of Queen Caroline had excited so much popular clamour against the Sovereign, Cannon was the first, on the termination of that affair, to get up and present an address from the inhabitants of the Isle of Wight to his royal master. Delighted at this seasonable exhibition of public approval, and not untouched, it may be, by the conduct of his former favourite, the King was all courtesy and condescension.

'You are not looking well, Cannon,' he observed, at length.

'I am not so well, sir, as I have been,' replied Cannon, with a meaning smile.

'Well, well! I must send Halford to prescribe for you,'

said the King. Nor did this prove to be an idle compliment ; in due time the physician of the household called, having it in command to tender to the invalid his professional assistance, and at the same time to intimate that he might expect to be received again at the royal parties. This honour Mr. Cannon bluntly and resolutely declined. On being pressed to give some explanation of his refusal, he merely answered,

' I have been early taught when I want to say " no " and can say " no," to say " no "—but never give a reason—' a maxim which he had learned from his early protector, Lord Thurlow, and a neglect of which, the latter used to boast, had enabled him to carry an important point with his late Majesty George III.

Thus it was : he had applied to that monarch on behalf of his brother for the Bishopric of Durham, and having somewhat unexpectedly met with a refusal, he bowed and was about to retire without pressing his suit, when the monarch, wishing to soften his decision as far as possible, added, ' Anything else I shall be happy to bestow upon your relative, but this unfortunately is a dignity never held but by a man of high rank and family.'

' Then, Sire,' returned Lord Thurlow, drawing himself up, ' I must persist in my request—I ask it for the brother of the Lord High Chancellor of England ! '

The Chancellor was firm, and the King was compelled to yield.

' He gave me his reasons,' said the former, ' and I beat him.'

With respect to Mr. Cannon, although he thought fit

to decline giving any explanation at the time, he was not so reserved on all occasions.

'The *creetur,*' he said, 'has turned me out of his house once—he shall not have the opportunity of doing so again.'

Of the many anecdotes of the Chancellor narrated by Cannon, I find but few preserved; the following, however, are given on his authority :—

'The great Lord Thurlow passed the latter part of his life at Brighton, and died there—it is said, while swearing at his servant. The present King (George IV.) having come down to the Pavilion, invited him to dinner, but knowing his man thought proper to offer a sort of half apology for some of the company, among whom were Sir John Lade, and several characters of sporting notoriety. The sturdy old Chancellor leaning upon his cane, and looking his Royal Highness full in the face, replied, " Sir! I make exceptions to no man. Sir John Lade, for instance, whom your Royal Highness has thought proper to mention by name, is an excellent character in his proper place, but that, with all due deference, I humbly conceive to be your Royal Highness's coach-box, and not your table."

Again :—

'A Mr. Sneyd, a tall, thin man, nicknamed by George IV. "the Devil's Darning Needle," was much about Lord Thurlow during his last years, and had a sort of roving commission from him to pick up any stray genius he could lay hold of and bring him to the old nobleman's table. Coming in the stage-coach one day to Brighton

Mr. Sneyd scraped an acquaintance with a fellow-traveller who turned out to be the celebrated J. P. Curran, and he eagerly invited his new friend to dine with Lord Thurlow, but some accident prevented his own attendance on the appointed day. Thurlow, who had heard much of Curran, when the cloth was removed, led the conversation to the state of the Irish bar which Curran, who was at that time red-hot against the Union, abused in the lump with great vehemence:

'"Timidity, my lord, and venality," said he, "are the bane of the Irish courts, and pervade them from the lowest to the highest."

'"Indeed!" said Thurlow, "pray what is the character of Lord ——?" (naming a particular friend of his own then on the Irish bench).

'"O," replied Curran, "never was man less fitted for his position; if he has any honesty in him, which is very problematical, he is infinitely too great a poltroon to let it appear."

'"Humph!" quoth the Chancellor—"a bad account of him indeed, Mr. Curran. And pray what do you think then of Lord ——?" (naming another old crony also in the same rank).

'"As to him," said the barrister, "he is ten thousand times worse than the other. The venality of that man is such that no person, however just and clear his case may be, can hope for a verdict where he presides, unless he has contrived to bribe his judge into justice. In fact these two form an admirable sample of Irish jurisprudence as it exists now—all venality and cowardice!"

' " In other words," said the Chancellor, "all the Irish lawyers are rascals ? "

" Pretty much so indeed, my lord."

' Here the conversation stopped. The next day Lord Thurlow attacked Mr. Sneyd for sending such a flippant fellow to his table, adding that he saw nothing whatever in him.

' " Ah, my lord," suggested Sneyd, "that might be because there was no one present to draw the trigger."

' " Sir," replied the old nobleman, with one of his inveterate frowns, "ask him to dine here again to-morrow, and be sure you are present and draw it yourself." '

Whatever version of Cannon's reply to Sir Henry Halford reached the King, and however much at first he may have been disposed to resent the rejection of his advances, the offender was nevertheless again forgiven and without being forgotten. One circumstance certainly deserves to be mentioned as tending, in its degree, to invalidate those charges of selfishness and want of feeling which have been so lavishly directed against the best abused of all earthly monarchs.

Many years afterwards, when Cannon, who, though of inexpensive tastes, was utterly regardless of money and almost ignorant of its value, and who generally carried all he received loose in his waistcoat pocket, giving it away to any one who seemed to need it, was himself severely suffering from the effects of ill-health and improvident liberality, the King, who accidentally heard of his melancholy condition, instantly made enquiries with a view of presenting him with some piece of preferment that might have served as a permanent provision; but ascertaining that his habits had become such as to render any advancement in the clerical profession inexpedient, he, entirely unsolicited, sent his old favourite a cheque for a hundred pounds.

This assistance proved most opportune and served to supply immediate necessities. Cannon was staying at the time at a small hotel on the banks of the Thames, near Twickenham, from which he was unable, or rather unwilling to depart, till his bill which had swollen to a somewhat formidable size was discharged. Mr. Barham, therefore, and another friend hastened down to release him from a position which most people would have deemed embarrassing in the extreme. They found him, however, perfectly happy in his retirement; clothed from head to foot in mine host's habiliments, and, altogether, appearing so much better in health and spirits than could have been anticipated, that Mr. Barham was led to address some compliment to the landlady on the good looks of her guest.

'Well, sir, to be sure,' replied that worthy personage, 'we have done our best to keep him tidy and comfortable, and if you had only seen him last Sunday, when he was *washed and shaved*, you really might have said he *was* looking well.'

He had formed, it appeared, a close intimacy with a monkey belonging to the establishment, and spent the principal portion of his time in its society, exchanging it occasionally for that of adventurous bipeds whom the steam-boats, then 'few and far between,' landed at the

Eyot, according as he found them more or less intelligent than his quadrupedal companion.

Like his friend, Cannon was one of those who gave full assent to the poet's doctrine,

> ' The best of all ways
>   To lengthen our days
>   Is to steal a few hours from night,' &c.

And so resolutely did he carry it out in practice when the opportunity offered, as at times to cause no little inconvenience to his entertainers. After a dinner, for example, given by Mr. Stephen Price of Drury Lane Theatre, all the guests, with the exception of Cannon and Theodore Hook, having long since retired, the host, who was suffering from an incipient attack of gout, was compelled to allude pretty plainly to the lateness of the hour. No notice, however, was taken of the hint, and, unable to endure any longer the pain of sitting up, Mr. Price made some excuse and slipped quietly off to bed. On the following morning he enquired of his servant—

' Pray, at what time did those gentlemen go last night?'

' Go, sir ! ' replied John ; ' they are not gone, sir : they have just rung for coffee ! '

It was not to be supposed that these eccentricities could altogether escape episcopal observation, and although they met with considerable indulgence, a rebuke was sometimes unavoidable. Cannon, however, resented the slightest attempt at interference with a warmth and jealousy, ill-advised, to say the least of it. His hostility indeed to his diocesan, Dr. Blomfield, was not altogether to be attributed to private feeling; and certainly it could not have been warranted by any treatment experienced at his hands. Many, however, of the bitter satires that appeared in the periodicals, directed against certain proceedings of this eminent individual, were from Cannon's pen. More than one of the more powerful and more personal of these Mr. Barham was fortunate enough to save from publication. He borrowed the copy, and that once in his possession, he knew that Cannon was too indolent a man either to write another, or to persevere in demanding the restoration of the original. Those, however, who have read the *Dives and Lazarus,* and *Lines written on the exclusion of ill-dressed persons from seats in the Chapel Royal,* though they can scarcely fail to admit that nothing produced by Byron or Churchill excelled them in pungency, will, nevertheless, consider their suppression justifiable even by an act of friendly felony.

That much of this caustic spirit sprang from blighted prospects, and was nurtured by the frequent supplies of his favourite 'ginnums and water,' there can be little doubt; his natural disposition was most amiable, and the kindness of his heart, and his complete freedom from selfishness in matters of importance, exhibited themselves in numberless instances, and never more conspicuously than in a case of self-denial which graced his declining days. He was summoned to the bedside of an old and valued friend; the lady (for a lady it was—like his 'double,' *Godfrey Moss,* he had been a lady-killer in his time) announced to him that believing her health to be rapidly giving way she had made her will, by which, at her demise, the whole of a considerable fortune was to be placed at his disposal.   Cannon looked at her doubtfully:

' I don't believe it ! ' he said, at length.

The lady assured him that she was incapable of trifling on such a subject, and at such a moment ; and added, that the document itself was lying in an escritoire in the room.

' I won't believe it,' persisted the other, ' unless I see it.'

Smiling at such incredulity, the lady placed the will in his hands.   Cannon took it, and read it.

' Well,' said he, ' if I had not seen it in your own hand-writing, I would not have believed you could have been such an unnatural brute ;' and he deliberately thrust the paper between the bars of the grate.

' What,' he continued, ' have you no one more nearly connected with you than I am, to leave your money to ? No one who has better reason to expect to be your heir, and who has a right to be provided for first and best ? Pooh! you don't know how to make a will.   I must send Dance, a very respectable man in his way, red tape and parchment and all that—he shall make your will; you may leave me a legacy, there's no harm in that.   I am a poor man, and want it; but I am not a-going to be d—— to please you.'

A new will was accordingly drawn up on Cannon's sug-gestion, bequeathing to him merely a sum of four thousand pounds.   It will scarcely be credited that advantage was afterwards taken of a technical informality (in ignorance, it is to be hoped, of previous circumstances) to resist his claim even to this. It appeared that two copies of the will were executed; one of which was retained in the custody of the testatrix, while the other was handed over to the care of a trustee. After a time, however, the lady sent for the duplicate, which was returned to her; and on her death the two documents were found in a drawer folded up together. From one every name except Cannon's had been snipped out with a pair of scissors; the other remained intact. Upon this it was contended that by mutilating one copy the testatrix had cancelled both; and a precedent was alleged to be found in the case of a gentleman who, taking with him to India one copy of his will, which he subsequently destroyed, left another in the charge of his solicitor at home. This on being produced was pronounced void in virtue of the cancelling of its fellow. It was urged in answer, that the precedent did not apply, inasmuch as in the latter case the gentleman had revoked and destroyed the only instrument which was within his power, whereas in the former, both papers being in the hands of the testatrix, there was nothing to prevent her destroying both if she wished to make the revocation complete; from her omitting to do so it was to be inferred that she repented of the change she had begun to make, and so reclaimed the uninjured copy of the will, to which she determined to adhere. After the delay of more than a year a decision was given in Cannon's favour, and the remainder of his life relieved from further apprehension on the score of pecuniary distress. He withdrew, shortly afterwards, to Ryde, in the Isle of Wight, taking his accustomed seat on the pier, with a pertinacity that gained

for him among the boatmen the sobriquet of the 'Pier
Gun.' Want of exercise, and the slow poison he became
a slave to, at length did their work. Like Swift—to
whom, in the general structure of his mind, in the power
of his reasoning, and in the peculiar bent of his humour,
he bore no little resemblance—his last hours were such as
might well have aroused

> ' The bitter pangs of humbled genius,'

they were those of one,

> ' Marked above the rest,
> For qualities most dear, plunged from that height,
> And sunk, deep sunk, in second childhood's night.

He died forgotten, and almost alone; and it was left for
a comparative stranger to raise the simple tablet that
pleads for the memory of Edward Cannon.

The acceptance of the living of St. Gregory involved
the necessity of a residence within the city walls, and to
this Mr. Barham very reluctantly yielded. It is true that
he might have claimed exemption on the ground of non-
suitability of the parsonage, but he found it impossible to
work the parish satisfactorily from a distance, and so, not
without misgiving, he pitched upon a house in St. Paul's
Churchyard adjoining the entrance to Doctor's Commons
and the Deanery. Here, in the constant hope of effecting
a change of preferment which would enable him to reside
a certain number of months in the country, he spent
about eighteen years of his life. Nor as regards his own
health had he any reason to complain, but the confine-
ment inseparable from such a situation told injuriously

upon that of his children. He had been established but a very short time in his new abode when he was visited by the first of a series of domestic afflictions, which proved the only troubled passages in a course, otherwise, fair and uniform. Devoted, too fondly perhaps, to his family, he felt most keenly the chastening of that hand which withdrew from him, at intervals, five of his little ones. For a time he was unmanned and prostrated by the blow ; the natural elasticity, however, of his mind, aided by that faith which bids us ' not sorrow as men without hope,' rapidly restored him to a cheerfulness not more constitutional, than the result of a thankful appreciation of the many blessings he was still permitted to enjoy. In the year 1825 he lost his eldest daughter, after a lingering disease, which from the first rendered recovery not only hopeless, but almost to be deprecated. Her constitution had received a severe shock from an accident which befell her at Warehorn. Purer air and plenty of exercise might have given her strength to outgrow the hurt. But it was not to be ; she was the first to succumb. The following lines, which appeared shortly after in *Blackwood's Magazine*, bear reference to that event :

ON THE DEATH OF A DAUGHTER.

'Tis o'er—in that long sigh she past—
The enfranchised spirit soars at last !

And now I gaze with tearless eye,
On what to view was agony.

That panting heart is tranquil now,
And heavenly calm that ruffled brow;
And those pale lips, which feebly strove
To force one parting smile of love,
Retain it yet—soft, placid, mild,
As when it graced my living child.

Oh! I have watched with fondest care
    To see my opening floweret blow,
And felt the joy which parents share,
    The pride which fathers only know.

And I have sat the long, long night,
    And marked that tender flower decay,
Not torn abruptly from the sight,
    But slowly, sadly, waste away.

The spoiler came, yet paused, as though
    So meek a victim checked his arm,
Half gave and half withheld the blow,
    As forced to strike, yet loth to harm.

We saw that fair cheek's fading bloom
The ceaseless canker-worm consume,
    And gazed on hopelessly;
Till the mute suffering pictured there
Wrung from a father's lip a prayer—
    Oh God! the prayer his child might die!
Ay, from his lip—the rebel heart
E'en then refused to bear its part.

But the sad conflict's past—'tis o'er;
That gentle bosom throbs no more!
The spirit's freed;—through realms of light
Faith's eagle glance pursues her flight
To other worlds, to happier skies—
Hope dries the tear which sorrow weepeth;
No mortal sound the voice which cries,
' The damsel is not dead, but sleepeth.'

CHAPTER III.

[1826–1828.]

Diary—Theatrical anecdotes—'Hot, Sir, Hot'—'Stolen or Strayed!'—
Cannon's snuff-box—Suicide of Mr. F——.—An amateur of Hanging—
Anecdote of Dignum—Introduction to Blackwood's Magazine—Anec-
dote by Sir Walter Scott—The Chalybeate—Excursion to Twicken-
ham—The two Geese—Death of Colonel Dalton—Epigram by Luttrel
—A Moravian Hymn—' Too Late '—The Duchess of St. Albans—
Theodore Hook—Mock Prologue and Epilogue—The Berners Street
Hoax—Hook's mock Burletta—Hook and Ingoldsby—Tom Hill—The
American Sea-Serpent—A paradox—Charades—Mr. Graham—Young
Norval—Cannon and Hook—Anecdote of Professor Wilson—The Literary
Fund—The Abbé Bertin—The original of Gervase Skinner—Hook and
Mr. H. Higginson—Hoax—Capt. Rock's Letters to the King—' The
Bride of Lammermoor '—' Meg Dodds '—Hook at Lord Melville's Trial—
' Martha the Gipsy'—The Villiers Ghost Story.

IN the course of the year 1826, Mr. Barham, in place
of the miscellaneous and unconnected notes he was wont
to throw together in any memorandum book that came to
hand, commenced a diary, which for some time was continued with considerable spirit and regularity; it is to be
regretted that it was not carried through with equal
diligence, the rather that the *hiatus* occur the more frequently, and are of wider extent, during that portion of
his life which was spent in constant and intimate intercourse with eminent men of whom every record is valuable. I shall avail myself of such passages in his journal
as may seem to bear a general interest, without trespass-

ing, it is to be hoped, in the slightest degree upon that social confidence, which every man is bound in common honesty to preserve inviolate.

'*Diary, July* 26, 1826.—Dined with Lord William Lennox. Mr. Fawcett of Covent-garden told a story of an old woman and her daughter in a provincial town in Yorkshire.

' " Mither," says the girl, " there do go Mr. Irby agen."

' " Ees, bairn, he be g'ween to ploy-house, I do suppose."

' " Mither, what do Mr. Irby do at ploy-house ? Him be never on steage ?"

' " Nay, girl, him be prompter."

' " What be prompter, Mither ?"

' " Why prompter, bairn, be mon wid book, and when all be fast on steage, he *lowses* 'em."

' He also gave us an anecdote of Cooper of C. G. T., when on a provincial tour. The prompter of the company was a drunken, one-eyed fellow, who, having been born at Kidderminster, was generally known at the theatre by the name of " Kiddy." From frequent attacks of rheumatic gout, he had become crippled in both his hands, and as the porter pot was never absent, was compelled to support it by applying the knuckles of both his clenched fists in order to get it to his mouth. One evening, during the performance of a new play, all the *dramatis personæ* on the stage came to a stand-still. " Kiddy " was loudly called on for the cue, but having been immersed for some minutes past, as usual, in contemplating the interior of his flagon, he had lost the place, and embarrassed at the same time with the mug, he cried out to the "call-boy," in a tone of voice which was heard, and caused no slight amusement in the stage boxes,

' "Little boy, little boy, come here and hold de pot, while I sees where these thieves be."

'Cannon, who was present, and in most entertaining mood, told, among other things, his story of a general officer who, having passed many years of his life in India, was taken by a friend, on his return, to dine with some common relation. All parties being anxious to conciliate the nabob, who was rich, old, and a bachelor, every attention was shown him during dinner-time. The General, however, either from paucity of ideas, or from his regards being riveted upon the good things before him, was invincibly taciturn.

' "Pray, General," said a female cousin on his left, " how did you like India ?"

" ' Hot, ma'am," said the commander, scarcely raising his eyes from his basin of mulligatawney, " Hot, very hot !"

'Another pause ensued, which was broken by her brother on his right :

' "General, we have heard much in England lately of the increase of Suttees in India ; may I ask if the burning of a Hindoo widow ever came under your personal notice ?"

' "Widow !—burning !— Oh, ay, it was very hot, sir, devilish hot, never so hot in my life !"

'An excellent curry had now engaged his attention, when the General was again addressed by a tall, thin, antiquarian-looking personage, from the lower end of the table,

' " Pray, General, during the many years you spent in Asia, did duty or inclination ever carry you into the neighbourhood of the celebrated caves of Elephanta ? "

' " Elephanta ! Oh, ah, Elephanta—the caves—of course. Why, sir, it was very hot, devilish hot; hot all the time I was there ; never was so hot in my life ; sir, it was as hot as H—— ! "

' This climax, delivered with the only spark of energy which the worthy officer had as yet exhibited, completely precluded any further attempt to engage him in conversation, and the observant veteran was permitted to relapse into silence ; several of the party, however, declaring the next morning that they had derived much pleasure from their relation the General's interesting description of the state of our Oriental empire.

' Repeated as much as I could recollect of the handbill respecting Cannon. The latter having gone off into the Isle of Wight with Vaughan, last Lent, without making any arrangement for the performance of his duty at St. George's, Hanover-square, a placard was, a few mornings after his arrival, affixed nearly opposite his window at the " Bugle Horn " Hotel, near the bottom of Ryde pier, to the following effect :—

' " STOLEN OR STRAYED !

' " A stout black horse, of the punch breed. Face tan, with a brown mark under the nostrils, coat rough, with brown spots, aged, but has the teeth of a young one. Fore-feet blacker than the hind. Is a little hard in the mouth, but gentle, having been ridden by a lady ; goes a little lame on one leg, from having been ill-driven in a buggy, and *shies at a Church bell*; supposed to have been carried off in Passion-week, by some itinerant musicians, who have been traced into Hampshire. Whoever will give information, &c." '

The brown mark under the nostrils, and the blackness of the fore-feet mentioned in the description, are allusions to the enormous quantity of snuff which Cannon was in the habit, partly of taking, and partly of scattering right and left over shirt, waistcoat, table, chair, carpet—everything that he approached. Once, at the Chapel Royal he set the Bishop of London sneezing through the whole of the Communion Service, and afterwards when the Bishop remonstrated with him on having produced an old, coloured, cotton handkerchief during the prayers, he merely asked in reply—' Pray, does your Lordship take snuff?'

'Not if I can help it, Mr. Cannon.'

' Ah, then, I do, my lord, a good deal.'

His friend, John Wilson Croker, gave him, in lieu of the fourpenny box which he commonly used, a very handsome substitute having a gold cannon on the lid, and as a motto—' *Non sine pulvere.*'

'*July* 28.—Went with Hawes to the rehearsal of Winter's "Das Unterbrochene Opferfest," translated by young Arnold, and to be brought out under the title of *The Oracle, or the Interrupted Sacrifice.* Met Cannon there ; was introduced by him to Banim, the author of *Tales of the O'Hara Family, The Boyne Water,* &c., and since, of adaptations of two stories from the former

novel to the stage, under the names of the *Last Guerilla*
and the *Death Fetch*. Heard from him a more detailed account of the suicide of poor young F—, the
artist, at whose apartments I had some little time since
seen Miss M. Tree, now Mrs. Bradshaw, sitting for her
picture. F— was said to have been the natural son of a
nobleman, and was much patronised by Mr. Croker of the
Admiralty. His pecuniary resources were more than ade-
quate to his wants, his spirits apparently good, and, in the
language of the newspapers, "no cause could be assigned
for the rash action." It seems, however, that a few of his
more intimate friends had observed something very like
aberration of mind as long ago as Easter, and from ex-
pressions which he had let fall, it is probable that an
unrequited affection had pressed strongly upon him,
which the marriage of the lady had brought to a crisis.
He left his lodgings in the morning, nor could any part
of his progress be traced till the same evening, when,
about nine o'clock, he entered a hotel at the West End of
the town (the Salopian coffee-house, Charing Cross), and
went to bed. From the state in which his candle was
found, he did not appear to have perpetrated the deed
which he meditated till about two in the morning, when
he blew out his brains with a horse pistol. The fellow to
the instrument he had used, was found lying loaded by
his side.

'*August* 10.—Preached at St. Martin's, Ludgate, to the
Stationers Company, and dined with them afterwards at
their annual livery dinner, Mr. Marsh of Canterbury,
brother to the Bishop of Peterborough, taking the chair

as Master. Mr. B——, the noted amateur of hanging, was present, the guest of his brother, who is a member of the court. Marsh informed me that on a former occasion of a similar description to the present, this gentleman, who was pledged to attend an execution on the following morning, got so sublimely elevated that he was obliged to be carried home, and put to bed by his friends, and that, to his lasting regret, he did not awake till the possibility of keeping his engagement was past.

'*August* 15.—Dined with the Girdlers' Company at their Hall, after preaching to them at St. Michael Bassishaw, Mr. Taylor in the chair. Among the professional singers on the occasion was poor old Dignum. Anecdote told of him which I first heard from Nield, the lay vicar of St. Paul's. Dignum, it seems, was complaining one morning to old Knyvett, the King's composer, that his health was much impaired, and what was very extraordinary, that so strong a degree of sympathy existed between him and his brother, that one was no sooner taken ill than the other felt symptoms of the same indisposition, whatever it might be. " We are both of us very unwell now," added Dignum, "and as our complaint is supposed to be an affection of the lungs, we are ordered to take asses milk, but unfortunately we have not been able to get any, though we have tried all over London; can you tell us what we had better do ? "

' " Do ? " answered Knyvett, " Why the deuce don't you suck one another ! "

'*August* 16.—Received a letter from Blackwood, with a copy of Nos. cxv. and cxvi. of his Magazine, thanking me for *The Ghost, a Canterbury Tale,* which appeared in the first of the two numbers, and which Mr. John Hughes (son of our Residentiary), had transmitted to him from me, informing him, at the same time, of the fact of its having appeared in sections, in three successive numbers of the *London Chronicle,* just before that paper was merged in the *St. James's Chronicle.* Of this journal Dr. Johnson was the first editor, and I the last. The causes of its decline may be inferred. Colonel Torrens the proprietor, sold it to Mr. C. Baldwin for 300*l.* He also enclosed a copy of the Poems of my old College acquaintance, Professor Wilson.

'*November* 26.—Dined at Doctor Hughes's. Sir Walter Scott had been there the day before ; and the Doctor told me the following anecdote, which he had just heard from the " Great Unknown.' A Scottish clergyman, whose name was not mentioned, had some years since been cited before the Ecclesiastical Assembly at Edinburgh, to answer to a charge brought against him of great irreverence in religious matters, and Sir Walter was employed by him to arrange his defence. The principal fact alleged against him was his having asserted, in a letter which was produced, that "he considered Pontius Pilate to be a very ill-used man, as he had done more for Christianity than all the *other nine apostles* put together." The fact was proved, and suspension followed.

'*December* 3.—Dined for the first time with Dr. Sumner, Bishop of Llandaff, who told me as a fact that Dr. R——, a fellow of Eton, had some time since ordered one of his ponds to be cleaned out. A great number of carp, tench, eels, &c., were taken in the course of the operation. The Doctor was at dinner with some friends who had been viewing the work, when a servant came in to inform him that in draining off the water the men had found a chalybeate, "Have they indeed?" cried he with much interest, "I am very glad to hear it. Tell them to put it along with the other fish for the present."

'1827. *May* 18.—Harry Sandford (of the Treasury), Cannon, Tom Hill, Sir Andrew Barnard, and myself, went up to Twickenham by the steamboat. On the way we talked all sorts of nonsense, and laughed at everything, and everybody. A queer-looking old gentleman served especially to amuse Sandford, who took a delight in quizzing him.

'"What is this bridge we're coming to?" asked the old gentleman of the skipper.

'"Kew, Sir," returned the man.

'"How dare you insult a respectable individual," cried Sandford, "by insinuating that he is a *Kew comer?*"

'One of the company asserting that he had seen a pike caught, which weighed thirty-six pounds, and was four feet in length.

'"Had it been a sole," said Harry, "it would have surprised me less, as Shakespeare tells us,

'"All the *souls* that are, were *four feet* (forfeit) once."

'On Hill's remarking on the number of publicans who had put up the Duke of Wellington's head over their doors, Sandford said, "Yes, let his grace's death come when, and how it may, you will never be able to say of him as King Henry does of Cardinal Beaufort,

> " ' He dies and makes no sign ! ' "

'September 1.—Lord William Lennox and Mr. George Hill (of the Blues) met Dick and myself at Parrock House, where we slept last night. Went out shooting this morning, killing eleven brace and a half of partridges ; dined at two, and returned at four by the steamboat. On the voyage we had our profiles taken by an artist on board for a shilling a head, which he executed in ten seconds by the help of a pair of scissors only. An old woman on board told some of her friends who were very merry that, while she was at Margate in the course of the summer, the friend at whose house she had been staying had gone into the market for the purpose of purchasing a goose. There were but two in the whole place, offered for sale by a girl of fourteen, who refused to part with one without the other, assigning no other reason for her obstinacy than that it was her mother's order. Not wishing for two geese, the lady at first declined the purchase, but at last finding no other was to be had, and recollecting that a neighbour might be prevailed upon to take one off her hands, she concluded the bargain. Having paid for and secured the pair, she asked the girl at parting if she knew her mother's reason for the directions she had given. " O yes ! mistress," answered the young poultry-merchant readily, "mother said that they had lived together *eleven years,* and it would be a sin and a shame to part them now!"'

By the death, in 1827, of Thomas Dalton, Colonel of

the West Kent Regiment of militia, his wife's uncle, Mr. Barham, who was left an executor and trustee, entered upon the administration of an estate considerable in value, and so fenced about with precautions that the provisions of the will remain up to this time (1870) unfulfilled, and the accounts unclosed. Among the matters demanding immediate attention was the home farm, which had been kept in hand under the care of a bailiff. Hence the visit to Parrock House mentioned in the foregoing entry.[1]

'*September* 20.—Walpole, Lord William, and Cannon dined here. Cannon repeated Luttrel's epigram on the illness of the King when Regent:—

> " The Regent, Sir, is taken ill,
> And all depends on Halford's skill.
> ' Pray what,' inquired the sage physician,
> ' Has brought him to this sad condition ? '

---

[1] During the absence of the Colonel from England, the preservation of the game on the estate had been entrusted to a most respectable farmer named Fothergill. He was an exceedingly eager sportsman, and what is commonly called a bit of a character. Some of his peculiarities are hit off in a parody upon a song, then all the fashion, which was jotted down during the return to London in the steamboat. The first verse is nearly all that is legible:—

> ' I'd be a Fothergill just turn'd of twenty,
>   In corduroy smalls and a velveteen vest,
> Roaming wherever the game is most plenty,
>   Claiming all birds that are wing'd by the rest,
> I'm not " tenashus " of smart detonators!
>   I should say flint and steel locks are the best,
> I'd be a Fothergill knee deep in " taturs,"
>   Claiming all birds that are shot by the rest!
>   I'd be a Fothergill,
>   I'd be a Fothergill,
> Claiming all birds that are shot by the rest,' &c.

When Bloomfield ventured to pronounce,
' A little too much Cherry Bounce.'
The Regent hearing what was said,
Raised from the couch his aching head,
And cried ' No, Halford, 'tis not so !
Cure us, O Doctor,—*Curaçoa !* ' "

' He then sat down to the piano, sang *The Bishop of Hereford*,[1] and finished by improvising half a dozen stanzas of what he called a Moravian hymn. The party afterwards went to the English Opera-house.' The stanzas are doubtless the following, which are entered elsewhere under the name of—

A MORAVIAN HYMN.

(By Cannon.)

There were two boys in ou-ur town,
　But born of different mothers ;
The Deuce-a-bit was one boy's name
　And *Oh-dear-me* the other's !

These two boys went into the field
　The old grey mare to find ;
The Deuce-a-bit got up before,
　And *Oh-dear-me* behind !

The Deuce-a-bit and *Oh-dear-me*
　Rode on to take the air ;
Their company did not agree
　With her—that old grey mare !

[1] *Robin Hood and the Bishop of Hereford* was Cannon's favourite ballad. He sang it with exquisite sweetness, to the tune afterwards borrowed by Hook for his song, *The Old Maid.*

> The old grey mare was lame and blind,
>   She kicked and reared full sore !
> *The Deuce-a-bit* fell off behind,
>   And *Oh-dear-me* before !
>
> Ye little boys, then, well beware !
>   And think what may betide !
> Nor mount upon an old grey mare
>   Till you have learned to ride !

' *October* 6.—Mr. Attwood, who had set to music my lines entitled *Too Late*, and published them in *The Harmonicon* last year, gave me to-day some verses, written, on perusing them by a lady, a friend of his.'

The song in question was elicited by an expression in a letter, from a dear and near relative. He was in the army, and had struggled on, many a weary year, unnoticed and a subaltern, happy, however, in the cheering companionship of an affectionate wife. At length the partner of his toils and hopes sank by the way, and was taken from him ; then, in quick succession, came wealth, honours, promotion ! But they had been ' delayed till he was indifferent, and did not care for them ; till he was solitary and could not impart them ; till he was (old) and did not want them.' In his own words it was—

TOO LATE.

Too late ! though flow'rets round me blow,
    And clearing skies shine bright and fair ;
Their genial warmth avails not now—
    Thou art not here the beam to share.

Thro' many a dark and dreary day,
 We journey'd on 'midst grief and gloom ;
And now at length the cheering ray
 Breaks forth, it only gilds thy tomb.

Our days of hope and youth are past,
 Our short-lived joys for ever flown ;
And now when Fortune smiles at last,
 She finds me cheerless, chilled—alone !

Ah ! no ; too late the boon is given,
 Alike the frowns and smiles of Fate ;
The broken heart, by sorrow riv'n,
 But murmurs now, ' Too late ! Too late ! '

STANZAS

ON READING THE ABOVE.

There came upon the sadness of my soul
 A strain of sorrow,
Sounding sweet Hope's death-toll,
 That has no morrow !
A voice it was that told how loveliest things
 Of earth and air
From her young grave upraise their wings,
 Or perish there !
That said how swiftly the immortal sprite
 Heaven sends below,
From Love's lorn heart must vanish quite,
 Or turn to woe !

Sweet song! I laud thee with a mourner's praise!
Thy voice spake true :
Woe shadows Earth! Joy's sunny rays
Are brief and few !

' *October* 28.—Dined at Dr. Hughes's. He read, from a letter of Southey, the Laureate, a humorous account of his first introduction to the Duchess of St. Albans, *ci-devant* Miss Mellon, alias Mrs. Coutts :—" I begin to think with Sir William Curtis that wonders will never have done ceasing. Here have I been hooked into an acquaintance with a duchess, and partaken of potatoe-pie of her grace's own making ! I could tell you much of her bonnet, which our vicar has already compared to a banyan-tree. I could say much of her lip, which would seem to bespeak her a Nazarite from her mother's womb," &c. This led the conversation to her grace's habits and manners, when it was mentioned that, while an actress, Miss Mellon was the terror of the green-room from her violence, and that on one occasion, having taken offence at something said about her by Horace Twiss, she went up to Mrs. Henry Siddons, while sitting on a sofa, and addressed her, to her no small consternation, " Madam, you may tell that rascal of a Twiss that the first time I meet him in a room I will shave his head with a poker !" '

About this time Mr. Barham found opportunities of renewing his acquaintance with one who, in many respects, was to be ranked among the most extraordinary men of his age—Mr. Theodore Hook. To say nothing of this gentleman's unequalled happiness in impromptu versification, conveying, as he not unfrequently did, a perfect epigram in every stanza—a talent, by the way, which sundry rivals have affected to consider mere knack, and one of whom long bore in his side the *lethalis arundo* of James Smith, for his bungling effort at imitation ; to pass by those practical jokes with which his name is so commonly associated, and in the devising and perpetration of which he was *facile princeps*, Mr. Hook possessed depth and originality of mind, little dreamed of, probably, by those who were content to bask in the sunshine of his wit, and to gaze with wonder at the superficial talents which he exhibited at table, but sufficient, nevertheless, to place him far beyond the position of a mere sayer of good things, or ' diner-out of the first water.' To those indeed who have never been fortunate enough to witness those extraordinary displays, no description can convey even a faint idea of the brilliancy of his conversational powers, of the inexhaustible prodigality with which he showered around puns, bon mots, apt quotations, and every variety of anecdote ; throwing life and humour into all by the exquisite adaptation of eye, tone, and gesture to his subject. His writings, admirable as they are, fail to impress one in any way commensurate with his society.

Of the few sketches of him that have been given in works of fiction, not one can claim the merit of being more than a most shadowy resemblance. It needs a graphic skill surpassing his own to draw his portrait with any approach to correctness. Nowhere, perhaps, is failure more conspicuous than in the miserable and meagre attempt in *Coningsby.* Not the faintest glow of humour, not one flash of wit, not an ebullition of merriment breaks forth from first to last; the author, apparently in utter incapacity for the task, contents himself with simply observing, 'Here *Mr. Lucian Gay* (the name under which Hook is introduced) was vastly amusing,' 'there he made the table roar,' &c., much in the manner of the provident artist, who, to obviate mistake, affixed the notice to his painting—'This is the lion—this is the dog!' Of the moral portraiture I will venture to say that it is as unjust as the intellectual is weak. As regards the great calamity —the defalcation at the Mauritius—which befell him in his youth, and which darkened the remainder of his career, shutting out hope, paralysing his best energies, and by consequence inducing much of that recklessness of living which served to embitter his privacy and hasten his end, it may almost be unnecessary to say, that one who continued to regard him with the feelings of affection which Mr. Barham entertained to the last, must have had full reason for believing him free from every imputation save that of carelessness, not wholly inexcusable in one so young, so inexperienced, and so constitutionally light-hearted.

Of what appears to have been his first interview with his old companion after their separation at college, my father gives a somewhat detailed account :—

'*November* 6.—Passed one of the pleasantest evenings I ever spent at Lord William Lennox's. The company, besides the host and hostess, consisted of Mr. Cannon, Mr. C. Walpole, Mr. Hill, generally known as "Tom Hill," Theodore Hook, and myself. It was Hook's first visit there, and none of the party but myself, Cannon, and Hill, who were old friends of his, had ever seen him before. While at dinner, he began to be excessively amusing. The subject of conversation was an absurdly bombastic prologue, which had been given to Cooper of D. L. T., to get by heart, as a hoax, beginning :—

> When first the Drama's muse, by Freedom reared,
> In Grecian splendour unadorn'd appeared,
> Her eagle glance, high poised in buoyant hope
> O'er realms restricted by no partial scope,
> Saw one vast desert horrify the scene ;
> No bright oasis showed its mingling green,
> But all around, in colours darkly rude,
> Scowled forth the intellectual solitude !
> And vain her art till Time's translucent tide,
> Like some sweet stream that scarcely seems to glide,
> The heaven-engendered embers fanned to flame,
> The ray burst forth ! Immortal Shakespeare came !
> 'Twas his with renovated warmth to glow,
> To feel that fire within ' that passeth show,'
> And nobly daring in a dastard age
> To raise, reform, and dignify the stage !
> To force from lids unsullied by a tear
> The pensive drops that bathe fond Juliet's bier,
> Bow the duped Moor o'er Desdemona's corse,
> Or bid the blood-stained tyrant cry " A horse ! "
> Waft the rapt soul with more than seraph flight
> From fair Italia's realms of soft delight,
> To mourn with Imogen her murdered lord,
> Or bare the patriot stoic's vengeful sword,
> To raise the poet's noblest cry " Be free ! "
> To breathe the tocsin blast of " Liberty ! " &c.

'Gattie, whose vanity is proverbial, was included in the joke. Wallack, the stage-manager, who had the arranging it, produced some equally ridiculous lines, which he said Poole, the author of the new comedy (*The Wealthy Widow*), had written for him, but that he had not sufficient nerve to deliver them.

' " No man on the stage has such nerve as I," interrupted Gattie.

' " Then it must be spoken in five characters ; the dresses to be thrown off one after the other."

' "No performer can change his dress so quickly as I can," quoth Gattie.

' " Then I am afraid of the French dialect and the Irish brogue."

' " I'm the only Frenchman and Irishman on the stage," roared Gattie.

'The hoax was complete, and poor Gattie sat up the whole night to learn the epilogue ; went through three rehearsals with 'five dresses on, one over the other, as a Lady, a Dutchman, a Highlander, a Teague, and lastly as "Monsieur Tonson come again." All sorts of impediments were thrown in his way, such as sticking his breeches to his kilt, &c. The time at length arrived, when the stage-manager informed him with a long face, that Colman, the licenser, instigated no doubt by Mathews who trembled for his reputation, had refused to license the epilogue ; and poor Gattie, after waiting during the whole of the interlude in hopes that the licence might yet come down, was obliged to retire most reluctantly and disrobe.

'Hook took occasion from this story to repeat part of a

prologue which he once spoke as an amateur before a country audience, without one word being intelligible from the beginning to the end. He afterwards preached part of a sermon in the style of the Rev. Mr. Fisher, of Norwich, of whom he gave a very humorous account. Not one sentence of the harangue could be understood, and yet you could not help, all through, straining your attention to catch the meaning. He then gave us many absurd particulars of the Berners-street hoax, which he admitted was contrived by himself and Henry H——, who was formerly contemporary with me at Brasenose and whom I knew there, now a popular preacher at Poplar. He also mentioned another of a similar character, but previous in point of time, of which he had been the sole originator. The object of it was a Mr. William Griffiths, a Quaker who lived in Henrietta Street, Covent Garden. Among other things brought to his house were the dresses of a Punch and nine blue devils, and the body of a man from Lambeth bone-house, who had the day before been found drowned in the Thames.

'In the evening, after Lady William had sung *I've been roaming,* Hook placed himself at the pianoforte, and gave a most extraordinary display of his powers both as a musician and an improvisatore. His assumed object was to give a specimen of the burlettas formerly produced at Sadler's Wells, and he went through the whole of one which he composed upon the spot. He commenced with the tuning of the instruments, the prompter's bell, the rapping of the fiddle-stick by the leader of the band, and the overture, till, the curtain being supposed to rise, he proceeded to describe—

'The first scene.—A country village—cottage (o. p.)—church (p. s.)—large tree near wing—bridge over a river occupying the centre of the back-ground. *Music.*—Little men in red coats seen riding over bridge. *Enter* Gaffer from cottage, to the symphony usually played on introducing old folks on such occasions. Gaffer, in recitative, intimates that he is aware that the purpose of the Squire in thus early

   —— 'a crossing over the water,
 Is to hunt, not the stag, but my lovely daughter.

Sings a song and retires, to observe Squire's motions, expressing a determination to baulk his intentions;

 'For a peasant 's a man, and a Squire 's no more,
 And a father has feelings, though never so poor.

'*Enter* Squire with his train.—Grand chorus of huntsmen—"Merry-toned horn—Blythe is the morn—Hark, forward, away!— Glorious Day," " Bright Phœbus," "Aurora," &c. &c.

'The Squire dismisses all save his confidant, to whom, in recitative, he avows his design of carrying off the old man's daughter, then sings under her window. The casement up one pair of stairs opens. Susan appears at it, and sings—asking whether the voice which has been serenading her is that of her

 'True blue William, who, on the seas,
 Is blown about by every breeze ?

'The Squire hiding behind the tree, she descends to satisfy herself ; is accosted by him, and refuses his offer ; he attempts force. The old man interferes, lectures the Squire, locks up his daughter, and *exit* (p.s.). Squire sings a song expressive of rage and his determination to obtain the girl, and *exit* (P.S.).

' *Whistle*—Scene changes with a slap.—Public-house door; sailors carousing, with long pig-tails, checked shirts, glazed hats, and blue trousers. *Chorus*—"Jolly tars— Plough the main—Kiss the girls—Sea again." William, in recitative, states that he has been " With brave Rodney," and has got " gold galore ;" tells his messmates he has heard a land-lubber means to run away with his sweetheart, and asks their assistance. They promise it :—

> ' Tip us your fin ! We'll stick t'ye, my hearty,
> And beat him ! Hav'n't we beat Boneyparty ?

Solo, by William, " Girl of my heart — Never part." *Chorus* of sailors—" Shiver my timbers," " Smoke and fire —D—n the Squire," &c. &c. (*Whistle*—scene closes— slap.)

' Scene—the village as before. Enter Squire; reconnoitres in recitative ; beckons on Gipsies, headed by confidant in red. *Chorus* of Gipsies entering — " Hark ? hark ? — Butchers' dogs bark !—Bow, wow, wow — Not now, not now." " Silence, hush !—Behind the bush-- Hush ! hush ! hush !"—" Bow, wow, wow."—" Hush ! hush ! —Bow, wow."—" Hush ! hush ! hush ! " *Enter* Susan from cottage. *Recitative*—

> ' What can keep father so long at market ?
> The sun has set, altho' its not quite dark yet.
>> —Butter and eggs,
>> —Weary legs.

'Gipsies rush on and seize her; she screams; Squire comes forward. *Recitative Affettuoso* — She scornful, imploring, furious, frightened! Squire offers to seize her; True Blue rushes down and interposes; Music *agitato*; Sailors in pig-tails beat off gipsies; Confidant runs up the tree; True Blue collars Squire. *Enter* Gaffer:—

> 'Hey-day! what's all this clatter;
> William ashore?—why, what's the matter?

'William releases Squire; turns to Sue; she screams and runs to him; embrace; "Lovely Sue—Own True Blue." She faints; Gaffer goes for gin; she recovers and refuses it; Gaffer winks, and drinks it himself; Squire, *Recitative*—" Never knew—About True Blue—Constant Sue." " Devilish glad—Here, my lad—What says dad?" William, *recitative*—" Thank ye, Squire—Heart's desire—Roam no more—Moored ashore." Squire joins lovers—" Take her hand—house, and bit of land, my own ground —

> " And for a portion here's two hundred pound!"

Grand chorus; huntsmen, gipsies, and sailors with pig-tails; *Solo*, Susan—" Constant Sue—Own True Blue." *Chorus*; *Solo*, William—" Dearest wife—laid up for life." *Chorus*; *Solo*, Squire—" Happy lovers—truth discovers." *Chorus*; *Solo*, Gaffer—" Curtain draws—your applause." *Grand chorus*; huntsmen, gipsies, sailors in pig-tails; William and Susan in centre; Gaffer (o. p.), Squire (p. s.), retire singing—

' Blythe and gay—Hark away !
    Merry, merry May ;
    Bill and Susan's wedding-day.'

Such is a brief sketch of one of those extemporaneous
melodramas with which Hook, when in the vein, would
keep his audience in convulsions for the best part of an
hour. Perhaps, had his improvising powers been restricted to that particular class of composition, the impromptu might have been questioned ; but he more
generally took for subjects of his drollery the company
present, never succeeding better than when he had been
kept in ignorance of the names of those he was about to
meet. But, at all times, the facility with which he
wrought in what had occurred at table, and the points he
made bearing upon circumstances impossible to have been
foreseen, afforded sufficient proof that the whole was un-
premeditated. Neither in this, nor in any other of his
conversational displays, was there anything of trickery or
effort. No abruptness was apparent in the introduction
of an anecdote ; there was no eager looking for an opportunity to fire off a pun, and no anxiety touching the fate
of what he had said. In fact, he had none of the artifice
of the professional wit about him, and none of that as-
sumption and caprice which minor ' lions ' exhibit so
liberally to their admirers. It may be fairly said, as he
knew no rival, so he has left no successor.'

Natura lo fece, e poi ruppe la stampa.

A kindred spirit and a similarity of style have been
found by critics in the writings—that is to say, in the

poetical compositions of Theodore Hook and Thomas Ingoldsby. And here the latter would probably have had little to fear from a comparison. Even in point of facility he was hardly, if at all, inferior to his friend. I am not aware indeed that my father, with a single exception,[1] ever attempted any extempore effusion, but pen in hand he would have hit off a dozen lively stanzas on a given subject, with a rapidity equal to that of any writer of the day. In conversation, dismissing all notion of equality between the powers of the two, it may be observed that, with some points of resemblance, a much greater diversity of manner separated them than when their pleasantries were expressed in rhyme. Mr. Barham uttered scarcely a dozen puns in the course of his life. He loved rather to play with a subject something after the manner of Charles Lamb; and his humour, always genial, was displayed in an agreeable irony (in the stricter and inoffensive sense of the term) which sometimes strangely perplexed matter-of-fact folks. Ready and fluent in conversation, and having at command an uncommon fund of anecdote, upon which he would draw largely, he possessed in addition one very valuable qualification—he was an excellent listener. In English literature he was well read, and moreover displayed just enough of that old-fashioned love of classical allusion and quotation to give a seasoning to his discourse, and a certain refinement to his wit, which, without exposing him to the charge of pedantry, bespoke the scholar and the man of taste.

---

[1] Once in the company of a few intimate friends, he was induced to improvise a song which, with very little correction, was afterwards published as *Mr. Barney Maguire's Account of the Coronation.*

It can be hardly necessary to remind the reader that the Mr. Hill mentioned in the preceding extract is the *Mr. Hull* of *Gilbert Gurney*, and also that this good-humoured and good-hearted, albeit somewhat inquisitive, personage furnished the subject of Mr. Poole's admirable comedy, *Paul Pry*. 'Pooh pooh! everybody must happen to know *that*.' It may not, however, be so generally known that to his spirit of inquiry was owing the discovery of the celebrated American sea serpent. Such was the fact! Hill was in the constant habit of visiting Mr. Stephen Price, the manager of Drury Lane, at his room in the theatre, and the latter soon found, to his surprise, that much that fell from him in conversation relating to en-gagements, the receipts of 'the house,' together with por-tions that he might have communicated of his American correspondence, appeared next day in the columns of the *Morning Chronicle*.

'When I discovered this, sir,' said Price, 'I gave my friend a lie a day!' and accordingly the public were soon treated with the most extraordinary specimens of Trans-atlantic intelligence; among the rest, with the first falling in with the body of a sea monster, somewhere about the Bermudas, and the subsequent appearance of his tail, some hundred miles to the north-east.

'Well, my dear boy,' used to exclaim the credulous visitor on entering the manager's sanctum, 'any news; any fresh letters from America?'

'Why, sir,' would reply Price, with the utmost gravity, 'I have been just reading an extract, sent under cover, from Captain Lobcock's log; they've seen, sir, that d—d

long sea-sarpant again; they came upon his head, off
Cape Clear, sir!'

And so the hoax continued, till the proprietors of the
journal which was made the vehicle for these interesting
accounts, finding they were not received with the most
implicit faith, unkindly put a stop to any further inser-
tions on the subject.

'*Diary.—November* 18.—Coming home in the evening
from the Chapel Royal, where I had been doing duty, I
overtook in the Strand two lads, having much the appearance of linendrapers' shopmen, and endeavouring to smoke
certain abominations under the semblance of cigars; both
of them very tipsy. The obliquity of their motions,
which resembled that sort of progress called by sailors
"tack and half tack," rendered it difficult to pass them,
and while thus kept, half voluntarily, half compulsorily,
following in their wake, I heard the following conundrum
put by the shorter one to his friend.

' "I say, Tom, do you know where that place is in the
world where two friends, let them be ever so intimate—
as good friends as you and me, Tom—can't be half an
hour together without quarrelling? Now there is a
paradox for you!"

' "A what? a Paradise?"

' "No, you fool, a *paradox*."

' "A paradox is it? Very well, and what's that?"

' "What, don't you know what a *paradox* is? Why, a
paradox is a—what a fool you must be not to know what's
a paradox; it's a sort of—oh, it's no good talking to a
chap that don't know what a paradox is!"

' Here the speaker relapsed into an indignant silence, which he maintained till I was obliged to pass them, and I remain to this hour as ignorant of the meaning, or rather solution (for meaning it may have none), of the conundrum, as his antiparadoxical ally.'

Mr. Barham, perhaps, was more fortunate in the weaving than in the disentangling knots of this description. A specimen or two from the same page as the foregoing are subjoined:

CHARADES.

I

My first on a schoolboy your bounty bestows,
Though 'tis commonly seen at the end of his nose;
My second you'll say, when my whole you explore,
Which once upon two legs walked proud at Mysore;
Now in town, less majestic, it capers on four.

Ans. Tippoo, an Italian greyhound.

II

Go, if my first you'd seek aright,
    And find her in yon dark-blue sky,
With many a starry gem bedight,
    In sweet but mournful majesty.

If on some dark and dismal shore,
    Through clouds and gloom your footsteps stray,
My second of my first implore,
    To guide thee on thy dreary way.

> And if, perchance, you'd find my whole,
>   See where it sleeps in soft repose,
> And to the contemplative soul
>   A thousand nameless charms bestows !

Ans. 'Moonlight.'

ENIGMA.

> To be called by my name you would highly disdain,
>   Though with titles of honour I rank in the list ;
> By law and by custom I single remain,
>   Though unless I am double I cannot exist.

Ans. 'A Fellow.'

On his first arrival in London, Mr. Barham had become acquainted with a young man named Graham, who may be remembered as moving some years ago in respectable literary circles ; he was possessed of considerable intellectual attainments, a prepossessing appearance, and very pleasing manners. The history of his career, detailed in the following extract, is not without interest, presenting, as it does, the melancholy spectacle of one endowed with great abilities, all blighted and rendered barren through want of principle.

'*December 2nd.*—Dined with Price, the manager of Drury Lane Theatre. The company were Const the magistrate, Tom Hill, Jerdan, Broderip, Braham the singer, and myself. Braham sang beautifully. . . . Had some conversation with Price respecting W. Graham, late editor of *The Literary Museum*, whom I knew well when he filled that situation. He was a tall, slight, gentlemanly

young man; rather, but not offensively,. dandified, and
with abilities and information which might have made
him anything he chose to be. He was, I found, on comparing notes with Price, an American by birth, and at the
age of seventeen had committed a forgery on a person
of high respectability at Philadelphia. He was detected,
but pardoned by the gentleman whom he had attempted
to defraud, on account of his youth, and out of regard to
his family, but on the express condition that he should
leave the country. Graham went, at first, no further than
New York, where Mr. Price was then practising at the
American Bar. The latter received a letter from the
gentleman alluded to, requesting him to call on the young
man, and either compel him to quit America forthwith,
or send him back in custody to Philadelphia. This commission Price executed to the letter, allowing him four
days for departure; and Graham, sailing for England,
landed at Plymouth. Here he was for a short time in the
company of Mr. Foote, the manager of the Plymouth
Theatre, and father to the (subsequently) celebrated Miss
Foote, of Covent Garden Theatre, to whose *Juliet*, I have
heard him say, he played *Romeo*; he also performed the
part of *Frederic* in *The School of Reform*, she playing the ˎ
heroine. With Miss Foote he was, according to his own
account, much "smitten" at the time, and to this early
attachment was owing several of his rhyming effusions
later in life; one I recollect ran the round of the newspapers, and was attributed to others, but I have heard
Graham claim it. The only verse I can call to mind runs:

> 'Had I the land that's in the Strand,—
> Gentles, I beg your pardon,—
> I'd give each Foot, and more to boot,
> For one of Covent Garden.'

'An opportunity occurring for a literary engagement in London, Graham came to town, when he distinguished himself as a contributor to the magazines, and other periodicals. It was about this time I first knew him. A gentleman with whom he had become acquainted in the course of business had, I understood, taken a great fancy to him, had sent him for a while to Cambridge, and at his death bequeathed him an annuity of 300*l.* This however was soon disposed of, and the sum raised was, according to some accounts, lost in speculation, while others said it was spent in debauchery. Of this I know nothing; the only reason I ever had for suspecting he was of a dissipated turn, was an account he himself once gave me, when we met accidentally—that a young woman had that evening called at his lodgings in a hackney-coach, and (I think on his declining to see her) had cut her throat on the spot. She was not dead at the time he mentioned this, and the result I never learned. The nature of this circumstance, and the want of feeling exhibited in the recital, were of course sufficient to check any favourable opinion I might have formed of him, and to replace our acquaintance on the most distant footing.

'When Mr Price first came to London, with the view of taking a lease of Drury Lane Theatre, he was walking one evening with a friend in the lobby of that house, when he met Graham, but without recognising him ; the latter, however, watched his opportunity, and drawing him aside, enquired if he did not recollect him.

' " Why, sir," said Price, " I have certainly seen you before, but where, and under what circumstances, I cannot at present call to mind. The impression I feel, however, respecting you is a painful one ; and it strikes me that either in my professional capacity, or otherwise, I have seen you involved in some disgrace."

' Graham did not hesitate to prompt a memory which further reflection might render less treacherous, but avowed himself at once, adding that he was now prospering and filling a respectable situation in the world, and begging Price not to betray that they had ever met before. This Price promised. Some short time after, the latter was called to dine with Mr. R——, to whom he had been recently introduced ; Graham was also asked for the same day, and had unhesitatingly accepted the invitation, but happening afterwards to hear that he would meet his countryman Mr. Price, he at once recollected " a previous engagement at Chelsea," and that in so marked a manner that his friend perceived it was a disinclination to meet the person he had just named which occasioned his retracting. He of course said no more to Graham ; but having a very slight acquaintance at the time with Mr. Price, actually went to a common friend to ask " if he were quite sure of Mr. Price's respectability, as Graham evidently would not meet him ? "

' The real state of the case he did not learn for a long

time after, when Graham, having run through all he possessed or could borrow, drew several forged bills on Mr. C. Knight, Mr. Whitaker, and others, and absconded with the money. He succeeded in returning to America, and there became sub-editor of a periodical paper, when a quarrel arising between him and a young man at a dinner party, Graham struck him ; a challenge was the consequence, and the assailant, being shot through the body at the first fire, died almost immediately. This happened in the autumn of 1827.'

'1828. *Sunday, February* 24.—Went for Cannon to St. George's, Hanover Square, and preached for him. Having dined at two, with the Bishop of Chichester (Dr. Carr), I was a few minutes behind my time, and service was on the point of commencing. Dr. Hodson, Dean of Carlisle, had begun to get fidgety at the non-appearance of the preacher. The Rev. John Sandford came into the vestry and asked the dean where Cannon was. "*Omne ignotum*," was the answer ; "that's all I can say."

'"If that's *all* you can say," returned Sandford, "of course you know nothing of the *magnifico*."'

'*March* 13.—Lord W. Lennox, Sir Andrew Barnard, Theodore Hook, Mr. Price, Capt. E. Smart, and Cannon dined here. The last told a story of a manager at a country theatre who, having given out the play of *Douglas*, found the whole entertainment nearly put to a stop by the arrest of *Young Norval* as he was entering the theatre. In this dilemma, no other performer of the company being able to take the part, he dressed up a tall, gawky lad who snuffed the candles, in a plaid and philabeg, and

pushing him on the stage, advanced himself to the foot-
lights with the book in his hand, and addressed the audience
with, " Ladies and Gentlemen,—

" This young gentleman's name is Norval. On the Grampian
    hills
His father feeds his flock, a frugal swain,
Whose constant care was to increase his store,
And keep his only son (this young gentleman) at home.
For this young gentleman had heard of battles, and he longed
To follow to the field some warlike lord ;
And Heaven soon granted what—this young gentleman's—sire
    denied.
The moon which rose last night, round as this gentleman's shield,
Had not yet filled her horns," &c.

And so on through the whole of the play, much to the
delectation of the audience. [1]

' In the evening Hook went to the piano, and played
and sang a long extempore song, principally levelled
against Cannon, who had gone up earlier than the rest,
and fallen asleep on the sofa in the drawing-room. Sir
Andrew Barnard, who now met the former for the first
time, expressed a wish to witness more of his talent as an
improvisatore, and gave him Sir Christopher Wren [2] as a
subject, on which he immediately commenced, and sang,

[1] In this anecdote, which rests on the authority of a celebrated singer
who told it to Cannon as having been herself present at the representation,
will be recognised the subject of one of the elder Mathews's most successful *scenas* ; it was repeated by Mr. Barham to Mr. Peake, who introduced
it in *Mathews's Comic Annual for* 1831.

[2] It will be remembered Mr. Barham's house was situated in St. Paul's
churchyard.

without a moment's hesitation, twenty or thirty stanzas to
a different air, all replete with humour.'

'*March* 23.—Dined at Sir Andrew Barnard's in the
Albany. The party consisted of Theodore Hook, Price,
Cannon, Lord Graves, Lord W. Lennox, Col. Armstrong,
Walpole and myself. Sir Andrew was called away to
attend the King, but returned before ten. In the meantime an unpleasant altercation took place between Cannon
and Hook, owing to an allusion, somewhat ill-timed, made
by the former to " treasury defaulters." This circumstance
interrupted the harmony of the evening, and threw a damp
upon the party. Hook made but one pun ; on Walpole's
remarking that, of two paintings mentioned, one was " a
shade above the other in point of merit," he replied, " I
presume you mean to say it was a *shade over* (*chef
d'œuvre*)." '

'*May* 14.—Acted as one of the stewards of the Literary
Fund dinner with Lord F. L. Gower, Mr. Buckingham the
traveller, Bishop of Winchester (Sumner), Hobhouse,
Colonel Fitzclarence and others. Duke of Somerset in
the chair. Fitzgerald the *poet* spouted as usual, and broke
down. Cannon observed " Poeta nascitur son *Fitz*—I beg
his pardon, I am afraid I am wrong in a letter ! " Supped
afterwards with Blackwood of Edinburgh, who dined with
us, at his rooms at the Somerset Coffee House. Jerdan,
Crofton Croker, Rev. M. Stebbing present, with whom was
passed an extremely pleasant evening, till " Ebony " fell
asleep. Amusing story told of John Wilson, the Professor
of Morality, editor of *Blackwood's Magazine*, and my old
college acquaintance. He had taken Mrs. Wilson, her

sister, and her sister's husband, in the summer of 1824, to the inn at Bowness for the purpose of viewing the Lake district. On the morning after their arrival the gentlemen walked out, leaving the ladies at their breakfast. Suddenly the latter were most unceremoniously broken in upon by Lord M——, a young nobleman recently expelled from Christ Church, and three of his companions, one of whom was in orders. In spite of the interference of the landlady, they acted very rudely, insisting on saluting the ladies, and in the scuffle overturned the table. Having been with much difficulty induced to quit the room, they next proceeded to stroll by the margin of the magnificent piece of water in the immediate vicinity. On his return, Mr. Wilson was made acquainted by the landlady with what had occurred in his absence, and became, as may be supposed, violently angry. In vain did his brother-in-law and the ladies endeavour to pacify him, and as they locked the door to prevent his going in search of the intruders, he sprang through the window, and made off to the shore of the lake, where he found the party amusing themselves with throwing stones into the water. Instantly addressing them, he insisted on knowing which was Lord M——. The gentlemen at first were silent, but on his declaring, if he were not informed, he should treat the person nearest as the object of his enquiry, his lordship avowed himself, and was immediately knocked down! The other three closed on the Professor; but he, being a very athletic man, as well as possessed of considerable skill in the art of boxing, soon gave the whole four a very severe drubbing, and compelled them to apologise for

their improper conduct. The next morning the clergyman, mounting a very respectable pair of black eyes, called
on him, having learnt his name in the interval, and renewing his excuses, hinted that for the sake of all parties
it would be better that the affair should be buried in
silence. Mr. Wilson replied that he was not in the least
ashamed of what *he* had done, and that if his Professor's
gown had been on his back at the time he should have
had no hesitation in laying it aside on such an occasion ;
but that his object of inflicting a due chastisement having
been accomplished, any publicity which might arise would
be owing only to their own indiscretion, as he should
think no more of the matter. And thus the affair
terminated.'

Of the admirable institution alluded to in the foregoing
memorandum, Mr. Barham remained for many years an
active and influential member. The peculiar sphere of
its beneficence, and the delicacy with which its assistance
was administered, were sufficient to enlist his best energies
in its cause. In the course of the long period during
which he continued on the council, scarcely a meeting
was held at which he was not present. Many a bereaved
family, ignorant perhaps of the existence of this Society
or of the mode of making application to it—many a
writer of education and ability, too sensitive to appeal to
vulgar charity, or to whom such degradation would be
ruin—has owed timely, and it may be invaluable relief to
his patient investigation and strenuous advocacy.

Having been instrumental on one occasion in obtaining
a donation of thirty pounds for a distressed author, he

resolved to make a *détour* on his way home, and inform
the poor man of the succour that had been awarded him.
The applicant was found in an upper room, containing
scarcely an article of furniture ; there was no fire in the
grate, but in one corner ' about as many coals as would fill
a pint pot.' The wife was sitting on an inverted tub,
nursing a dying child, and one great source of misery appeared to be the fear that the poor infant would expire
without the benefit of baptism. This anxiety was at once
removed by Mr. Barham, who immediately proceeded to
administer that sacrament. The child died on the day
following, but the parents were restored by the Society's
bounty, and subsequently enabled to regain their position
in the world.

' *May* 29.—Dined with the Bishop of Winchester in
Portland Place. Rather dull party, but chatted a good
deal with my old college friend W. Borradaile, Vicar of
Wandsworth, who had just returned from Paris. He told
me that the Abbé Bertin, whom I knew at Oxford endeavouring to pick up a living as a teacher of French,
and whom Nugent and Rookwood Gage were so perpetu-
ally tormenting, was now reinstated in his preferment at
Abbeville, and fond of receiving the English. Poor Abbé
Bertin! he deserves to be commemorated as one of the
few emigrés who in their subsequent prosperity did not
treat their former benefactors with ingratitude.'

' *September* 6.—Called at Hook's on my return from
the Isle of Thanet. Mr. Powell there ; then came in a
Mr. E——, an Irish barrister, rich and stingy, from whom
Hook afterwards told me he had taken his character of

Gervase Skinner, in the third series of *Sayings and Doings*. He mentioned, in proof of the saving propensities of this gentleman, that on a visit to Dover Castle with the Crokers he was about to leave without offering anything to the sergeant who had attended them, when Mrs. Croker, observing the omission, borrowed half a crown from her friend, in the absence of her husband, for the purpose of rewarding the man. This she repaid at the hotel before going down to dinner. But Mr. E——, making many excuses, affected to be half-affronted at her insisting on discharging the debt, and with becoming indignation threw the coin upon the table. There it lay till the waiter announced dinner, when offering his left arm to the lady, he contrived in passing to slip the piece of money—unobserved as he thought—off the table with his right hand, and deposit it in his breeches pocket.

'Hook told us an amusing story of his going down to Worcester, to see his brother the dean, with Henry Higginson (his companion in many of his frolics). They arrived separately at the coach, and taking their places in the inside, opposite to each other, pretended to be strangers. After some time they begin to hoax their fellow-travellers—the one affecting to see a great many things not to be seen, the other confirming it and admiring them.

' "What a beautiful house that on the hill!" cried Higginson, when no house was near the spot; "it must command a most magnificent prospect from the elevation on which it stands."

' "Why, yes," returned Hook, "the view must be extensive enough, but I cannot think these windows in good taste ; to run out bay windows in a gothic front, in my opinion, ruins the effect of the whole building."

' " Ah ! that is the new proprietor's doings," was the reply, " they were not there when the Marquis had possession." Here one of their companions interfered; he had been stretching his neck for some time, in the vain hope of getting a glimpse of the mansion in question, and now asked,

' " Pray, sir, what house do you mean ? I don't see any house."

' " That, sir, with the turrets and large bay windows on the hill," said Hook, with profound gravity, pointing to a thick wood.

'" Dear me !" returned the old gentleman, bobbing about to catch the desired object, " I can't see it for those confounded trees."

' The old gentleman, luckily for them, proved an indefatigable asker of questions, and the answers he received of course added much to his stock of authentic information.

' " Pray, sir, do you happen to know to whom that house belongs ? " enquired he, pointing to a magnificent mansion and handsome park in the distance.

' " That, sir," replied Hook, " is Womberly Hall, the seat of Sir Abraham Hume, which he won at billiards from the Bishop of Bath and Wells."

' " You don't say so !" cried the old gentleman, in pious horror, and taking out his pocket-book begged his informant to repeat the name of the seat, which he readily did, and it was entered accordingly—the old gentleman shaking his head gravely the while, and bewailing the profligacy of an age in which dignitaries of the church practised gambling to so alarming an extent.

' The frequency of the remarks, however, made by the associates on objects which the eyesight of no one else was good enough to take in began at length to excite some suspicion, and Hook's breaking suddenly into a rapturous exclamation at "the magnificent burst of the ocean !" in the midst of an inland country—a Wiltshire farmer, who had been for some time staring alternately at them and the window, thrust out his head, and after reconnoitering for a couple of minutes drew it in again, and looking full in the face of the sea-gazer exclaimed with considerable emphasis,

' " Well, now then, I'm d—d if I think you can see the ocean, as you call it, for all you pretends "—and continued very sulky all the rest of the way.'

' *November* 17.—Called with Lord W. Lennox on Mr. Jerdan, at Grove House, Brompton. He showed me the suppressed book of which the whole five hundred copies were burnt in Ireland, with the exception of this, and said that he was about to send it as a present to the King, having had a hint from Mr. O'Reilly that it would be acceptable in that quarter. The book was a tolerably thick duodecimo, neatly bound, had no title-page, but on the tops of the pages was printed *Captain Rock's Letters to the King.* The introductory letter commenced, " My Brother;" many of the others "Sir," " My Cousin." It was very strongly written, and among other things contained a list of the present Irish peers, with a history of their families, the means by which their honours were acquired, and especially the conduct of the representatives of most of the noble families during the insurrection of 1798, which it depicted with great bitterness. Jerdan also read to me a key to the characters in the *Anglo Irish*, a recently published novel, said to be by Sir J. C. Morgan. Of these I only recollect that my friend Cannon is *Mr. Gunning*; the late Marquis of Londonderry the minister; *Lord Harmer*, Lord Farnham; and the Bishop, Archbishop Magee.'

'*November* 20.— Carried a letter addressed by Sir Walter Scott to Mrs. Hughes, on the subject of a benefit for Mr. Terry the actor, lately afflicted with a paralytic stroke, to Stephen Price at Drury Lane Theatre. Price promised me to let him have a benefit at the proper season, if he wished it; Sir Walter undertaking to write a prologue or an epilogue. Mrs. H., in a conversation respecting the *Bride of Lammermoor*, told me that she had been informed by Sir Walter, when she was last at Abbotsford, that the main incidents of that story were true; that the *Lucy* of the tale was a Miss Dalrymple; *Bucklaw*, who marries her, was Dunbar of Dunbar; and her lover, Hamilton of Bungany, who, however, survived her many years. The expression used by *Lucy*, 'So ye have taken up your bonnie bridegroom,' is historically correct; as is the whole circumstance of her stabbing her new-made husband, and her subsequent insanity. The catastrophe of *Ravenswood's* being overwhelmed in the sand is founded on an occurrence which took place before

the eyes of Sir Walter's son, Major Scott, who saw three
Irish horsedealers disappear in the manner described.   A
similar accident is said to have happened to the son of
the celebrated Mrs. Trimmer.

'*Meg Dodds*, described in *St. Ronan's Well*, is a
Mrs. Wilson, who keeps the inn at Fushie Bridge, the
first stage from Edinburgh on the road to Abbotsford.
She adores Sir Walter, and when Dr. and Mrs. Hughes
were detained for want of horses, finding out accidentally
that they were friends of his, she without any scruple
ordered those which were bespoken for a gentleman, then
on his way to dine with Lord Melville, to be put to their
carriage.   Mrs. Wilson is a strict Presbyterian, and once
complained to Sir Walter that "though he had done just
right by being so much with Arnieston (Mr. Dundas of
Arnieston), yet that the latter had grievously offended
her.   He had pit up," she said, "in the kirk the Lord's
Prayer and the Ten Commandments, and when a remonstrance was sent to him against such *idolatry*, he just
answered, that if they did not let him alone he would
e'en pit up a "Belief" into the bargain!'

'*December* 8.—Called on Hook.   In the course of
conversation he gave me an account of his going to Lord
Melville's trial with a friend.   They went early, and were
engaged in conversation when the peers began to enter.
At this moment a country-looking lady, whom he afterwards found to be a resident at Rye, in Sussex, touched
his arm, and said,

' " I beg your pardon, sir, but pray who are those gentlemen in red now coming in ? "

' " Those, ma'am," returned Theodore, " are the Barons of England ; in these cases the junior peers always come first."

' " Thank you, sir ; much obliged to you. Louisa, my dear ! (turning to a girl about fourteen), tell Jane (about ten) those are the Barons of England, and the juniors (that's the youngest, you know) always goes first. Tell her to be sure and remember that when we get home."

' " Dear me, Ma ! " said Louisa, " can that gentleman be one of the *youngest ?* I am sure he looks very old."

' Human nature, added Hook, could not stand this ; any one, though with no more mischief in him than a dove, must have been excited to a hoax.

' " And pray, sir," continued the lady, " what gentlemen are these ? " pointing to the Bishops, who came next in order, in the dress which they wear on state occasions, viz. the rochet and lawn sleeves over their doctor's robes.

' " Gentlemen, madam ! " said Hook, " these are not gentlemen : these are ladies—elderly ladies—the dowager peeresses in their own right."

' The fair enquirer fixed a penetrating glance upon his countenance, saying, as plainly as an eye can say, " Are you quizzing me or no ? " Not a muscle moved ; till at last, tolerably well satisfied with her scrutiny, she turned round and whispered,

' " Louisa, dear, the gentleman *says* that these are elderly ladies, and dowager peeresses in their own right; tell Jane not to forget that."

' All went on smoothly till the Speaker of the House of

Commons attracted her attention by the rich embroidery of his robes.

' " Pray, sir," said she, " and who is that fine-looking person opposite ? "

' " That, madam," was the answer, " is Cardinal Wolsey!"

' " No, sir!" cried the lady, drawing herself up, and casting at her informant a look of angry disdain, " we knows a little better than that; Cardinal Wolsey has been dead many a good year!"

' " No such thing, my dear madam, I assure you," replied Hook, with a gravity that must have been almost preternatural; " it has been, I know, so reported in the country, but without the least foundation; in fact, those rascally newspapers will say anything."

' The good old gentlewoman appeared thunderstruck, opened her eyes to their full extent, and gasped like a dying carp; *vox faucibus hæsit*—seizing a daughter with each hand, she hurried without another word from the spot.'

Mr. Hook has been accused of a tolerably strong leaning to superstition; one instance in particular is given by Mrs. Mathews, in the memoirs of her husband, of the ludicrous advantage taken by the latter of this weakness, to turn the tables on his former tormentor. His biographer in *The Quarterly* also alludes to indications of a similar feeling apparent in the diary to which he had access; but for these concurrent testimonies, one might be apt to refer the following statement to that love of mystification in which this singular being was so profound an adept. Mr. Barham, however, always believed him to have spoken in perfect good faith; and certainly the circumstances of the story in question, supported, as they are, by most respectable authority, have more than common claims on the attention of the sceptical.

The date of the interview is not given, but it must have been between September 6 and December 8 of this year.

'Met Hook in the Burlington Arcade; walked with him to the British Museum. As we passed down Great Russell Street, Hook paused on arriving at Charlotte Street, Bedford Square, and, pointing to the north-west corner, nearly opposite the house (the second from the corner) in which he himself was born, observed,

' " There, by that lamp-post, stood Martha the gipsy!" [1]

' " Yes," I replied, " I know that is the spot on which you *make* her stand."

' " It is the spot," rejoined Hook, seriously, "on which she actually did stand;" and he went on to say that he entertained no doubt whatever as to the truth of the story; that he had simply given the narrative as he had heard it from one (Major Darby) who was an eye-witness of the catastrophe, and was present when the extraordinary noise was heard on the evening previous to the gentleman's decease. He added, that he was intimately acquainted with the individual who had experienced the effects of Martha's malediction, and whose name was Hough. He said, further, that he had merely heightened the first accident, which had been but a simple fracture of the leg, occasioned by his starting at the sight of the

[1] Vide First Series of *Sayings and Doings.*

gipsy, and so slipping off the curb-stone; but that in all
other main incidents he had adhered strictly to fact.'

With his vivid imagination, and appreciation of the
marvellous, it is not to be altogether wondered at if Mr.
Barham himself appeared a little disposed to give cre-
dence to the existence of things undreamed of in our
philosophy.

People who heard him narrate some tale of mystery
with a dramatic power and flow of impressive language
that riveted the attention of a youthful audience, whom
he always loved to amuse and with whom he loved to be
amused, might easily allow the undercurrent of humour
to escape their notice.   And really he seemed at times to
endeavour to persuade himself into credulity, much in
the way that some people strive to convict themselves of
a bodily ailment.   He sought, as it were, to lull reason to
sleep for awhile, and leave an uninterrupted field for the
wildest vagaries of fancy.   Unlike poor Lady Cork, whose
enjoyment of ' her murders' sensibly declined, he never
lost his relish for a ' good ghost story; ' nothing delighted
him more than to listen to—unless it were to tell—one
of those 'true histories,' properly fitted with the full
complement of names, dates, and locale, attested by 'living
witnesses of unblemished reputation,' and hedged in on
all sides by circumstantial evidence of the most incontro-
vertible nature; one, in short, of those logical *culs de sac*
which afford no exit but by unceremoniously kicking down
the opposing barrier.   It was Sir Walter Scott, I believe,
who was thus driven to extricate himself from a dilemma
of this sort, when, being asked 'how he accounted' for

some strange tale he had related on no less authority than that of his own grandmother, he was forced to reply, after some deliberation,—'Aiblins my grandmither was an awfu' leear!'

That the lovers of well-authenticated ghost stories owe a good deal of their delectation to the ingenuity of the 'awfu' leears' is, I fear, not to be gainsaid. The diary seems to supply an instance with which this chapter may conclude:

'It is a singular thing that, of all the numerous writers who have told this celebrated ghost story (that of Sir George Villiers[1]), not one that I have ever seen has alluded to a story precisely similar in all its details which is recorded by the Duc de St. Simon, in the first volume of his memoirs, as having happened to Louis XIV. A man brings the same message of secret advice, together with a secret known only to the King himself, which he declares he has received three different times from a phantom representing the late Queen, in the forest of St. Germain, and which had been confided to the speaker

---

[1] The particulars of the Villiers story are briefly these: A certain Mr. Twose, an old schoolfellow of Sir George Villiers, father of the first Duke of Buckingham, being asleep in his lodging in Drury Lane was disturbed by the apparition of the knight, who enjoined him to visit the Duke and admonish him as to his conduct and policy, and assure him, if he attended to the warning, of life and prosperity, but to predict his death before St. Bartholomew's day if he neglected it. The man not obeying, the visit was repeated thrice, and on the last occasion the ghost told him certain secrets to be used as credentials. Mr. Twose, having with difficulty obtained access to the Duke, delivered the message. The Duke, on receiving it, consulted with his mother, who was much affected, but paid himself no further heed to the admonition, and was soon after assassinated at Portsmouth by Felton, as he was about to set out for the relief of Rochelle, then besieged by the French.

for the purpose of securing attention to his message. The King receives the man more than once, rebukes his ministers for thinking him mad, and treats the whole business very gravely, ordering the messenger to be provided for comfortably in his own sphere of life for the rest of his days. This happened in 1691, and St. Simon conjectures it to have been a trick of Maintenon's to induce Louis to own their marriage. It is difficult to believe that one of these stories is not a mere variation of the other.'

CHAPTER IV.

[1829-1831.]

Dr. Hume—The advertisement—Romantic history of the Rev. Mr. G——
——Letter to Dr. Hume—Dr. Hughes and his family—Correspondence with
Mrs. Hughes—'The London University'—'King's College'—Mr. Ma-
thews the elder—Irish Story—Characters in the Waverley Novels—
Stealing Gooseberries —Curious Dream—The Portsmouth Ghost—Fracas
in the Queen's Bench Prison—O'Connell and Lord Anglesea—Lord
Anglesea and his cook—Funeral of Sir Thomas Lawrence—The Medico-
Botanico Society—The Director and the Dukes of Wellington and
St. Albans—The College of Arms—The Pedigree of Cato—Sir George
Nayler—Epistle in verse.

ONE of the earliest and closest intimacies which Mr.
Barham contracted, after his settlement in London, was
with Dr. Thomas Hume, who, like Cannon, had been for
many previous years a constant guest of Dr. Bond, the
husband of Mrs. Barham's sister, at Hanwell. Hume
must have been naturally a man of strange temper, and
time and circumstances had combined to deepen his
peculiarities. Tall, upright, stern, with a cold, colourless,
impassive face over which a smile rarely flitted, he was
assuredly not one either to invite or to accept any hasty
demonstration of friendship. There was indeed something cynical about him which had the effect of keeping
people in general at a distance; and at a distance
people in general were best pleased to keep. The absence

of all outward show of geniality, and the seeming want of sympathy which he displayed, rendered it impossible for mere acquaintances to feel at ease in his company. And yet, notwithstanding his repellent manner, he was blessed with a heart warm, true, and largely generous—qualities which endeared its possessor to a chosen few, among whom may be numbered Thomas Moore and my father. Moreover, he was a perfect gentleman—an Irish gentleman, and endowed with a courteous gravity of demeanour which lent an uncommon force to anything of a sarcastic turn to which he might be provoked into giving utterance.

One instance, in particular, of his dry humour my father used to relate. They had walked together to the office of one of the morning newspapers, and there the doctor silently placed upon the counter an announcement of the death of some friend, together with five shillings, the usual charge for the insertion of such advertisements. The clerk glanced at the paper, tossed it on one side, and said gruffly, ' Seven and six ! '

' I have frequently,' replied Hume, ' had occasion to publish these simple notices, and I have never before been charged more than five shillings.'

' Simple ! ' repeated the clerk without looking up, ' he's universally beloved and deeply regretted ! Seven and six.'

Hume produced the additional half-crown and laid it deliberately by the others, observing as he did so, with the same solemnity of tone he had used throughout— ' Congratulate yourself, sir, that this is an expense which your executors will never be put to.'.

Dr. Hume was, as I observed, an Irishman : he was in

the army, had done some service, and had attained, I believe, the rank of physician to the forces. He was married twice : in his first choice he was not fortunate ; and to this early disappointment of his hopes something of the sternness of his disposition is in fairness to be attributed. His first wife was the daughter of a clergyman, rector of a parish which now may almost be reckoned in the suburbs of London, whose tragic end shocked the town some sixty years ago, and has since been introduced in at least one work of fiction. The particulars, as my father heard them on good authority, are certainly remarkable. The gentleman, whom I need designate no further than by the initial G——, was a tolerably well-known, and accomplished member of society, an elegant scholar distinguished for much of that facility in the composition of Latin verse which has rendered Father Prout famous, and one who called great folks—even royal dukes—his friends. More than one of these illustrious personages occasionally did him the honour of visiting his rectory. As may be supposed, he was not long in finding out that the entertaining royalty is a sort of hospitality far too splendid for the fortune of a simple clergyman. Perhaps, like so many men under the like circumstances, and yet without reason, he vaguely hoped that something would be done for him. But whether or not he had been beguiled by others, or by himself, in this respect, one thing was clear—the something was too long a-doing ! Ruin was inevitable, and was at hand ! Resolving to anticipate the wreck, he got together all that was available of his remaining property and departed suddenly and secretly for London. It so happened that one of his friends, residing at Hanwell, had invited him to join a party at dinner on the following day. The guests, with the exception of Mr. G——, arrived in due time. At first there was the usual disposition shown, on the part of the host, to await his coming; then a little whispering among the gentlemen took place; and by degrees a gloom, felt but not comprehended by all, stole over the company, who sat down to table without the rector and quitted it at an unusually early hour. It was not till the next morning that the hostess (a near relative of my own) was informed of the cause of her friend's absence. A rumour of its nature had reached the village the day before, and had been communicated to her husband in the drawing-room; the report was now confirmed, and there was no further use in maintaining silence on the subject. Mr. G——, it appeared, had reached London safely and had been driven to one of the large coaching inns in the city; I believe it was 'The Spread Eagle,' in Gracechurch Street. Here he supped and retired, as it was supposed, to rest, having given orders to be called in the morning in time to enable him to start off by the first stage bound for Dover. Noises, it came out afterwards, were heard in the course of the night proceeding from his room, but as they probably had not reached the ears of any of the servants of the house, no notice was taken of the occurrence. At the appointed hour 'boots' rapped at the traveller's door. No answer was returned: the summons was repeated, but in vain. The man became alarmed, called his master, under whose directions the door was forced, and a strange and shocking sight was disclosed. Suspended from the bedstead, strangled and long dead, hung the occupant of the apartment. Bed and bedding were tumbled in confusion on the floor; every article of clothing, the curtains, even the sheets, were torn to shreds and scattered in all directions; the furniture was over-thrown and broken, and the work of destruction was com-pleted by the self-murder of its perpetrator. For some little time no clue to the mystery could be gained, but ere long a discovery was effected by means the most unlooked for. A hackney coachman was taken into cus-tody for drunkenness. On being examined by the police, there was found in his possession a pocket-book containing bank notes for a very large amount. Enquiry elicited the fact that he had lately obtained change for others; and, finding evasion impossible, the man confessed that he had a few days before driven a gentleman to the inn in question, and that, on examining the carriage after depositing his fare, a pocket-book lying among the straw at the bottom caught his eye, and that he could not resist the temptation to appropriate its contents. Mean-while the wretched owner evidently had not become aware of his loss till he had reached his bed-room. Then there must have flashed upon him the hopelessness and horror of his position—a penniless fugitive, with disgrace and ruin confronting him turn which way he would! One may well imagine the despair and agony which accompanied the frantic search for his treasure, and finally the mania which drove him to his death.

To return to the intimate relations existing between

his son-in-law and Mr. Barham. It is not to be supposed that the latter, with the large amount of work he had to get through, found much time to carry on a gossiping correspondence with his friends. His rule was to write to no one except on business—a rule waived indeed in one notable instance, that of a lady who will presently be introduced, and one to which Dr. Hume supplied another, I might perhaps say *the* other, exception. A few of the letters addressed to him by my father have been preserved, and these will be given under their respective dates.

To Dr. Hume.

'January 15, 1828.

'My dear Doctor,—What has become of you? I am afraid you have been waiting in expectation of hearing from me respecting the book; but with shame and confusion of face I confess I have lost your note, and with it all clue to the title; only that I recollect it is of or belonging to Burke, but whether the Sublime and Beautiful man, or the little hero of the same name now figuring away at the Surrey, the mental hallucination which has succeeded renders me unable to call to mind. I searched everywhere for it the first time I saw Edwards, but in vain, and conclude it is certainly in the moon,

'"Since all things lost on earth are treasured there,"

or else in the recesses of Dick's room, a great receptacle in its way, and as inaccessible as the other. Pray give me a second set of credentials and I will do your bidding forthwith.

'They came and told me that you had been fighting a duel; but it turned out that it was another Dr. Hume,[1] a sort of *Double-goer* of yours, as the Germans call it, who haunts one at every turn. It is a great pity he was not killed, it would have saved so much confusion. But after all it is to be feared he was never in danger, as I find he was second and not principal in the affray, which turned out bloodless. When will you come and dine with us? Talking of that—"Why is the railroad in Dr. Hume's brick-field like a good dinner? D'ye give it up?"—"Because its a Line of Wheel!"—Billy Curtis[2] for ever! Find a worse if you can, and till then

'Believe me, yours inconceivably,

' R. H. B.'

Since the publication of this memoir four-and-twenty years ago, the name of Hughes, at that time well known in literary circles and by those conversant with the lives of modern writers, has become a household word among us. To pass by all political claims, the production of such a work as *Tom Brown's School Days* must alone entitle its author to the thanks of his countrymen. No work has appeared, certainly in the present generation, better calculated to delight and at the same time to purify and brace the mind of the youthful reader. It is a work to do much and real good. And in it may be traced the fruits of a father's manly teaching who, to use his own ⌣

---

[1] This was Dr. Hume, the friend of the Duke of Wellington, who attended his grace in his duel with Lord Winchelsea, at Battersea Fields.

[2] Sir William Curtis, the alderman, to whom is attributed the celebrated toast, ' The three R's.'

words, desired that his sons should learn early, like the Persians of old, to ride, to shoot with bow and arrow, and to speak the truth! It was with the grandfather of the present member for Frome, Dr. Hughes, Canon Residentiary of St. Paul's, that Mr. Barham became first acquainted. Of the comparative intimacy which ensued and of the many acts of kindness, being mostly of a professional character, which he received at his hands it is unnecessary further to speak. Not so as regards his intercourse with the son and widow of that excellent and amiable man. Between them and my father a warm and enduring friendship sprang up. Kindred tastes, identity of political opinions, mutual respect, and a regard for a knot of common associates bound them together.

Mrs. Hughes, even at the time of my father's introduction to her, was a lady well advanced in years, but possessed of a surprising activity of mind and body, an excellent memory, and a knowledge of what may be called the curiosities of county history unequalled so far as my experience goes. She is mentioned by Lockhart as the frequent correspondent of Sir Walter Scott and Southey, and for nearly a quarter of a century she kept up with unflagging vivacity a regular interchange of letters with Mr. Barham. To her he was indebted not only for a large proportion of the legendary lore which forms the groundwork of the 'Ingoldsby' poems, but also for the application of a stimulus that induced him to complete many papers which diffidence, or that aptitude, previously spoken of, to turn aside at the faintest suspicion of 'a lion in the way,' would have left unfinished. The

distich, inscribed in the copy of the *Ingoldsby Legends,*
presented to the lady in question, conveys no more than
the actual fact :—

> ' To Mrs. Hughes, who *made* me do''em,
> Quod placeo est—si placeo—tuum.'

Thanks are due to the same good friend, long since departed, for much that forms material of the present volume.
To the lively interest indeed exhibited by her, so long as
she lived, in everything relating to Mr. Barham and his
family the production, in its original form, of this memoir
is almost entirely to be attributed. In the first instance my
father's correspondence with this lady was given curtailed,
such specimens only being printed as seemed sufficient to
convey a notion of that happy temperament and involun-
tary flow of humour which distinguished the writer ; in the
present edition, all the letters which the kindness of
Mr. Thomas Hughes has placed at my disposal are, with
trifling exceptions, given at length.

To Mrs. Hughes.

'April 15th, 1828.

' My dear Madam,—Nothing has afforded me greater
regret than that, though I called three times at the
deanery, I missed seeing Dr. Hughes on his visit. I had
a story of an old acquaintance of his (as I believe), Bishop
G. Beresford, which I think would have amused him, but
it must rest *altâ mente repôstum* (I make no apology for
being learned to you), till I have the pleasure of seeing
him in the autumn. I have little news to tell you, except

that Mrs.—— the *auctioneeress*, if there be such a word, is likely to die, and that the sorrowing widower *in posse* is said to have already made arrangements to take the beautiful (Oh! that I could add prudent) Miss Foote, as her successor. He, at least says green-room scandal, wears a watch riband she has given him, as the decoration of a military order; while others add, that though the gentleman is unquestionably anxious to become a "Knight Companion," the lady is still "Grand Cross."

'I enclose a set of rhymes, as yet in a chrysalis state; should *John Bull* get hold of them, after they have thrown off the grub, I am afraid they are too well adapted for his purpose for him to refrain from appropriating what is now a mere embryo.

THE LONDON UNIVERSITY;

OR,

STINKOMALEE TRIUMPHANS.

AN ODE TO BE PERFORMED ON THE OPENING OF THE NEW COLLEGE OF GRAFTON-STREET EAST.

'Whene'er with pitying eye I view
   Each operative sot in town,
 I smile to think how wondrous few
  Get drunk, who study at the U-
           niversity we've Got in town,
           niversity we've Got in town.

'What precious fools "The People" grew,
   Their *Alma Mater* not in town;

The "useful classes" hardly knew
Four was composed of two and two,
Until they learned it at the U-
        niversity we've Got in town.

' But now they're taught by JOSEPH HU-
    ME, by far the cleverest Scot in town,
Their *items* and their *tottles* too ;
Each may dissect his sister Sue,
From his instructions at the U-
        niversity we've Got in town.

' Then LANSDOWNE comes, like him how few .
    Can caper and can trot in town,
In *pirouette* and *pas de deux*—
He beats the famed *Monsieur Giroux*,
And teaches dancing at the U-
        niversity we've Got in town.

' And GILCHRIST, see, that great Gentoo-
    Professor, has a lot in town
Of Cockney boys, who fag Hindoo,
And *larn Jem-nasties* at the U-
        niversity we've Got in town.

' SAM ROGERS' corpse of vampire hue,
    Comes from its grave to rot in town ;
For Bays the dead bard's crowned with Yew,
And chaunts The Pleasures of the U-
        niversity we've Got in 'town.

' FRANK JEFFREY, of the Scotch Review,—
    Whom MOORE had nearly shot in town,—
Now with his pamphlet stitched in blue
And yellow, d—ns the other two,
But lauds the ever-glorious U-
                    niversity we've Got in town.

' [1] Great BIRKBECK, king of chips and glue,
    Who paper oft does blot in town,
From the Mechanics' Institu-
tion, comes to prate of wedge and screw,
Lever and axle at the U-
                    niversity we've Got in town.

' Lord WAITHMAN, who long since withdrew
    From Mansion-house to cot in town ;
Adorned with chair of ormolu,
All darkly grand, like Prince Lee Boo,
Lectures on *Free Trade* at the U-
                    niversity we've Got in town.

' Fat FAVELL, with his coat of blue,
    Who speeches makes so hot in town,
In rhetoric spells his lectures through,
And sounds the V for W,
The *vay they speaks* it at the U-
                    niversity we've Got in town.

---

[1] Stanzas 8, 9, 12, 13, were added in the copy which subsequently appeared in the *John Bull.*

' Then HURCOMBE comes, who late at New-
 gate-market, sweetest spot in town !
Instead of one clerk popped in two,
To make a place for his ne-phew,
Seeking another at the U-
     niversity we've Got in town.

' There's Captain Ross, a traveller true,
 Has just presented, what in town-
's an article of great *virtu,*
(The telescope he once peep'd through,
And 'spied an Esquimaux canoe
On Croker Mountains), to the U-
     niversity we've Got in town.

' Since MICHAEL gives no roast nor stew,
 Where Whigs might eat and plot in town,
And swill his port, and mischief brew—
Poor CREEVY sips his water gru-
el as the beadle of the U-
     niversity we've Got in town.

' There's JERRY BENTHAM and his crew,
 Names ne'er to be forgot in town,
In swarms like Banquo's long is-*sue*—
Turk, Papist, Infidel, and Jew,
Come trooping on to join the U-
     niversity we've Got in town.

' To crown the whole with triple queue,—
  Another such there's not in town,
Twitching his restless nose askew,
Behold tremendous HARRY BROUGH-
AM! Law Professor at the U-
                        niversity we've Got in town.
                        niversity we've Got in town.

Grand chorus :
' Huzza! huzza! for HARRY BROUGH-
AM! Law Professor at the U-
                        niversity we've Got in town.[1]

' I have room for no more than to say that I am most
sincerely and truly yours,   ' R. H. B.'

As a *pendant* to the above may be subjoined the following hint to a rival establishment :—

ON THE WINDOWS OF KING'S COLLEGE REMAINING BOARDED.

Loquitur Discipulus Esuriens.

' Professors, in your plan there seems
  A something not quite right,
'Tis queer to cherish learning's beams,
  By shutting out the light.

---

[1] ' I well recollect,' writes Mr. Hughes, ' the success of his song,
                    "The U-
            niversity we've Got in town."

Sir Walter Scott, who was in London when this humorous extravaganza
appeared in the *John Bull*, was most anxious to ascertain the author ; and

'While thus we see your windows block'd,
    If nobody complains ;
Yet every body must be shock'd,
    To see you don't take pains.

'And tell me why should bodily
    Succumb to mental meat ?
Or why should ητα, βητα, πι,
    Be all the pie we eat ?

'No *Helluo librorum* I,—
    No literary glutton,—
Would veal with Virgil like to try,
    With metaphysics, mutton.

Leave us no longer in the lurch,
    With Romans, Greeks, and Hindoos ;
But give us beef as well as birch,
    And *board us*—not your windows.'

In 1829, Mr. Barham appears to have met for the first
time, at the table of their common friend, Theodore
Hook, Charles Mathews the elder. Their acquaintance
was of some years' duration, but never reached intimacy ;
it was accompanied, nevertheless, certainly on the part of
Mr. Barham, by feelings of no ordinary regard. It may,
indeed, be questioned whether the golden opinions won

having learnt it from my father, expressed a particular desire to make his
acquaintance. A breakfast party was accordingly arranged at Dr. Hughes's
house, where Mr. Barham had the gratification of being introduced to Sir
Walter.

by this accomplished actor in his professional career upon the stage were more than commensurate with the esteem which he inspired in private life.

'*Diary: May* 5, 1829. — Dined at Hook's. Horace Twiss, Lord W. Lennox, Jerdan, Cannon, Mathews, Yates, Professor Millington, Allan Cunningham, Price, Denham, brother to Colonel Denham the traveller, Milan Powell, F. Broderip, Doctors Arnott and Whimper, with myself, formed the party. Sir A. Barnard being engaged with the king, Lockhart with his wife, and Charles Kemble laid up with a bilious attack. Mathews told an excellent story of an Irish surgeon named Maseres, who kept a running horse, and who applied to him on one occasion for his opinion respecting a disputed race.

'"Now, sur," commenced the gentleman, "Mr. Mathews, as you say you understand horse-racing, and so you do, I'll just thank ye to give me a little bit of an opinion, the least taste in life of one. Now, you'll mind me, sur, my horse had won the first *hate*, well, sur, and then, he'd won the second *hate*, well—"

'" Why, sir," said Mathews, " if he won both the heats, he won the race."

'"Not at all, my dear fellow, not at all. You see he won the first *hate*, and then, somehow, my horse fell down, and then the horse (that's not himself, but the other), came up—"

'" And passed him, I suppose," said Mathews.

'' Not at all, sur, not at all; you quite mistake the gist of the matter. Now, you see, my horse had lost the first *hate*—"

' " Won it, you mean—at least, won it, you said."

' " Won it ! of course, I said won it ; that is, the other horse won it, and the other horse, that is, *my* horse, won the second *hate*, when another, not himself, comes up and tumbles down—but stop ! I'll demonstrate the circumstances ocularly. There—you'll keep your eye on that decanter ; now, mighty well ; now, you'll remember that's *my* horse, that is, I mane it's not my horse, it's the other, and this cork—you observe this cork—this cork's my horse, and my horse, that is this cork, had won the first *hate*—"

" ' Lost it, you said, sir, just now," groaned Mathews, rapidly approaching a state of complete bewilderment.

" ' Lost it, sur, by no manes ; won it, sur, I maintain— 'pon my soul, your friend [1] there that's grinning so is a mighty bad specimen of an American—no, sur, *won* it, I said ; and now I want your opinion about the *hate*, that is, not the *hate*, but the race, you know, not, that is, the first *hate*, but the second *hate*, that would be the race when it was won."

' " Why, really, my dear sir," replied the referee, " I don't precisely see the point upon which— "

' " God bless me, sur ! do ye pretind to understand horse-racing, and can't give a plain opinion on a simple matter of *hates?* Now, sur, I'll explain it once more. The stopper, you are aware, is my horse, but the other horse —that is the other *man's* horse,' &c. &c.

' And so poor Maseres went on for more than an hour, and no one could tell at last which horse it was that fell ;

---

[1] Mr. Stephen Price.

whether he had won the first *hate*, or lost it; whether his horse was the decanter or the cork; or what the point was, upon which Mr. Maseres wanted an opinion.

'Mathews afterwards sang a very amusing song in his best manner, descriptive of a Lord Mayor's day. Yates was no less entertaining, and on his health being drunk, returned thanks in an imitation of Young which was perfect. Hook had hung a piece of black crape over Peel's picture, which was on one side of his room, and H. Twiss, being Under Secretary of State, thought it incumbent on him to endeavour to remove it. The piece of mourning, however, was more strongly fastened than he had imagined, which induced Lennox to say, on seeing him bungling in his attempt; "It's of no use, Horace; you'll never be able to get him out of his scrape." [1]

'*September*, 1829.—Mrs. Hughes told me that the person whose character was drawn by Sir Walter Scott as *Jonathan Oldbuck* was a Mr. Russell, and that the laird whom he mentions as playing cards with Andrew Gemmell

---

[1] This refers, of course, to Mr. Peel's change of opinion on the question of Catholic Emancipation. The indignation which his conversion aroused in the hearts of the *ultra* Tories may be sufficiently understood from the following passages extracted from *Blackwood, March* 1829:—'It is our sincere belief, that he is the object of a more unmitigated abhorrence than can have attended any political renegade in any history, not excepting Sir Thomas Wentworth, in the age of Charles I.' 'All hearts are turned against him with scorn, even the hearts of those for whom he has made shipwreck of his honour and his conscience. And with reason; for the aggravating circumstances of his case are these: first, that he had been more indebted to the cause which he has betrayed than any other apostate of our times; and secondly, that he of all apostates has the most eminently failed to make out any shadow of a case for himself, or any colourable show of expedience for the new policy he has adopted.'

(the prototype of *Edie Ochiltree*) through the window was Mr. Scott of Yarrow.

'Snivelling Stone, about two miles and a half from the cromlech known as Wayland Smith's Cave, in Berkshire, is a large stone, which it is said that Wayland, having ordered his attendant dwarf to go on an errand, and observing the boy to go reluctantly, kicked after him. It just caught his heel, and from the tears which ensued, it derived its traditionary appellation. It is singular that when Mrs. Hughes, who had this story from a servant, a native of that part of the country, first told it to Sir Walter Scott, he declared that he had never heard of Wayland's having had any attendant, but had got all the materials for his story, so far as that worthy is concerned, from Camden. His creation of *Dicky Sludge*, a character so near the traditionary one of which he had never heard, is a curious coincidence.

'So also is his description of Sir Henry Lee and the dog in *Woodstock*. There is a painting in the possession of Mr. Townsend, of Trevallyn, in Wales, representing, according to a tradition long preserved in his family, Sir Henry Lee of Ditchley, with a large dog, the perfect resemblance of Bevis. Mr. Townsend, however, thinks he flourished about a century earlier than the Woodstock hero, and was the same with the Sir H. Lee whose verses to Queen Elizabeth, on his retiring from the tilt yard in consequence of old age, are preserved in Walpole's *Antiquities*. The strange thing is that Sir Walter knew nothing of this picture till after *Woodstock* was published.

'Told her the story of old Steady Baker, the Mayor of

Folkestone, whom I well remember. A boy was brought
before him for stealing gooseberries. Baker turned over
Burn's Justice, but not being able to find the article he
wanted in the book, which is alphabetically arranged, he
lifted up his spectacles, and addressed the culprit thus:
' My lad, it's very lucky for you that instead of stealing
gooseberries, you were not brought here for stealing a
goose; there is a statute against stealing geese, but I
can't find anything about gooseberries in all *Burn*; so
let the prisoner be discharged, for I suppose it is no
offence.'

There is another entry in the diary made in the course
of this month containing two stories of the supernatural
order, the latter of which was furnished by Mrs. Hughes.
To this lady's extensive acquaintance with family history,
as I have said, Mr. Barham was frequently indebted for
the subject of his poetical legends, the manner in which
she herself delivered these ' undoubted facts' leaving little
room for embellishment within the limits of prose. For
some reason the following was never incorporated with
the Ingoldsby revelations, and it is given accordingly
much in the way in which it fell from the lips of the original narrator.

The anecdote which serves as an introduction rests on
the authority of an intimate friend, who had it from the
veracious dreamer of dreams himself.

' *September*, 1829.—A Mr. Philipps, Secretary to Mr.
Abbott, Speaker of the House of Commons, stated to my
friend Mr. Wood, that, about the year 1805, he woke
one night in some perturbation, having dreamt that he

had been sentenced to be hanged, when the agony of his situation roused him at the very moment they were in the act of pinioning his arms in the press-yard. Heartily pleased at finding it but a dream, he turned and fell asleep again, when precisely the same scene was repeated, with the addition that he now reached the foot of the gallows, and was preparing to mount, before he awoke. The crowd, the fatal tree, the hangman, the cord, all were represented to him with a frightful distinctness, and the impression on his mind was so vivid that he got out of bed and walked about the room for some minutes before he could reconcile himself to the attempt at seeking rest on his pillow again.

' He was a long while before he could close his eyes, but towards morning he fell into a perturbed slumber, in which precisely the same tragedy was acted over again ; he was led up to the scaffold, placed upon the drop, the rope was fitted to his neck by the executioner, whose features he distinctly recognised as those of the man whom he had seen in his former vision ; the cap was drawn over his face, and he felt the trap giving way beneath his feet, when he once more awoke as in the very act of suffocation, with a loud scream that was heard by a person sleeping in a neighbouring apartment.

' Going to rest again was now out of the question, and Mr. Philipps described himself as rising and dressing, though it was then hardly daybreak, in a state of the greatest possible nervous excitement. Indeed, so strong a hold had this dream, so singularly repeated, taken upon his imagination, that he found it almost impossible to

shake off the unpleasant feeling to which it gave rise, and
had almost resolved to send an excuse to a gentleman
with whom he had engaged to breakfast, when the reflection that he must by so doing defer the settlement of
important business, and all on account of a dream, struck
him as so very pusillanimous a transaction, that he determined to keep his appointment.

'He might, however, as well have staid away, for his
thoughts were so abstracted from the matter they met to
discuss, and his manner was altogether so *distrait*, that
his friend could not fail to remark it, and speedily closed
the business by an abrupt enquiry if he was not unwell.
The hesitation and confusion exhibited in his answer drew
forth other questions, and the matter terminated in Mr.
Philipps fairly confessing to his old acquaintance the unpleasant impression made upon his mind, and its origin.
The latter, who possessed good nature as well as good
sense, did not attempt to use any unwarrantable raillery,
but endeavoured to divert his attention to other subjects,
and, their meal being concluded, proposed a walk. To
this Mr. Philipps willingly acceded, and, having strolled
through the park, they at length reached the house of
the latter, where they went in. Several letters had arrived
by that morning's post, and were lying on the table,
which were soon opened and read. The last which Mr.
Philipps took up was addressed to him by an old friend.
It commenced :—

'Dear Philipps—You will laugh at me for my pains, but I
cannot help feeling uneasy about you; do pray write and let me
know how you are going on. It is exceedingly absurd, but I

really cannot shake off from my recollection an unpleasant dream I had last night, in which I thought I saw you *hanged* ——'

' The letter fell from the reader's hand ; all his scarcely-recovered equanimity vanished ; nor was it till some weeks had elapsed that he had quite recovered his former serenity of mind.

' It is unfortunate for the lovers of the marvellous that five-and-twenty years have now elapsed, and Mr. P. has not yet come under the hands of Jack Ketch. I suppose we must take it, " *Exceptio probat regulam.*"

' A story with much more of the supernatural about it was related to me by Mrs. Hughes the other day which·is, I think, one of the best authenticated ghost stories in existence. It was narrated to her by Mrs. Hastings, wife of Captain Hastings, R.N., and ran to the following effect:—

' " Captain and Mrs. Hastings were driving into Portsmouth one afternoon, when a Mr. Hamilton, who had recently been appointed to a situation in the dockyard there, made a third in their chaise, being on his way to take possession of his post. As the vehicle passed the end of one of the narrow lanes which abound in the town, the latter gentleman, who had for some little time been more grave and silent than usual, broke through the reserve which had drawn a remark from the lady, and gave the following reason for his taciturnity :—

' " It was," said he, " the recollection of the lane we have just passed, and of a very singular circumstance which occurred to me at a house in it some eighteen years ago, which occupied my thoughts at the moment, and which,

as we are old friends and I know you will not laugh at me,
I will repeat to you.

' " At the period alluded to, I had arrived in the town
for the purpose of joining a ship in which I was about to
proceed abroad on a mercantile speculation. On enquiry,
I found that the vessel had not come round from the
Downs, but was expected every hour. The most unpleasant part of the business was, that two or three king's
ships had just been paid-off in the harbour, a county
election was going on, and the town was filled with
people waiting to occupy berths in an outward-bound
fleet which a contrary wind had for some days prevented
from sailing. This combination of events, of course, made
Portsmouth very full and very disagreeable. To me it
was particularly annoying as I was a stranger in the place,
and every respectable hotel was quite full. After wandering half over the town without success, I at length
happened to enquire àt a tolerably decent-looking public-
house situate in the lane alluded to, where a very civil,
though a very cross-looking landlady at length made me
happy by the intelligence that she would take me in, if I
did not mind sleeping in a double-bedded room. I certainly did object to a fellow-lodger, and so I told her,
but, as I coupled the objection with an offer to pay hand-.
somely for both beds though I should occupy only one of
them, our bargain was settled, and I took possession of
my apartment.

' " When I retired for the night I naturally examined
both beds, one of which had on a very decent counterpane,
the other being covered with a patchwork quilt, coarse,

but clean enough. The former I selected for my own use, placed my portmanteau by its side, and having, as I thought, carefully locked the door to keep out intruders, undressed, jumped beneath the clothes, and fell fast asleep.

' I had slept, I suppose, an hour or more when I was awakened by a noise in the lane below; but being convinced that it was merely occasioned by the breaking-up of a jolly party, I was turning round to recompose myself, when I perceived, by the light of the moon which shone brightly into the room, that the bed opposite was occupied by a man, having the appearance of a sailor. He was only partially undressed, having his trousers on, and what appeared, as well as I could make it out, to be a Belcher handkerchief, tied round his head by way of nightcap. His position was half sitting, half reclining on the outside of the bed, and he seemed to be fast asleep.

' I was, of course, very angry that the landlady should have broken her covenant with me and let another person into the room, and at first felt half disposed to desire the intruder to withdraw; but as the man was quiet, and I had no particular wish to spend the rest of the night in an altercation, I thought it wiser to let things alone till the morning, when I determined to give my worthy hostess a good jobation for her want of faith. After watching him for some time, and seeing that my chum maintained the same posture, though he could not be aware that I was awake, I reclosed my eyes and once more fell asleep.

' It was broad daylight when I awoke in the morning, and the sun was shining full in through the window. My slumbering friend apparently had never moved, for there he was still, half sitting half lying on the quilt, and I had a fair opportunity of observing his features, which, though of a dark complexion, were not ill-favoured, and were set off by a pair of bushy black whiskers that would have done honour to a rabbi. What surprised me most, however, was that I could now plainly perceive that what I had taken in the moonlight for a red handkerchief on his forehead was in reality a white one, but quite saturated in parts with a crimson fluid, which trickled down his left cheek, and seemed to have run upon the pillow.

'At the moment, the question occurred to me—how could the stranger have procured admission into the room? as I saw but one door, and that I felt pretty confident I had myself locked on the inside, while I was quite positive my gentleman had not been in the chamber when I retired to bed.

'I got out and walked to the door, which was in the centre of one side of the room, nearly half-way between the two beds; and as I approached it, one of the curtains interposed for a moment so as to conceal my unknown companion from my view. I found the door, as I had supposed it to have been, fastened, with the key in the lock, just as I had left it, and, not a little surprised at the circumstance, I now walked across to the farther bed to get an explanation from my comrade, when to my astonishment he was nowhere to be seen! Scarcely an instant before I had observed him stretched in the same position which he had all along maintained, and it was difficult to conceive how he had managed to make his exit so instantaneously, as it were, without my having perceived or heard him. I, in consequence, commenced a pretty close examination of the wainscot near the head of the bed, having first satisfied myself that he was concealed neither under it nor by the curtain. No door nor aperture of any kind was to be discovered, and, as the rawness of the morning air began by this time to give me a tolerably strong hint that it was time to dress, I put on the rest of my clothes, not, however, without occasionally pausing to muse on the sailor's extraordinary conduct.

' I was the first person up in the house ; a slipshod, ambiguous being, however, in whom were united all the various qualities and functions of " boots," chambermaid, waiter, and potboy, soon made its appearance, and yawning most terrifically began to place a few cinders, &c., in a grate not much cleaner than its own face and hands, preparatory to the kindling a fire. From this combination I endeavoured to extract some information respecting my nocturnal visitor, but in vain ; it " knowed nothing of no sailors," and I was compelled to postpone my inquiries till the appearance of the mistress, who descended in due time.

' After greeting her with all the civility I could muster —no great amount by the way as my anger was in abeyance only, not extinct—I proceeded to inquire for my bill, telling her that I certainly should not take breakfast, nor do anything more " for the good of the house," after her breach of promise respecting the privacy of my sleeping room. The good lady met me at once with a " Marry come up ! " a faint flush came over her cheek, her little grey eyes twinkled, and her whole countenance gained in animation what it lost in placidity.

' " What did I mean ?   I had bespoke the whole room, and I had had the whole room, and, though she said it, there was not a more comfortable room in all Portsmouth ; she might have let the spare-bed five times over, and had refused because of my fancy ; did I think to ' *bilk* ' her ? and called myself a gentleman she supposed ! "

' I easily stopped the torrent of an eloquence that would have soon gone near to overwhelm me, by depositing a guinea (about a fourth more than her whole demand) upon the bar, and was glad to relinquish the offensive for the defensive.   It was therefore with a most quaker-like mildness of expostulation that I rejoined; that certainly I had not to complain of any actual inconvenience from the vicinity of my fellow-lodger, but that, having agreed to pay double for the indulgence of my whim, if such she was pleased to call it, I of course expected the conditions to be observed on the other side ; but I was now convinced that it had been violated without her privity, and that some of her people had doubtless introduced the man into the room, in ignorance probably of our understanding.

' " What man ? " retorted she briskly, but in a much more mollified tone than before the golden peace-maker had met her sight—" There was nobody in your room, unless you let him in yourself ; had you not the key, and did not I hear you lock the door after you ? "

' That I admitted to be true ; " nevertheless," added I, taking up my portmanteau and half turning to depart, as if I were firing a last stern-chaser at an enemy whom I did not care longer to engage, "there certainly was a man —a sailor—in my room last night; though I know no more how he got in or out than I do where he got his broken head, or his unconscionable whiskers."

'My foot was on the threshold as I ended, that I might escape the discharge of a reply which I foreboded would not be couched in the politest of terms. But it did not come, and as I threw back a parting glance at my fair foe, I could not help being struck with the very different expression of her features from that which I had anticipated. Her attitude and whole appearance were as if the miracle of Pygmalion had been reversed, and a living lady had been suddenly changed into a statue; her eyes were fixed, her cheek pale, her mouth half open, while the fingers, which had been on the point of closing on the guinea, seemed arrested in the very act.

'I hesitated, and at length a single word, uttered distinctly but lowly, and as if breathlessly spoken, fell upon my ear; it was " WHISKERS ! ! "

' " Ay, *whiskers*," I replied; "I never saw so splendid a pair in my life."

' " And a broken —— For Heaven's sake come back one moment," said the lady, whom I now perceived to be labouring under no common degree of agitation.

'Of course I complied, marvelling not a little that a word, which though, according to Mr. Shandy, it once excited a powerful commotion in the Court of Navarre, is usually very harmless in our latitudes, should produce so astounding an effect on the sensorium of a Portsmouth landlady.

' " Let me entreat you, sir," said my hostess, " to tell me, without disguise, who and what you saw in your bedroom last night."

' " No one, madam," was my answer, " but the sailor of whose intrusion I before complained, and who, I presume, took refuge there from some drunken fray, to sleep off the effects of his liquor, as, though evidently a good deal knocked about, he did not appear to be very sensible of his condition."

' An earnest request to describe his person followed, which I did to the best of my recollection, dwelling particularly on the wounded temple and the remarkable whiskers, which formed, as it were, a perfect fringe to his face.

' " Then, Lord have mercy upon me ! " said the woman, in accents of mingled terror and distress, " it's all true, and the house is ruined for ever ! "

' So singular a declaration only whetted my already excited curiosity, and the landlady, who now seemed anxious to make a friend of me, soon satisfied my inquiries in a few words which left an impression no time will ever efface.

' After entreating and obtaining a promise of secrecy, she informed me that, on the third evening previous to my arrival, a party of sailors from one of the vessels which were paying off in the harbour were drinking in her house, when a quarrel ensued between them and some marines belonging to another ship. The dispute at

length rose to a great height, and blows were inter-
changed. The landlady in vain endeavoured to inter-
fere, till at length a heavy blow, struck with the edge
of a pewter pot, lighting upon the temple of a stout
young fellow of five-and-twenty, who was one of the most
active on the side of the sailors, brought him to the
ground senseless and covered with blood. He never
spoke again, but, although his friends immediately conveyed him up-stairs and placed him on the bed, endeavouring to stanch the blood and doing all in their power
to save him, he breathed his last in a few minutes.

'In order to hush up a circumstance which could
hardly fail, if known, to bring all parties concerned " into
trouble," the old woman admitted that she had consented
to the body's being buried in the garden, where it was in-
terred the same night by two of his comrades. The man
having been just discharged, it was calculated that no
inquiry after him was likely to take place.

'" But then, sir," cried the landlady, wringing her hands,
" it's all of no use. Foul deeds will rise, and I shall never
dare to put anybody into your room again, for there it
was he was carried ; they took off his jacket and waistcoat,
and tied his wound up with a handkerchief, but they never
could stop the bleeding till all was over ; and, as sure as
you are standing there a living man, he is come back
to trouble us, for if he had been sitting to you for his
picture, you could not have painted him more accurately
than you have done."

'Startling as this hypothesis of the old woman's was, I
could substitute no better, and as the prosecution of the

inquiry must have necessarily operated to delay my voyage, and, perhaps, involve me in difficulties, without answering, as far as I could see, any good end, I walked quietly, though certainly not quite at my ease, down to the Point; and my ship arriving in the course of the afternoon, I went immediately on board, set sail the following morning for the Mediterranean, and though I have been many years in England since, have never again set foot in Portsmouth from that hour to this.

' Thus ended Mr. Hamilton's narrative.

' The next day the whole party set out to reconnoitre the present appearance of the house, but some difficulty was experienced at first in identifying it, the sign having been taken down, and the building converted into a greengrocer's shop about five years before. A dissenting chapel had been built on the site of the garden, but nothing was said by their informant of any skeleton having been found while digging for the foundation, nor did Mr. Hamilton think it advisable to push any inquiries on the subject. The old landlady, he found, had been dead several years, and the public-house had passed into other hands before the withdrawal of the licence and its subsequent conversion to the present purposes.'

The following letter contains an acknowledgment of a present — annually repeated — of one of those beguiling Berkshire delicacies so fraught with peril to the inexperienced or unwary :—

To Mrs. Hughes.

'St. Paul's Churchyard, January 5, 1830.

'My dear Madam,—

'"I know not how to thank you.   Rude I am
In speech and manner: never till this hour "
'Tasted I such a dainty!

'But young *Norval* never had such a " pig's head " to
be thankful for ; it is truly delicious—almost too much so
indeed, for it tempted me last night to do what I very
seldom do, and never ought to do, viz., eat a hearty supper ;
the consequence was that I " dreamt of the d—l, and
awoke in a fright ":—

'Methought I was seated at church,
    With Wellington acting as clerk,
And there in a pew,
Was Rothschild the Jew,
    Dancing a jig with Judge Park ;
Lady Morgan sat playing the organ,
    While behind the vestry door,
Horace Twiss was snatching a kiss
    From the lips of Hannah More.

'In short I cannot tell you half the vagaries I was
carried through, at least within any moderate compass in
a letter, but I mean to put as much of it down as I can
call to remembrance, and, following the example of Mr.
Bottom the weaver, get some good-natured Peter Quince
to " make a ballad of it," and " it shall be called Barham's
dream," not because " it hath no bottom," but because it

proceeded from a pig's head, a metaphor in which Mrs. B. sometimes speaks of mine, when, more than usually persevering, I resist unto the death some measure which I consider wrong and she right, or *vice versâ*, as the case may be. Let me not forget to add, however, that in the present instance she is to the full as much inclined to be pig-headed as myself, and begs me to join her thanks to my own.

'With respect to our whereabouts at St. Paul's, you will be pleased to hear that we are as tranquil as heart can wish. The Dean has not made B——eat dirt, but has taken the duty entirely himself, except last Sunday evening, when the new Prebendary, Mr. [Sydney] Smith—who read himself in to the Chiswick stall that day—preached for him. In the meantime our coffee-coloured friend— may his shadow increase!—is looking out, I hear, very sharp after the living in the city of which he is the curate. His rector is very infirm, and within these few weeks has broken apace; should he die therefore, "as there is hopes he will," a fierce attack is to be made on the Chancellor. The way I hear is even now paving, and if perseverance, or assurance, or any other " ance," will give a man a chance, I think he has it.

'Your old friend Mr. Thomas Welsh, of the Royal *Harmonic* Institution, is again in hot water. His action against D'Egville stands over for reference, and in order to while away the interval of this piping time of peace, he has commenced a couple more; one against Hawes's brother-in-law, Molineux, the other against John Tate; both arising out of the "unholy alliance," originally cemented at the Argyle Room Congress. Indeed there seems to be something of a malignant aspect in the heavenly bodies just at present with respect to musical men. Mr. (or I believe I should say Signor) B—— hath had the sanctity of his person much outraged. Certain obdurate tailors and butchers have lately given him an opportunity of sitting quietly down over the water, "The King, heaven bless him, finding him a bench." Now it so happens that my Lord G——, Captain G——, of mysterious box noto-riety, and two or three other lively lads holding the King's commission, are at this moment enjoying themselves in that *séjour*. The other evening, hot, not with the Tuscan grape, but with quite as good a thing, viz., whisky toddy, and the fumes of real havannahs, they took it into their heads to satisfy a very natural curiosity, and to ascertain, if possible, by ocular demonstration whether Mr. B—— had actually undergone the unpleasant ceremony of being stamped with a red-hot F, as so confidently alleged by his unfriends, or no. For this purpose, they proceeded in a body to his room, and commenced, not in the most polished manner, stripping him of his habiliments, in spite of remonstrances, yells, and struggles. They succeeded, I believe, so far as to ascertain that he was no Freemason, but it having escaped their recollection, in the first in-stance, that the shoulder is the part where the forçats are usually marked, so much time was lost from their having begun the business at the wrong end, that the marshal made his appearance *cum suis*, stopped this very interest-ing investigation, and placed most of the philosophical inquirers in the strong-room for the rest of the evening.

The main question therefore—much to the regret of all musical savants—remains still enveloped in mystery. I know of no other private news; the public, I think, notwithstanding the cloud in the Irish horizon, is more favourable than it has been; the necessity of repressing the mob seems now to be so universally felt that no danger exists any longer from that, the most formidable source.

‘Spence's plan is too wild even to be attempted by any above the very lowest of the low. Part of it is, I believe, the allotment of all the surface of the land in equal portions. Happy man be his dole who gets his share located on the top of Plynlimmon! Seriously, I entertain no apprehension now of “revolt;” the crisis is, I verily believe, over. In Ireland there may and probably will be a few broken heads. O'Connell, I understand, waited on Lord Anglesea before he left town, and told him that, as he had received personal marks of attention from him when last in Ireland, he thought it right and fair to call and say that he was now going over, with a determination to agitate the country, and that he begged Lord A. to believe that, while he felt it his duty to oppose the Government in every possible way, yet personally he felt a great respect for his lordship.

‘The peer was quite as civil and to the full as open as the commoner. He replied that he thanked Mr. O'C. for his candour; that he, too, was uninfluenced by motives of personal opposition to that gentleman, but that he was going over with a firm determination to repress agitation, *coute qui coute*; and that, if the boundaries laid down by law were once overstepped, he would embody a special commission instantly, and hang every agitator in his power. My informant adds that O'Connell retired very much crestfallen, and seemed to think himself that he had taken nothing by his motion. Lord A. is quite the man to do the thing if he has the opportunity. The country people in Kent and Sussex are quite quiet and beginning to listen to reason. The addresses and Goodman's 'confession have done much good. ·

> ' And now, my dear Madam, etc. ·
>
> ' Most faithfully and truly yours,
>
> ' R. H. BARHAM.'

Another anecdote of Lord Anglesea may here be added, having occurred about the time of that narrated in the preceding letter. ' The marquis had in his service as cook, while he was Lord Lieutenant of Ireland, a young man of good figure and prepossessing appearance generally, and who certainly was by no means unconscious of the gifts the gods had bestowed upon him. One day one of the Ladies Paget, being in a carriage with some friends in the Phœnix Park, encountered the gentleman riding on a showy horse, when he had the impudence to kiss his hand to her. The young lady on her return told her father, who rang the bell and desired Mr. —— to be sent up.

' " Mr. ——, I believe you were in the Park to day ? "

' " Yes, my lord "

' " On horseback ? "

' " Yes, my lord."

' " You bowed to some ladies in a carriage ? "

' " Yes, my lord,—bowed to several."

' " Perhaps, sir, you are not aware that my daughter was one of them ? "

' Then the young lady, willing to spare what she thought would be his confusion, interfered :—

' " I dare say, papa, he did not see me when he rode up."

' " Oh dear yes ! I did, my lady—I knew you ! "

' The Marquis again rang the bell :—

' " Pack up all Mr. ——'s things immediately, turn him into the street, and never suffer him to put his foot into this house again.   Begone, sir ! "

' The discomfited cook quitted not only the house, but the profession, in disgust.   He afterwards went upon the stage, and made some impression on the town as an actor and singer at the minor theatres.'

' *Diary.—January* 21, 1830.—Attended the public funeral of Sir Thomas Lawrence.   An immense throng, but all conducted with great order and splendour.   The coffin was carried into the vaults and brought under the brass plate in the centre of the dome, after the part of the service usually performed in the choir had been gone through.   The mourners formed a large outer circle, in the centre of which, close round the plate, was an inner one composed of the members of the cathedral.   Among the mourners were Sir G. Murray, Peel, Lord Aberdeen (who seemed almost frozen while bearing the pall from the west door), C. Kemble, Horace Twiss, Derham, Gwilt, T. Campbell, John Wilson Croker, conspicuous in a black velvet cap, and old Nash, the architect, still more so in a

Welsh wig. My poor little Emma being very ill, I had some doubt as to going, but Dr. Bowring and Mr. Rothwell with the Crombies coming, I was obliged to conduct them, and we got in with no little difficulty through the crowd, already assembled at twelve, though the funeral was not appointed to take place till two o'clock. Dr. Hughes, a very old friend of the deceased, was so affected that it was with the greatest difficulty he got through the lesson. After the ceremony the body was conveyed to a brick grave under the south aisle, where it lies, thus :—

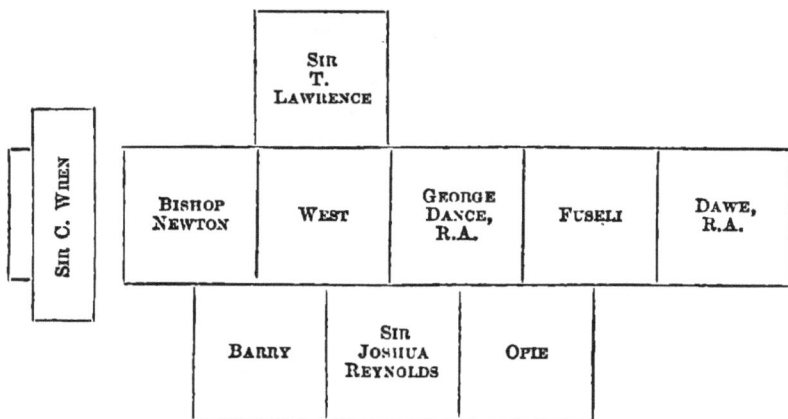

	SIR T. LAWRENCE			
BISHOP NEWTON	WEST	GEORGE DANCE, R.A.	FUSELI	DAWE, R.A.
	BARRY	SIR JOSHUA REYNOLDS	OPIE	

SIR C. WREN

' Mrs. Hughes mentioned to me a singular story respecting the deceased, which she had from his intimate friend, Miss C——. This lady told her, while in the gallery during the ceremony, that the evening before his decease she had seen him. He seemed, she said, a little out of spirits, and asked her somewhat abruptly if she had ever heard a death-watch ? She replied that she had ; on which he requested her to describe the noise it made, which she did. On hearing her description he replied, " Ay, that is it exactly!" and relapsed into a thoughtful silence which he scarcely broke during the rest of her visit.'

'All the papers of this date [*January*, 1830] were full of the quarrel between the Medico-Botanico Society and its Director, as he was called, and founder, Mr. John Frost, a gentleman remarkable equally for his modest assurance and the high estimate he had formed of his own pretensions, on what many persons thought singularly insufficient grounds. The Royal Society, as a body, were unquestionably of this opinion, as, on his name being submitted to the ballot, he was almost unanimously blackballed. His perseverance, however, in beating up for recruits for his favourite society was unparalleled. It was his custom to run about with a highly ornamented album to every distinguished person, British or foreign, to whom he could by any possibility introduce himself, inform them that they were elected honorary members of the Medico-Botanico Society, and give a flourishing account of its merits; and as one of the rules required that a member should write his own name in their book, Mr. F. procured by these means a valuable collection of autographs.

'The best of the joke was, that, having written to several foreign princes through the medium of their ambassadors, and under Lord Aberdeen's government franks, procured through the interest of Lord Stanhope, the President and head of the Society (for the high-sounding office of Director was, in fact, that of Secretary), he contrived to get no less than a dozen potentates of various grades to consent to their enrolment, and to acknowledge

the compliment. Two indeed of them—the Emperor of
the Brazils was one—went so far as to enclose the insignia
of one of their minor orders, addressed to " the Director,"
as they had never heard of any higher officer, and these
Jacky Frost, as he was commonly called, lost no time in
mounting upon his coat, much to the annoyance of Lord
Stanhope and the rest of the body.

'It was determined, in consequence, to get rid of Mr.
Frost, by doing away with the office of Director altogether ;
the orders, however, and the album he could not be induced
to part with. His honours after all were dearly purchased,
as the Royal Humane Society, thinking, perhaps, that it
was sadly *infra dig.* for a chevalier with two crosses on
his breast to be holding the bellows to the nose of every
chimney sweeper picked out of the Serpentine, dismissed
him from the employment he held under them, whereby
he lost 200*l.* a year and a good house in Bridge-street.

'Among the cool stratagems which he occasionally
made use of to procure signatures to his book, was one
which he played off on the Duke of Wellington, which,
had it not been vouched for by Mr. Wood, F.R.S., I should
hardly have credited. Having failed in repeated attempts
to get with his quarto into Apsley House, he heard by
good luck that his Grace, then Commander-in-chief, was
about to hold a levee of general officers. Away posted
Jacky to a masquerade warehouse, and hired a Lieut.-
General's uniform, under cover of which he succeeded in
establishing himself fairly in the Duke's anteroom, among
thirteen or fourteen first-rate Directors of strategetics.

'Everybody stared at a General whom nobody knew,

and at length an aide-de-camp, addressing him, politely requested to know his name.

‘ “ What General shall I have the honour of announcing to his Grace ? ”

‘ “ My name is Frost, Sir.”

‘ “ Frost, General Frost ! I beg your pardon, but I really do not recollect to have heard that name before ! ”

‘ “ O, Sir, I am no general, I have merely put on this costume as I understood I could not obtain access to his Grace without it ; I am the Director of the Medico-Botanico Society, and have come to inform his Grace, that he has been elected a member, and to get his signature.”

‘ “ Then, Sir, I must tell you that you have taken a most improper method and opportunity of so doing, and I insist upon your withdrawing immediately.”

‘ Jacky, however, was too good a general to capitulate on the first summons, and he stoutly kept his ground, notwithstanding a council of war at once began to deliberate on the comparative eligibility of kicking him into the street, or giving him in charge to a constable. Luckily for him the aide-de-camp thought his grace had a right to a voice in the matter, as the offence was committed in his own house. On the business, however, being mentioned to him, the Hero of Waterloo, not choosing perhaps to risk the laurels he had won from Napoleon in a domestic encounter with so redoubtable a champion, said, “ Let the fellow in,” cut short Jacky’s oration by writing his name hastily in the book, and gave the sign to “ show him out again.” It was doubtful, however, whether any other sanctuary than the house he was in would have sheltered him from the indignation of the *militaires* in waiting, at the sight of what they considered a degradation of the national uniform.

'Quite as amusing was this gentleman's interview with the Duke of St. Albans. The " Director " easily got his grace's consent to be elected a member, and the book was produced for his signature. The latter took up a pen, and commenced " *Du*—," when he was interrupted by his visitor,

' " No, I beg pardon, it is your Grace's title we require, written by your own hand."

' " Well, my title is Duke of St. Albans, is it not ? "

' " Yes, your Grace, undoubtedly, but your signature merely—the way in which your Grace usually signs." —Here the Duchess interfered, and " St. Albans " was soon written, in a large German-text, school-boy hand, the " *Du* " having been previously expunged by a side wipe of his grace's forefinger. Mr. Frost bowed, pocketed the subscription, pronounced all to be *en règle*, congratulated his noble friend on having become a brother Medico-Botanico, and quitted Stratton Street in high glee.

'Not long afterwards it was his good fortune again to encounter his grace, on some public occasion. Of course he paid his respects, and equally of course the Duke inquired of " Mr. *Thingumee*," as he called him, how that " medical thing " that he belonged to, went on.

' " Exceedingly prosperous, indeed, my Lord Duke," was the answer ; " we are increasing both in numbers an respectability every day; I have got twelve Sovereigns down since the commencement of the present year."

' " O, if you have only got twelve *sovereigns* in all that time, I don't think you are getting on so very fast; you know I gave you *five guineas* of them myself."

This anecdote may easily be believed of a duke who soon after his wedding wrote to the editor of *Debrett's Peerage*, then Mr. Townshend, Rouge Dragon, saying, ' Sir, I have to inform you that I am married to Mrs. Coutts, and Mrs. Coutts desires you will put it into your next edition.' This Townshend told me himself.

On the south side of St. Paul's churchyard a street narrow and none of the sweetest, called at the upper end, Paul's Chain, and at the lower Bene't Hill, leads down by a sufficiently steep descent to the river bank. Somewhere about the middle of the thoroughfare a gateway on the left admits the visitor to a respectable-looking paved court. Strange devices may catch his eye on entering, but he is probably disposed to be struck more by the lightness and cheeriness of the spot, hidden away in a huge maze of dingy lanes and foul alleys, than by any eccentricity in the way of ornament. Round this quadrangle are ranged the buildings attached to the Heralds' College, or more correctly, the College of Arms. On the left stand the hall and library; and here are preserved, among other relics, the turquoise ring and sword taken, so say the heralds, from the body of James IV. of Scotland as it lay dead on the field of Flodden. Here are stored those dusty tomes and emblazoned parchments—records that could throw a curious light upon the history of many a noble name—so dear to the eye of the antiquarian ; and here, in the company of 'Rouge Dragon' aforesaid, *Clarence-shoes,*[1] and, above all, his dear friend the late Sir Charles Young, sometime ' Garter,' but at the date of which I am writing, holding the office of York Herald, Mr. Barham was wont to spend hours in the patient disentanglement of some knotty point of genealogy—in the fruitless endeavour perhaps to make a square Sir Thomas fit the round hole vacant in some imperfect pedigree—a mode of relaxation of which I have spoken before. Of course there was a certain amount of gossip going on. The Heralds, like the lawyers and the doctors, are pretty deep in family secrets, and can tell odd stories when they choose. Once they were a power in the realm ; but the good old days are past when they could stop a man's carriage on the king's highway, and daub out the spurious bearings on his panels. Now when every Bugg can become a Howard by advertisement, and at the small annual charge of one guinea, obtain a licence to mount coat armour of any pattern that may take his fancy, there really appears little left for the chivalry of Bene't Hill but an application for a winding-up order under the Court of Chancery, or the sharper but less prolonged torture of the 'Happy Despatch.' Forty years ago business was tolerably brisk at the College. One instance I have heard my father relate as having been communicated to him by his friend Townshend. A well known claimant to `

---

[1] 'Then the guns' alarums, and the King of Arums,
    All in his garters and his Clarence shoes.'

See *Mr. Maguire's Account of the Coronation.*

a certain peerage in abeyance came to the latter for the purpose of obtaining assistance in the getting up his case. ' Rouge Dragon ' went carefully through the papers submitted to him, and after a reasonable time spent in searching and sifting, pointed out to his client the utter groundlessness of his claim.

' Look here,' he said, ' this entry proves distinctly, not only that you are not the representative of the branch you assume to be, but that you come of another family altogether.'

' Well but,' suggested the other coolly, ' that difficulty perhaps may be got over. The entry may disappear; at all events we are not bound to produce it, and it is ten to one the blot is not hit ! '

The gentleman was requested to walk down stairs. He complied, but prosecuted his suit nevertheless; happily meeting with the success which he deserved. At times people would come to the office on missions yet more hopeless. Take, for example, an

Extract from the Books of the Heralds' College.

' Cato of Jamaica, but anciently of Tusculum in Latium and Rome. A search for the arms of Marcus Portius Cato, or those borne by his grandson Marcus Cato Uticensis, the famous patriot. The inquirer is a gentleman in Jamaica, and says he is their lineal heir male and descendant.

'N.B.—He is to produce his pedigree and call again, as none of the posterity of these celebrated Romans ever exemplified their arms in this office.—2s. 6d.'

The gravity with which the application appears to have been entertained is delightful. I will venture to add another piece of trifling with the sacred subject of genealogy, perpetrated by my father, in the shape of a

PEDIGREE

SHOWING HOW A MAN MAY BECOME BY MARRIAGE HIS OWN
GRANDFATHER AND GRANDSON.

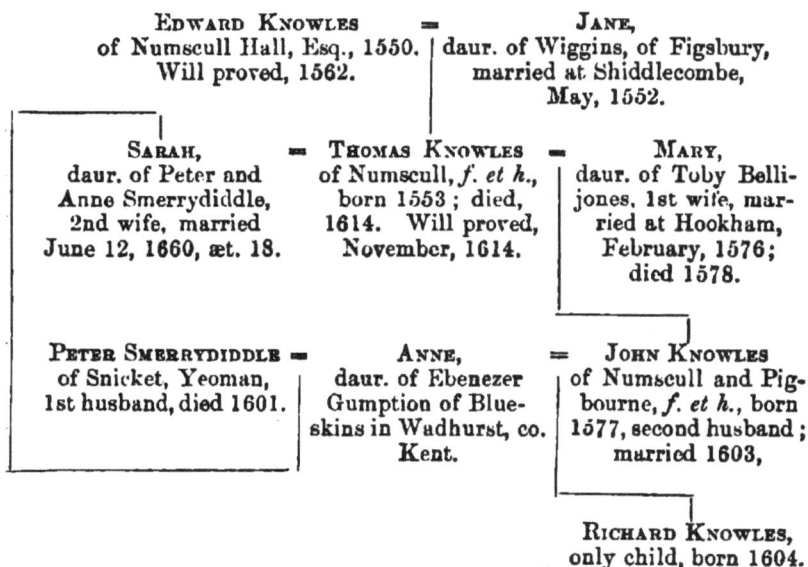

EDWARD KNOWLES of Numscull Hall, Esq., 1550. Will proved, 1562.	=	JANE, daur. of Wiggins, of Figsbury, married at Shiddlecombe, May, 1552.

SARAH, daur. of Peter and Anne Smerrydiddle, 2nd wife, married June 12, 1660, æt. 18.	= THOMAS KNOWLES of Numscull, *f. et h.*, born 1553 ; died, 1614. Will proved, November, 1614. =	MARY, daur. of Toby Belli-jones, 1st wife, married at Hookham, February, 1576; died 1578.
PETER SMERRYDIDDLE = of Snicket, Yeoman, 1st husband, died 1601.	ANNE, daur. of Ebenezer Gumption of Blue-skins in Wadhurst, co. Kent.	= JOHN KNOWLES of Numscull and Pig-bourne, *f. et h.*, born 1577, second husband ; married 1603,

RICHARD KNOWLES,
only child, born 1604.

Thomas Knowles is grandfather to the daughter of his son's wife ; he is also grandfather to that daughter's husband ; he is also that daughter's husband himself ; therefore he is his own grandfather. He is also his daughter's son, therefore he is his own grandson. Q. E. D.

The following extract refers to the gentleman who at this time held the office of Garter King at Arms :—

' Sir George Nayler was an ensign in the (East ?) York

Militia, where he made himself useful to the radical Duke of Norfolk, who was Lord-Lieutenant of the Riding till dismissed by Pitt for toasting " The Sovereignty of the People." The Duke made him a Pursuivant in the Heralds' College, and by the catastrophe at the Haymarket Theatre, on the occasion of the visit of George III., when Pingo and two other members of the college were squeezed to death, he obtained promotion. Afterwards his *History of the House of Guelph* brought him into favour with the Duke of York. When the Garter was to be sent to St. Petersburg to the Czar, Nayler tried his best to get the commission, but the Duke of Norfolk created Henry Stephenson Falcon Herald for that purpose. Nayler was much disappointed, and complained that it was at least a thousand pounds taken out of his pocket. At the levee soon after, the Regent said, " Nayler, stop ! I have something to say to you." And when the levee broke up, the Prince asked for a sword and knighted him. The Duke of York told him he had asked this as a favour to himself, and observed that Sir Isaac Heard owed half his business in the College to his title, and that therefore he had got one for him as an assistance.'

There is nothing further under the date of 1830 worth producing, unless it be a ' familiar epistle ' in easy verse addressed to me, then a boy of fourteen. Some slight difference of opinion I remember to have arisen between my father and myself respecting the comparative merits of the box-seat and a place inside the coach, which was to convey me to Tunbridge. My fare paid, I was handed, under protest, into the interior of the ' machine,' and on

my naturally availing myself of the opportunity offered
by the first stoppage to mount the roof, in which position
I accomplished the remainder of the journey, some mistake arose respecting my identity and the sum disbursed
on my behalf.   Thence ensued, to my confusion, a disclo-
sure of the masterly movement that had been effected,
and a consequent remonstrance conveyed in terms more
indulgent than, I fear, I deserved :—

To R. H. D. Barham.

'St. Paul's, July 5, 1830.

'I find, Mister Dick,
    That you've played me a trick,
For which you deserve a reproof—
    Not to say a reproach ;
    You got out of the coach,
And settled yourself on the roof.

'You knew you'd a cough,
    And when you set off,
I cautioned you as to your ride,
    And bade you take care
    Of the damp and cold air,
And above all to keep withinside.

'This they tell me that you
    Did not choose to do,
But exchanged with some person, they said ;
    And so Easton mistook
    Your name in his book,
And charged you what he should have paid.

‘ I found them quite willing
To refund every shilling,
And render to Cæsar his due ;
  They gave me back three,
  Which I take to be
The overplus forked out by you.

‘ Now don't do this again ;
Indeed, to be plain,
If you mount, when you come back to town,
  Your namesake the ‘ Dicky,’
  I shall certainly lick ye,
And perhaps half demolish your crown.

‘ Mamma means to enclose
Two white ‘ wipes ’ for your nose ;
As your purse may be run rather hard,
  I shall also attack her
  To augment your exchequer
With a sovereign stuck in a card.

‘ But my note I must end it,
Or 'twill be too late to send it
To-day, which I much wish to do ;
  So remember us, mind, enough
  To our friends who are kind enough
To be bored with such a nuisance as you.

‘ Write as soon as you can,
That's a good little man,

And direct your epistle to me ;
    Meanwhile I remain,
    Till I see you again,
Your affectionate sire,—R. H. B.'

CHAPTER V.

[1831—1835.]

Letter from Rev. E. Cannon—The Dulwich Fellowship—Opening of London Bridge—Letter to Mrs. Hughes—'Deady's Gin'—Poetical Report of Harris v. Kemble—Establishment of the Garrick Club—Mr. Sydney Smith at St. Paul's—Townsend and the Jew Boy—Sir Walter Scott—Anecdotes—Bishop the Murderer—Death of Mr. Barham's second son—Letter to Mrs. Hughes—Miss Richards's Ghost Story—Motto—Lord Alvanley's bon mot—Mr. Samuel Arnold—Scott's Review of himself—Visit to Mrs. Hughes—Anecdotes—Correspondence—Summer Hill—Death of Cannon—Dinners at the Garrick—Anecdotes—'My Cousin Nicholas'—'My Grandfather's Knocker'—Letter to Mrs. Hughes—Visit to Oxford—Hook's improvisation—Appointment to the Chaplaincy of the Vintners' Company—Criticism on Macbeth—Letter to Mrs. Hughes—Bishop Copleston—'O no, we never mention him'—Roasted Turbot—Visit to Strand or Green—'Lines left at Hook's House'—Anecdotes—The Foreign Counts—Letter to Mrs. Hughes—Mr. Smith's advice—Southey's affliction—'The Two M.P.'s'—Dinner at Sydney Smith's—'Receipt for Salad'—Letter to Mrs. Hughes.

In the Spring of 1831, Mr. Cannon became a candidate for a vacant fellowship at Dulwich College, and addressed a highly characteristic letter to my father on the subject. A comparison of its style with that of *Godfrey Moss* before mentioned will show that the caricature, as it has been termed, is in no degree an exaggeration of the grotesque humour of the original :—

Edward Cannon to R. H. B.

'March, 1831.

' My dear Dickums,—Dr. Moss is all for Dulwich; the circumstances thereof suit me very well—salary paid quarterly and nothing to do. I had thought the election was pulling papers out of a hat, and the successful boy drew out one on which "*Donum Dei*" was written. If it depends on people, get their names and I dare say we can get at them. I suppose six and eight-pence is at the bottom of the thing as at the bottom of every thing else in this world; meanwhile your zeal becomes you, although I do not see so strongly as you do the necessity of my showing my old face to the creeturs. I can't run after them all over the town, but I have written—"Ah! *written*," you'll say—stop a bit—to Linley, to ask him about it all. If introduction is necessary, he shall be the introducer. The Pope was too cool about it in his converse on Sunday. Whatever Linley thinks is right to be done, I'll awake and rise and do it. That I think will satisfy you. Did you send *Intelligence*? It came to-night. I see your claw in it—Poetizums and Puffum Devilums. Do send me *Valpergis* by "twopenny;" I will repay thee.

'Yours always,

'Deanums.'

Mr. Barham did what he could in the way of canvassing, but his efforts, as appears in his communication with Dr. Hume, were not seconded by the faintest show of activity on the part of his principal, whose indolence proved insuperable. As might be expected, Cannon was not even one of the two returned to try the curious *sortes* by which the election is determined:—

To Dr. Hume.

‘April 1, 1831.

‘ My dear Doctor,—I have not answered your note before, because I have been too much vexed and annoyed about this business to do it as I ought to have done, and even now, as you will easily perceive, the amiable serenity of my temper is not perfectly restored. Never man had friends (yourself among the number) more disposed to aid and abet than Cannon; but his own inveterate laziness—I had almost written selfishness—will not allow him to move so much as a finger to help them to help himself. Will you believe it, that up to this moment he has not so much as written to these people to announce himself as a candidate, or to solicit their most sweet voices? still less has he called upon them ! Atwood by appointment went down, much to his inconvenience, to Dulwich on Monday to meet him there, and introduce him personally to the Fellows. Having waited for about an hour he went home, and is not best pleased at having been made a fool of. He (Cannon) is very angry with me, because I would not write to Dr. Crotch, a man whom I do not know from Adam, to ask him to write testimonials as to the musical qualifications of a man whom he has known intimately for five-and-forty years, and when there was no earthly reason to prevent said man from writing himself. Would not Crotch naturally answer, if he answered at all,—“ Pray, Sir, who the deuce are you ? Are you one of these Dulwich Fellows that require these testimonials ?” “ No !” “ Then if Mr. Cannon wants anything of me, can’t he write and tell me so without employing an amanuensis of whom I know nothing and care less?" But however I have done with the business; everything has been done that could be done by proxy, and if he will content himself with praying to Hercules without putting his shoulder to the wheel, why he has no right to grumble if he continues sticking in the mud. As to the poet (Moore), I did not think a man of the world like him had been so sensitive, or so alarmed at the ghost of a repulse, as he professes to be. But small blame to him for that same! Cannon has certainly no claim on him whatever; although to be so easily "sent to the right about" by anticipation would seem to savour more of the "cold-hearted Saxon" than Green Erin. As it happens, there is every reason to believe that Allen is pledged body and soul, to Blanco White. Perhaps he knew that, and did not choose to ask at a *certainty* of being refused. With all these drawbacks, I still hope Cannon will be one of those returned: the rest is, as you know, literally a "toss up." When shall we see you?—Yours ever,

'R. H. BARHAM.'

'*Diary.—August* 1.—The King opened London Bridge. I had read prayers to him and the Queen at the Chapel Royal the day before. Princess Mary (Duchess of Gloucester) there, the Duke of Devonshire as Lord Chamberlain, and the Bishop of Chichester as Clerk of the Closet. Lord Augustus Fitzclarence, who was to have preached, neither came nor sent any notice of his intended absence. Great consternation in consequence as neither I nor Holmes had come prepared with a sermon. Fortunately Lupton, deputy for Packe, had one in his pocket which he preached.'

A similar defalcation occurred subsequently, when my father for the first and last time, I believe, in his life was compelled to preach before the King *extempore.*

To Mrs. Hughes.

'Park Cottage, Hanwell, August 8, 1831.

'My dear Madam,—I hasten, as in justice bound, to acquit Mr. Sharpe of the charge of negligence. The fact is I have been running all over Kent, while my menagerie of animals, wild and tame, have been recruiting their health here—

Far from the world, its commerce and its cares,

as the poet hath it. As I was wandering about on strictly a journey of business, and had to visit Canterbury, Dover, and even that *ultima Thule* of abomination, Margate, in the course of my pilgrimage, I did not have my letters sent after me, consequently did not receive yours till I found them installed on my mantelpiece when I returned. As to that unfortunate man, C——, I hardly know what to say. It is impossible not to feel pity for the melancholy degradation of such talent as he, once at least, possessed, and if embarrassed circumstances and the anxiety and misery of mind necessarily attendant upon them be any excuse for intemperance, I fear he may plead it with too much truth. That he is harassed to death by money matters there can be no doubt. Bentley told me that he owes them a thousand pounds, and talked of taking serious steps against him. Now when we see

the projectile force of—say five hundred duns—impelling
on one side, and the seductive allurements of "Deady's
imperial, full proof Old Tom" sucking one down like a
Charybdis on the other, both urging with united energy.
in the same direction, it is a matter of regret, perhaps
rather than surprise, that a person originally, may be,
of a convivial temperament should be whelmed in a vortex
of gin and bitters.   That there is something inexplicably
soothing in these "compounds" when all the usual sources
of consolation are cut off is unquestionable.   *Tilburina*
tells us—and truly—that "when the soul is sunk in com-
fortless despair it cannot taste of merriment;"—but it
may of gin! while, if we are to believe Tom Moore,
Lord Byron himself owed at least as much of his inspiration to Hodges as to Helicon.   My own sentiments on
the subject stand, or did some fifteen years ago, recorded
on the wainscot of the "worst inn's worst room," in the
village of Nettlebed,—whither I was driven by a storm of
rain for shelter,—written and composed under the immediate inspiration of "something short!"

> ' If torn from all we hold most dear,
>   The tedious moments slowly roll,
> Can Music's tenderest accents cheer
>   The silent grief that melts the soul?

> ' Or can the Poet's boasted art,
>   To breasts that feel corroding care
> The healing balm of peace impart,
>   And pluck the thorns engendered there?

' Ah no ! in vain the verse may flow,
In vain the softest strain begin ;
The only balm to soothe our woe
And hush our grief is—Deady's Gin !

' By this time, my dear madam, I dare say a lurking
suspicion has crept into your mind that I am myself
slightly under the influence of this favourite Hippocrene,
and have been partaking somewhat too plentifully of the
" great sublime I draw." At the risk, however, of confirming you in the impression, I cannot resist copying a stanza
of one of our most loyal songs, which I was lucky enough
to hear in passing through town, on the memorable 1st
of August, while His Majesty was on his way to open the
new bridge.   That it was composed under the inspiration
of a " Muse of fire," i. e. gin, we cannot doubt, and I have
transmitted it to Blackwood, *inter alia,* that it may find
a place in his account of that august ceremony in the
next *Noctes.*   Would I could have retained the whole,
but the following lines are all I could carry away ; they
formed the chorus of the ballad :—

God save our great King William,
Be his name for ever blest ;
He's the father of *all his people,*
And the guardian of *all the rest !*

' As Tom Moore has left off writing verses except for
the *Times,* and O'Connell is incapable of perpetrating
" Poethry," the credit of the authorship must remain at
present in abeyance between O'Gorman Mahon and Dick

Shiel, both lovers of the Muses—and of gin ! Adieu, my dear Madam, and believe me to be

> 'Yours very faithfully,
> 'R. H. BARHAM.'

A True and Particular Report of the case, Harris *v.* Kemble, *as* not *heard in the House of Lords, September* 5, 1831.[1]

> Lord Mulgrave sat there,
> With his fine head of hair,
> While the Chancellor's look was so glum,
> That on t'other side Plunket
> Appeared much to funk it,
> And Lyndhurst kept biting his thumb.
>
> In front Sir Edward,
> His brief who had read hard,
> Began to address these great men ;
> While behind, Mr. Pepys
> Sat drawing little ships
> On the back of his brief with his pen.
>
> Messrs. Pulman and Currie
> Came up in a hurry,
> In bag-wigs, knee-breeches, and swords,
> As two gentlemen more
> Set open a door,
> And let in three queer-looking lords.

[1] The subject of this action was the validity of a lease granted by the proprietors of Covent Garden Theatre to Mr. Charles Kemble.

King Norroy, so great
In his tabard of state,
To the Chancellor then made a bow;
In a kind of a growl, he
Says, 'Here's my Lord Cowley,
Who is come here to *promise and vow!*'

Lord Brougham, for the Crown,
Says, 'My lord, pray sit down,
You're quite welcome—I never dissemble.'
So Lord C., after that,
Puts on his cocked hat,
And goes and sits down near Miss Kemble.

Then was heard a sad rout
In the lobby without,
As if twenty or more were a-talking;
And in came a summons,
'A message from the Commons!'
Says the Chancellor, 'Pray let 'em walk in.'

Then Sir John Milley Doyle,
With a score more who toil
In committee, to wait longer scorning,
Came and said, 'We agree
Mrs. Turton to free
From her husband.   We wish you good morning.'

'Then,' says my Lord Brougham,
'It's high time to go home;

Sir Edward, pray stop your red rag!'
Then Counsellor Pepys
Never opened his lips,
But popped his brief into his bag.

Then Sugden, so sly,
Gave a wink with his eye,
And shut up *his* brief without sorrow,
Saying, ' Earned with much ease,
This morning, my fees,
And hey for ten guineas to-morrow!'

Among the various departments of literature in which
Mr. Barham sought relaxation, the drama occupied a very
considerable portion of his attention. From the Greek tragedians to Shakespeare and the more modern playwrights,
there was scarcely an author possessed of any pretensions
to merit with whose writings he was not familiar. His
acquaintance, indeed, with the works of Shakespeare was
such as to enable him, at one time, when his memory was
in its full vigour, to supply the context to almost any
quotation that could be made from them, to mention the
play, the act, and generally the very scene from which it
had been taken. Nor was his admiration for this species
of composition confined merely to the *litera scripta* ;
from a boy his cry had been with Hamlet,

' The play, the play's the thing.'

In early life, his own amateur performances had attracted
the favourable notice of several ' regulars,' one of whom,
an eminent actress, seriously assured him that with a little

study he might soon arrive at a respectable position in the profession, and at all events make a very satisfactory stage villain.

Under these circumstances, and firmly believing, as he did, that the stage, which afforded the most intellectual public amusement of the day, might also be made to conduce materially to moral progress, he naturally looked with great interest on the formation of the Garrick Club, which was established, mainly by the exertions of Mr. Frank Mills, with the design of constituting a society in which actors and men of education and refinement might meet on equal and independent terms. The club was intended to be an inexpensive one, and conversational rather than culinary excellence was the object to be aimed at. By the promoting easy intercourse between artists and patrons, by raising the tone of criticism, by the collection of a library of reference, especially of scarce and valuable works on costume, and by the exercise of a salutary influence upon authors as well as managers and actors, it was hoped, as was expressed in the song commemorating the origin of the club,

‘ To bring back the drama to glory again ! ’

How far this end was attained or kept in view, it is not necessary here to inquire, but something was certainly done to elevate the *status* of a profession which, more than any other, suffers from the effects of prejudice and misrepresentation. Of the ‘ Garrick ’ Mr. Barham was one of the original members, and the following lines, composed by him and set as a glee by Mr. Hawes, were sung at the opening dinner in November 1831 :—

ON THE ESTABLISHMENT OF THE GARRICK CLUB.

> Let poets of superior parts
> Consign to deathless fame
> The larceny of the Knave of Hearts,
> Who spoiled his Royal Dame.
>
> Alack! my timid muse would quail
> Before such thievish cubs,
> But plumes a joyous wing to hail
> Thy birth, fair QUEEN OF CLUBS!

The appointment of Mr. Sydney Smith to one of the canonries of St. Paul's proved the means of introducing Mr. Barham to the society of that distinguished individual, and circumstances led afterwards to a pretty frequent correspondence between them, chiefly indeed bearing reference to matters of business, but abounding, on the part of the latter, with instances of that decided spirit and peculiar humour inseparable from his writings and conversation. At first, I believe Mr. Barham looked upon the introduction of the great Whig wit into the chapter with some feeling of misgiving, but the thorough honesty and kindheartedness of the new canon soon made themselves manifest to the apprehension of the candid observer. And differing, as they always did more or less, in political opinion, an appreciation of each other's worth gradually sprang up sufficient to induce a greater degree of intimacy than might, under the circumstances, have been expected.

The first appearance of Mr. Smith at the Cathedral, for the purpose of taking possession of his stall, is thus briefly noted :—

'*Oct.* 2, 1831.—Rev. Sydney Smith read himself in as Residentiary at St. Paul's; dined with him afterwards at Dr. Hughes's. He mentioned having once half offended Sam Rogers by recommending him, when he sat for his picture, to be drawn saying his prayers with his face in his hat.

'Cannon called in the evening, and told us an adventure of his with Townsend, the Bow-street officer, at Brighton. A little Jew boy had been plaguing him the day before to buy pencils, saying that he had a sick mother, thirteen brothers and sisters, and that his father was dead, &c. Cannon gave him a trifle, but desired him not to bother him again. The next day, however, the little Israelite attacked him as before, when he called to Townsend, standing on the Steyne, and told him not to be rough with the lad, but to prevent his continuing to annoy him.

'Townsend commenced a regular examination of the youth. "Do you know Mr. Goldsmith? Do you know Houndsditch?" &c., till he made Cannon open his eyes by asking, "When were you last at Purim?"

'The boy's answer was satisfactory, and when he was dismissed Cannon turned to the officer and inquired how *he* came to know anything about the Jewish festivals.

'"Why God *blesh* you," says Townsend, "Purim's one of these rascals' grand feasts; the High Priest wets his thumb, and the fellows fall a knocking as if they was all at Bartle-my fair. Why blesh your soul! there was a Queen Easter, you know, once, and if it had not ha' been for her, all these scamps would have been hanged altogether. Now you know how I respect 'The Establisment,' so you won't be offended at what I am going to say, which is this

—you remember these *Smouches* are said to be 'whited sepulchres,' well enough to look at outside, but good for nothing within—well, so they continues to be to this very day—and I'm blessed if you'll find any lead in that chap's pencils !"—The illustration proved perfectly correct.'

'*October.*—Sir Walter Scott came to town on his way to Malta, and visited Dr. Hughes. Is much sunk in spirits, and told the doctor, on taking leave, that "he saw a broken man !"—in spirit, of course, as his circumstances are now reviving. He still, however, retains gleams of his former humour, and told with almost his usual glee the story of a placed minister, near Dundee, who, in preaching on Jonah, said: " Ken ye, brethren, what fish it was that swallowed him ? Aiblins ye may think it was a shark— nae, nae, my brethren, it was nae shark; or aiblins ye may think it was a saumon—nae, nae, my brethren, it was nae saumon; or aiblins ye may think it was a dolphin—nae, nae, my brethren, it was nae dolphin "——

' Here an old woman, thinking to help her pastor out of a dead lift, cried out, " Aiblins, sir, it was a dunter !" (the vulgar name of a species of whale common to the Scotch coast).

' " Aiblins, madam, ye're an auld witch for taking the word o' God out of my mouth !" was the reply of the disappointed rhetorician.

' Mr. Lonsdale, late chaplain to the Archbishop, dined there, and, in a conversation which ensued, mentioned his having, in a late tour, fallen in with the original Dominie Sampson. This gentleman was a Mr. Thompson, the son of the placed minister of Melrose, and himself in orders, though without a manse. He had lived for many years as chaplain in Sir Walter's family, and was tutor to his children, who used to take advantage of his absence of mind to open the window while he was lecturing, get quietly out of it and go to play, a circumstance he would rarely perceive. Sir Walter had many opportunities of procuring him a benefice, but never dared avail himself of them, satisfied that his absence of mind would only bring him into scrapes if placed in a responsible situation. Mr. T. was once very nearly summoned before the Synod for reading the " Visitation of the Sick " service from our Liturgy to a poor man confined to his bed by illness.'

No atrocity perpetrated of late years—not even, I will venture to say, the Clerkenwell explosion—has produced an excitement more intense and general than that aroused by the murder of the Italian boy, in 1831, by the resurrectionists Bishop and Williams. The former was, by his own confession, the contriver of the scheme, and the chief actor in carrying it out.[1] It was to his house the boy was lured ; he procured the laudanum to stupify the lad ; he it was who carried out his victim heavy with sleep into the garden, and, with the assistance of Williams, suffocated him in the well. Upon him therefore was the indignation of the town naturally concentrated, and almost equally as a matter of course was his sin visited upon the members of his family, although there was no just cause

---

[1] It was a singular retribution that the body of Bishop was handed over for dissection to the anatomists of King's College, the very place to which he and his accomplices had brought ' *the thing*,' as they termed the corpse of their victim, for a like purpose. ' *Things*,' in those days, appear to have been worth from eight to ten guineas a-piece.

for suspecting them to have been cognisant of the crime or crimes committed beneath their roof. People supposed to be his widow and daughter were attacked in the street, and with difficulty, and not always without serious injury, rescued by the police. Meanwhile, Mrs. Bishop herself having quitted the slaughter-house in Bethnal Green was living, under a feigned name, in the parish of Mr. Barham, who, as the annexed memorandum shows, was soon engaged in rendering her such assistance as was in his power :—

'*Memorandum respecting Bishop's widow and child,* *December* 28, 1831.

'The Rev. R. H. Barham presents his compliments to Mr. C——, and begs to say that he has called on Mr. A—— of Kingsland Road, with whom the boy John Bishop lived several months, and that the result of his inquiries as to the lad's character is very satisfactory. A——, who seems a very respectable man, and his wife agree in stating that the boy was a good boy; that he was honest, civil, and active; and that the only fault they ever had to find with him was a difficulty in getting him up in the morning sufficiently early to attend his master, who keeps an eating-house, to market. Mr. Barham has subsequently seen Mrs. B—— of Shepperton Street, Islington, respecting the mother. Mrs. B—— informs him that Mrs. Bishop has been in her employ during the last nine years both as charwoman and occasionally as nurse, in which latter capacity she nursed Mrs. B—— through her accouchement, that she always showed herself a mild, strictly honest, and sober woman, but appeared latterly almost heart-broken from the ill-treatment of a bad husband. Mrs. B—— added that the woman first informed her about three years since that she had found out the trade which her husband had adopted of resurrectionist, by his having been sent to jail for an offence of that description; she having for some time before suspected what courses he was following, from the discovery of certain implements, and from the circumstance of his continual absence from home at night. She declared, however, that nothing had ever occurred to induce her to suspect the yet more horrible acts he was in the habit of committing. Mrs. B—— further assured me that she is fully satisfied that the bare apprehension of such a crime would have been sufficient to deter the woman, out of sheer terror, from returning home to her husband, whose violence kept her in great fear of her life, even without any such suspicion. Mrs. B—— said that she shall without hesitation continue to employ Mrs. Bishop in her own family as heretofore, and that several persons of respectability in the neighbourhood will bear equal testimony to her character, some of whom, however, decline to employ her from the fear that, if it be known, their houses may be attacked by the mob. Mr. Barham begs leave to add that the various stories circulated in the papers of the woman Bishop and her daughter having been found drunk and assaulted in the streets are from his own knowledge absolutely false; that the women have been residing quietly under the protection of a brother-in-law, and under the woman's maiden name, ever since the execution of Bishop; and that on one occasion, when they

were reported in several of the journals to have been assaulted while in a state of intoxication, in Shoreditch, they
were at that very time in Mr. Barham's own parlour.'

July 1832 brought with it a sudden and severe shock
to Mr. Barham's domestic happiness ; his second son was
smitten by the cholera, then raging fearfully in London.
The peculiar phenomena of this dreadful disease were
developed in all their horrors in the case in question.
Within the short space of four-and-twenty hours was
compressed the sad succession of events, embracing health,
sickness, death, and burial.

To Mrs. Hughes.

'Herne Bay, July 19, 1832.

'My dear Madam,—So kind a friend as you have ever
proved yourself will, I am confident, rather have anticipated the occurrence of something extraordinary to
account for my silence, than have accused me of ingratitude or neglect. I have, indeed, another and most melancholy call on you for that sympathy which your kind
heart is so ready to extend to all. A week has now
elapsed since it pleased Almighty God to visit me with a
severe affliction—to take from me my poor boy George,
of whom perhaps I was too fond ; and that in a manner
the most terrible and astounding. It was nearly two in
the morning when I went into his room and kissed him,
as I had always been in the habit of doing before retiring
to rest. He awoke, was in high spirits, and apparently,
as I had seen him in the daytime, in the highest health.

At five Mrs. Barham, who had been aroused by his calling from the adjoining room, woke me and told me he was in violent pain. Five minutes were sufficient to satisfy me that he was attacked by cholera, and, I had every reason to fear, in its most alarming form. My eldest boy flew to Mr. Burn, our apothecary, while I proceeded to Dr. Pearce's, in St. Helen's Place. He was at home, but, on being informed of the supposed nature of the complaint, declined coming " for an hour or so, as he never visited a cholera patient before he had had his breakfast." Happily, as I then thought, Dr. Davies of Broad Street was less cautious, and in the kindest manner accompanied me back. His language, however, was anything but cheering, as he told me the disease had made tremendous progress in London within the last forty-eight hours, and with a character of far greater malignancy than it had exhibited on its first visit. He had himself, he said, seen eight patients in the evening previous, of not one of whom did he entertain any hopes. An hour had not elapsed from his first seizure when we reached my poor little sufferer, to whom Mr. Burn had for more than half that time been administering the most active medicines. I cannot describe to you the shock I experienced on now looking at him. The poor little fellow was so changed that none but a parent could have recognised his identity, and up to this moment I dare not recall his appearance to memory. My kind friend Dr. O'Shaughnessy, who witnessed the ravages of this horrible pest at Warsaw, and was afterwards employed by Government, both at Paris and Sunderland, and who has perhaps more knowledge and experience of it than any man in Europe, was with us by eleven. The efforts of these gentlemen were at one time so successful that at half-past twelve we began to hope a reaction had taken place, and O'Shaughnessy, on taking leave, told me that he did hope the poor boy was one of a thousand, and that we had seen the worst. Poor George was at this moment even cheerful, and chatted, begging me to tell him stories, which I did till about four, when he fell into a gentle sleep, from which we augured the most favourable results. Poor child!—he never woke again, but dozed away, and slept out of life so gently that his mother continued rubbing his chest with a strong embrocation full twenty minutes after his gentle and affectionate spirit had quitted its tenement, without either of us being aware of the circumstance. Mr. Burn, however, who knew what had taken place, called me out, and informed me of it. I received the intelligence, not only with incredulity, but almost indignation; it was, however, too true. Of what passed afterwards, I can give you no account—it is a perfect blank in my memory— the suddenness of the blow was stunning. But a few hours before, the question had been whether we should take him with us to the theatre, and now they asked me about his funeral—his *immediate* interment! God's hand pressed indeed heavily upon me, and I fear my heart was not right towards Him, even when I said, " His will be done!" They told me to take comfort and example from my wife, who had never quitted the poor child's bedside, and who now bore up with a fortitude that surprised them. But I was not to be deceived; I saw that it was not so much resignation as to the dead as alarm for the living that kept her up, and I knew from experience what the reaction would be when that fear was quieted.

' To my eldest son, I verily believe, I owe it that I am at this moment alive. He managed everything with an intelligence and sympathy far beyond his years ; and two hours after they had placed my boy in the house appointed for all living, we found ourselves on the road to Parrock House. A severe attack which I had in the night caused the medical man to be sent for from Gravesend. We at first thought it was the same complaint, but it proved only a violent nervous affection, and the perfect quiet we experienced soon restored my bodily health ; my mind will, I hope and pray, soon recover its tone also, although I fear this letter will give you no very favourable specimen of its present condition. I know my duty, however, and with the aid of that good God who even in His wrath thinketh upon mercy, will endeavour, and do endeavour, to perform it. In the meantime, as I had foreboded, my wife, when the necessity for exertion was over, sank into an abstraction which tells me that her grief is indeed deeply seated. From his quiet, domestic, and affectionate habits, the poor boy who is gone had perhaps wound himself closer round our hearts than some other of our children whose bolder and more independent habits seemed less to require that constant and affectionate attention without which he was unhappy. Many a care and fear, as well as many a hope, are now buried with him in his early grave ; but it is in sincerity and truth that I am now enabled to say, " It is the Lord, let Him do what seemeth Him good."

'We have been now four days at this place, the retirement of which and the absence of all other society than that of our remaining children, all of whom are with us, have done much to tranquillise the minds of both of us. Twice before I have attempted to address you, but could not succeed. Ordinary occupation is, I am convinced, not only beneficial but necessary to me, and I shall endeavour to resume mine forthwith. Fortunately there are several things which call upon me for immediate exertion. The proofs of Mr. Hughes's poem have been forwarded to me here. I return them to Moyes by this post, with directions to him to send the copies when corrected to Mr. Hogan Smith. May I trust to Mr. Hughes's kindness to make my excuses to that gentleman for my neglect of his last letter. I am sure he will forgive me when he knows how I have been situated.

'I am sorry to say, from letters received from town this morning, that this horrible plague continues its ravages in the city. Of Dr. Davies's eight patients, four died the same day with my poor boy, and the others since; and I learn that twelve are now lying dead in the immediate neighbourhood of St. Paul's Churchyard. In the meantime Government are using all their influence with the Press to make as light as possible of the business, in order to prevent the necessity of declaring London a foul port. God bless you, my dear madam, and preserve you and all dear to you from this and all other calamities—is the sincere prayer of your ever obliged

'R. H. BARHAM.'

'*Diary.—November* 4, 1832.—Mrs. Hughes told me the following ghost story. Her own grandfather had carried on a flirtation with Miss Richards of Compton, one of the richest heiresses in his native country, but being, for a gentleman, in comparatively narrow circumstances did not venture to propose for her; nor was it till after he had engaged himself to another lady that he discovered the heiress might have been his but for the faint heart which prevented him from winning the fair lady. Miss Richards, however, remained a spinster for his sake, formed a strict intimacy with his sister, whom she prevailed upon to live with her, and when he had children adopted one of them—a girl—aunt to the lady from whom I had this story, and from whom she had it.

'At the death of her father, Miss Richards inherited, among other possessions, the home farm called Compton Marsh, which remained in her own occupation under the management of a bailiff. This man, named John ——, was engaged to be married to a good-looking girl, to whom he had long been attached, and who superintended the dairy.

'One morning Miss Richards, who had adopted masculine habits, was going out with her greyhounds, accompanied by her *protégée*, and called at the farm. Both the ladies were struck by the paleness and agitation evinced by the dairymaid. Thinking some lover's quarrel might have taken place, the visitors questioned her strictly respecting the cause of her evident distress, and at length, with great difficulty, prevailed upon her to disclose it.

'She said that on the night preceding she had gone

to bed at her usual hour, and had fallen asleep, when she was awakened by a noise in her room. Rousing herself she sat upright and listened. The noise was not repeated, but between herself and the window, in the clear moon-light, she saw John standing within a foot of the bed, and so near to her that by stretching out her hand she could have touched him. She called out immediately, and ordered him peremptorily to leave the room. He re-mained motionless, looking at her with a sad countenance, and in a low but distinct tone of voice bade her not be alarmed, as the only purpose of his visit was to inform her that he should not survive that day six weeks, naming at the same time two o'clock as the hour of his decease. As he ceased speaking, she perceived the figure gradually fading, and growing fainter in the moonlight, till, without appearing to move away, it grew indistinct in its outline and finally was lost to sight.

'Much alarmed she rose and dressed herself, but found everything quite quiet in the house, and the door locked on the inside as usual. She did not return to bed, but had prudence enough to say nothing of what she had seen, either to John, or to any one else. Miss Richards com-mended her silence, advising her to adhere to it, on the ground that these kinds of prophecies sometimes bring their own completion along with them.

'The time slipped away, and, notwithstanding her un-affected incredulity, Miss Richards could not forbear, on the morning of the day specified, riding down to the farm, where she found the girl uncommonly cheerful, having had no return of her vision, and her lover remaining still in full health. He was gone, she told the ladies, to Wantage market, with a load of cheese which he had to dispose of, and was expected back in a couple of hours. Miss Richards went on and pursued her favourite amusement of coursing. She had killed a hare, and was returning to the house with her companion, when they saw a female, whom they at once recognised as the dairymaid, running with great swiftness up the avenue which led to the mansion.

'They both immediately put their horses to their speed, Miss Richards exclaiming, "Good God! something has gone wrong at the farm!" The presentiment was verified. John had returned looking pale and complaining of fatigue, and soon after went to his own room, saying he should lie down for half an hour while the men were at dinner. He did so, but not returning at the time mentioned, the girl went to call him, and found him lying dead on his own bed. He had been seized with an aneurism of the heart!'

'*November* 17.—Dined with Mr. (Sydney) Smith. He told me of the motto he had proposed for Bishop Burgess's arms, in allusion to his brother, the well-known fish-sauce projector:

" *Gravi* jamdudum *saucia* curâ ! "

'*February* 9, 1833.—Dined, for the first time, at the Beefsteak Club, held at the Bedford till the rebuilding of Arnold's theatre. The members present were Mr. Lewin (in the chair), Stephenson (vice), the Duke of Leinster, Lord Saltoun, Sir Andrew Barnard, Sir Ronald Ferguson, Sir John Cam Hobhouse, Messrs. Hallett, Peake, Linley, and Arnold. All very amusing. Jokes of Lord Alvanley mentioned. At the late fête at Hatfield House, *tableaux vivants* were among the chief amusements, and scenes from *Ivanhoe* were among the selections. All the parts were filled up but that of *Isaac of York*. Lady Salisbury begged Lord Alvanley "to make the set complete by doing the Jew." "Anything in my power your ladyship may command," replied Alvanley, "but though no man in England has tried oftener, I never could *do a Jew* in my life."

'He half affronted Mr. Greville, with whom he was dining. The dining-room had been newly and splendidly furnished, whereas the dinner was but a very meagre and indifferent one. While some of the guests were flattering their host on his taste, magnificence, &c., "For my part," said his lordship, "I had rather have seen less gilding and more carving."'

Of the Mr. Samuel Arnold just mentioned, Mr. Barham observes elsewhere: 'I first met him at Hawes's, several years before the institution of the "Garrick," where he was a member of the committee at the same time with myself. I encountered him the morning after his theatre (the English Opera-house, afterwards the Lyceum) was burnt down, by which he lost 60,000*l.*, and never saw a man meet misfortune with so much equanimity. His new theatre, which was raised by subscription, completely failed, and when Osbaldiston took Covent Garden in 1835, and reduced the admission to the boxes to four shillings, Arnold reduced his price to two, but this did not succeed, while the property was materially depreciated by the measure. Arnold was one of the leading members of the Beefsteak Club, where he was called "the Bishop."'

To authors' oaths, as well as to those of lovers, Jove, it is to be hoped, is particularly indulgent; for, assuredly, whatever amount of affirmative perjury may be incurred by the latter, it is to the full paralleled by the ample negations put forth by the former. Southey distinctly denied the authorship of *The Doctor*. But, perhaps, a greater degree of 'nerve' was exhibited by Mr. Sydney Smith, who, positively disowning all connection with the *Plymley Letters* in one edition, actually published them in a collection of his acknowledged works some few months after. The mystery that hung so long around the Wizard of the North is yet more notorious; the anecdote which follows may serve to show the anxiety of the 'Great Unknown' to preserve his incognito :—

'*February* 11.—Dined with Sir George Warrender at his house in Albemarle Street. Met Lord Saltoun, John Wilson Croker, Sir Andrew Barnard, Mr. Barrow of the Admiralty, John Murray, the publisher, Mr. Littleton, Sir Charles Bagot, Mr. Lee, an artist, Francis Mills, and James Smith.

'Murray told me that Sir Walter Scott, on being taxed by him as the author of *Old Mortality*, not only denied having written it, but added, "In order to convince you that I am not the author, I will review the book for you in the *Quarterly*,—which he actually did, and Murray still has the MS. in his handwriting.

'Sir George Warrender said that, returning once from Windsor with the Duke of Wellington in his cab, the Duke drove so furiously and so badly, narrowly escaping collision with several drags, &c., that he, Sir George, was much alarmed, and begged him not to drive so fast. "Pooh, pooh!" said his Grace, "where there is no fear there is no danger!" "My dear Duke," returned Sir George, "if fear is the criterion of danger, for Heaven's sake stop and let me out, for I never was in such a funk in my life!"'

'*July* 3, 1833.—Visit to Mrs. Hughes at Kingston Lisle. From letters of Sir Walter Scott, it appears that Lord Webb Somerset, brother to the Duke of Beaufort, was the author of the note to *Rokeby* containing the legend of Littlecote Hall, and that Miss Hayman furnished him with the ballad, "The spirit of the blasted tree" in *Marmion*.

'*Dandie Dinmont* was one Jamie Davison, who lived in Liddesdale, and died in September 1823. When the minister, who had paid him several visits during his illness, called for the last time on the morning of his death, the good man inquired as to the state of his mind :—

' " Eh minister, ye're vara gude and Ise muckle obleeged to ye; eh, sir, it's a great mercy that I sulde be able to look out of window the morn and get a sight o' the hounds; it's just a mercy they sulde rin this way. 'Twad ha' bin too much for a puir sinner like me to ha' expeckit a sight o' the tod ! sae thank the Lord for a' things ! "

' The circumstances attending *Tony Foster's* death as described in *Kenilworth* are taken from a real incident recorded in the third volume of the Duc de St. Simon's memoirs. There an account is given of the death of an avaricious Master of Requests at Lyons, named Pecoil, who had contrived a recess within his cellar closed by a heavy iron door, within which he was in the habit of depositing his hoards. By some means the lock at last got hampered, and on one of his visits he was unable to let himself out again. He was eventually discovered lying on his treasures dead, and having previously begun to gnaw one of his arms.

'Mrs. Hughes repeated several anecdotes which she had heard from the mouth of Sir Walter himself; among them one of Lady Johnson, sister to the late Earl of Buchan and Lord Erskine, and widow of Sir J. Johnson. When on her death-bed, a few hours prior to her dissolution, she had her notice attracted by the violence of a storm which was raging with great fury out of doors. Motioning with her hand to have the curtains thrown open, she looked earnestly at the window through which the lightning was flashing very vividly, and exclaimed to her attendants: "Gude faith, but it's an unco awfu' night for me to gang bleezing through the lift!"

'Another story told by Sir Walter was of a drunken old laird who fell off his pony into the water while crossing a ford in Ettrick.

'"Eh, Jock," he cried to his man, "there's some puir body fa'en into the water; I heard a splash; who is it, man?"

'"Troth, laird, I canna tell; forbye it's no yersell," said John, dragging him to the bank. The laird's wig meanwhile had fallen off into the stream, and John in putting it on again placed it inside out. This, and its being thoroughly soaked, annoyed the old gentleman, who refused to wear it:—

'"Deil ha' my saul, it's nae my ain wig; what for do ye no get me my ain wig, ye ne'er-do-weel?"

'"Eh then, laird, ye'll no get ony ither wig the night, sae e'en pit it on again. There's nae sic a wale of wigs in the burnie I jalouse."

'Another of his stories was of a party of Highland gentlemen who continued drinking three whole days and nights successively, without intermission :—

' " Hech, Sirs," cried one at last, " but McKinnon looks gash ! "

' " What for should he no," returned his neighbour, " has na' the chiel been dead these twa hoors ? "

' " Dead ! " repeated his friend, " an ye did na 'tell us before ! "

' " Hoot, man," was the answer, " what for should I ha' spoiled gude company for sic a puir bit bodie as yon ? " '

To Mrs. Hughes.

'St. Paul's Churchyard, July 27, 1833.

' My dear Madam,—Here we are at last, once more returned to the immediate vicinity of the " Wren's Nest," where I am happy to find that all things have gone on tolerably smoothly in the main, and that order has once more sprung out of confusion.

'Packe has got the stall he was desirous of, and B— after, I believe, something very like an admonitory lecture from Sydney Smith, succeeds to that which is relinquished, and which is by no means a bad one. This amiable young gentleman was a long time in making up his mind, and indeed trifled with the Dean and Chapter so long that the Dean, I am told, actually determined on giving it to L——, but for the interference of Mr. Smith, who begged to be allowed to give the foolish fellow a true insight into his position first. " What is heavier than lead, and what is the name thereof but a fool?" Dr. Blomberg is fully installed at Cripplegate, where his parishioners have given him a public dinner on his remitting three hundred a year from their tithes. Of course he is at present very popular there, and goes to reside immediately. A long, flourishing account of the banquet appeared next day in the *Times*, furnished no doubt by Mr. W——, who was present on the occasion and pronounced a panegyrical oration with sufficient emphasis, I say nothing of discretion. Altogether it appears to have been a mighty silly affair, and I much fear the worthy Doctor may hereafter find himself inconvenienced, when called upon, as he assuredly will be—for radicals give no quarter—to redeem some of the pledges of hospitality and good-fellowship which escaped from him in the overflowing of his heart. To wind up the whole, his coffee-coloured friend has at last carried his favourite point, and is to be " his worship's representative, factotum, locum tenens " at the cathedral, *residing in the Residentiary House*, and *presiding* at the weekly dinners! Adkins has, I believe, given up all thoughts of further proceedings at law or otherwise; so you will not have to fear another *subpœna*. Not that I should feel so much for you on a third as I did on the first and second times of your appearance *coram nobis*. The account you gave me of your sensations on the latter occasion put me very much in mind of Beaumont and Fletcher's little French lawyer, excessively alarmed in the first instance and dragged with difficulty into fighting, but afterwards quite eager for a rencontre with every one he met; nor have I the least doubt that a summons or two more would make you not only dumbfound the counsel, but bully the judge himself in all the majesty of *Domini Regis*.

'Vivian starts to-morrow for Venice, Packe is off to Walton in Essex, the Dean, reversing young Lochinvar's line of march, is gone *into* the West, and Mr. Smith is on the high road to—— Heaven knows where! so that, as is usual at this time of the year, the birds of passage are all migratory and "leave St. Paul's to Lingard and to me !" All my clan accompanied me back to town, and are all, thank God, in excellent health. The children, of course, miss their fields and gardens very much at present, and I own I should not myself have been grieved at being able to run about a little longer among the groves of Summer Hill, which I think I described to you as the seat of Charles the Second, and since of Mr. James Alexander, the East India Director, and immediately adjoining our grounds. As you encourage me to bestow all my tediousness on your worship, I shall make no apology for enclosing a copy of "an effusion" which burst from a heart overflowing with nonsense when I quitted it, for the last time, on my return to the "Wells." Will it do for another number of *Family Poetry* ? [1]

'And now, having surfeited you with rubbish enough for one dose, let me conclude with my best acknowledgments to you and Mr. and Mrs. Hughes, for the kindness with which you have made me spend some of

---

[1] The poem enclosed was *An Ode on a Nearer Prospect of Summer Hill.* It was printed in *Blackwood,* and will be found under the title of *The Country Seat,* in *The Annotated Edition of the Ingoldsby Legends,* vol. ii. p. 404.

the pleasantest days that have lately fallen to my lot.
I shall never think of Berkshire and the White Horse-men
but with the warmest feelings.   Mrs. Barham and Dick
(who by the way *has* gained the prize) beg to unite in
every good wish with,

'Dear Madam, your much obliged

'R. H. Barham.'

The principal events of 1834 of which Mr. Barham has
left any note are the death of his friend Cannon, and the
appearance, in the pages of *Blackwood* of his novel,
My Cousin Nicholas.   Of the former occurrence he gives
a brief account in a letter to Dr. Hume :—

To Dr. Hume.

' March 4, 6 o'clock, 1834.

'My dear Hume,—When I wrote to you this morning
from the " Garrick," I did not think to address you so soon
again, but on my return home I found a letter from poor
Cannon's niece, with the information that he died yesterday between twelve and one.   Although, in the state
he was, this dispensation cannot be lamented, yet the
impression which the news has made upon me is much
stronger than I expected under all the circumstances it
would have been. "Auld lang syne " comes over me strongly,
and all recent occurrences are lost in the remembrance of
what has been.   Poor fellow! with all his infirmities he
had a warm heart, and even to those he disliked his bark
was worse than his bite.   His little property is not, I
believe, wholly swallowed up ; a few hundreds must remain,

and I hope they are properly disposed of. I know he made a will in favour of his sister, which Moore still has, but it is not impossible that designing people—and I fear that he has had some such about him—have induced a different disposition. The moment I learn anything certain I will let you know, as I am sure it is a subject in which you will take an interest. Alas, poor Yorick!

'Yours as ever,

'R. H. BARHAM.'

'*Diary.—March* 24, 1834.—Dined at the "Garrick;" Mr. Williams, the banker, in the chair, Fladgate, croupier, Charles Mathews (the father), E. Parrott, Westmacott, the sculptor, Mortimer Drummond, T. Clarke, Tom Hill, J. R. Durrant, W. Beloe, myself, and John Murray. We twelve were seated when Hook arrived. He looked at first very blank on finding himself the *thirteenth*, but being told that Charles Young the actor was expected immediately took his seat, and we had a very pleasant evening. C. Mathews gave a very amusing account of poor Dicky Suett's funeral which he had attended as a mourner. Suett lies buried in St. Paul's Churchyard, in the burial-ground belonging to St. Faith, nearly opposite the shop of Dollond the optician, and just within the rails. Suett had been brought up originally as a boy in the choir. Mathews and Captain Caulfield (whom I have often seen perform, and whose personation of Suett, Mathews said, was much more perfect than his own) were in the same coach with Jack Banister and Palmer. The latter sat wrapt up in angry and indignant

silence at the tricks which the two younger *mourners*
(who, by the way, had known but little of Suett, and were
invited out of compliment) were playing off; but Banister,
who was much affected by the loss of his old friend,
nevertheless could not refrain from laughing occasionally
in the midst of his grief and while the tears were actually
running from his eyes. Mr. Whittle, commonly called
" Jemmy Whittle," of the firm of Laurie and Whittle,
stationers, in Fleet Street, was an old and intimate friend
of Suett's. As the procession approached, he came and
stood at his own door to look at it, when Caulfield called
out to him from the mourning-coach in Suett's voice,

' " Aha! Jemmy—O la! I'm going to be buried! O,
la! O lawk! O dear!"'

' Whittle ran back into the house absolutely frightened.
Similar scenes took place the whole of the way. The
burial service was read, when, just as the clergyman had
concluded it, an urchin seated on a tombstone close by the
rails began clapping his hands. The whole company were
struck by this singular conclusion to a theatrical funeral;
but the boy when questioned and taken to task for the
indecency said,

' " La! there was only them two dogs outside as wanted
to fight, and was afraid to begin, so I did it to set 'em on."'

' Mathews also gave a very entertaining account of his
having been recommended by Mr. Lowdham, a member
of the club, to stop at a particular inn in Nottingham,
when upon his last theatrical tour. He found it, however,
quite a third-rate inn, and could get no attendance.
Half-a-dozen different people successively answered the

bell when he rang, stared at him, said "Yes, sir!" and went away; nor could he get anyone to show him into a private room, though he had bespoken one. At last a great lubberly boy came blubbering into the room, when Mathews addressed him very angrily :—

' " *M.*—When am I to have my private room ?

' " *Boy.*—We ha'n't got none but one, and that's bespoke for Mathews the player.

' " *M.*—Well, I am Mathews the player, as you call him.

' " *Boy.*—Oh, then you may come this way !

' " He was ushered at length into a room with a fire just lighted, and full of smoke ; still there was nothing to be got to eat, while Mathews, who had travelled between forty and fifty miles that day, was very hungry.

' " *M.*—Send me up the master of the house ! Where is the master ?

' " *Boy.*—He's dead, sir !

' " *M.*—Then send the mistress.

' " *Boy.*—Mother's gone out !

' " *M.*—Well, do let me have something to eat at all events; can you get me a mutton chop ?

' " *Boy.*—Not till mother comes home.

' " *M.*—Well, then, some cold meat—anything. Confound it, boy, have you got nothing in the house ?

' " *Boy.*—Yes, sir !

' " *M.*—Well, what is it then ?

' Here the poor boy burst into a flood of tears and blubbered out—" An execution, sir ! "

' Late in the evening Young did come, and sang with great taste and feeling Sheridan's *When 'tis night.*

Hook improvised, as usual with him, on the company, but was not altogether so happy as I have sometimes heard him.'

The completion and publication of *My Cousin Nicholas* were immediately owing to the kindly interference of Mrs. Hughes. Having read *Baldwin,* and having learnt that another tale was lying unfinished in Mr. Barham's desk, she prevailed upon him to lend her the manuscript. So favourable was her opinion of its merits that without more ado she submitted it to the inspection of Mr. Blackwood, and the first intimation the author received of the circumstance was conveyed in the shape of a packet containing the proof-sheets of the opening chapters. As his zealous friend had pledged her word for the continuation of the work all retreat was cut off; there was nothing for it but diligently to take the matter in hand, and endeavour to surmount those obstacles that had caused him to lay his pen aside. Whatever the difficulties may have been, they were speedily overcome, ' My Cousin's ' adventures were carried on monthly with spirit, and the catastrophe was worked up in a manner that certainly brought no discredit on the earlier portions of the novel.

Mr. Barham always asserted that he was singularly deficient in the faculty of invention. ' Give me a story to tell,' he would say, ' and I can tell it, in my own way ; but I can't invent one !' and although *My Cousin Nicholas* might, I think, be fairly cited as a witness to the injustice of the disclaimer, there is no doubt that the character of his hero's escapades was suggested by an event which occurred in the life of the author's father, and which the former once thought of producing under the title of *My Grandfather's Knocker*! The circumstances, as nearly as I can recollect them, were as follows :—

Somewhere about a century ago, rather more than less, Richard Barham, of Parmstead, became by marriage the owner of some property—principally hop-gardens—lying in close vicinity to Canterbury, and also of a large red-brick house situated within the city walls. It is, I believe, still in existence, enclosed by its high garden walls, above which the tops of a few trees look down refreshingly upon the narrow streets of Burgate. But in addition to house and land, Mrs. Barham brought her husband in due time a son and heir—Richard Harris, the father of the subject of this memoir. Having reached man's estate, Richard Harris declined longer residence in the red-brick house— which was only occasionally inhabited by his father, who spent a good deal of his time at Tapton Wood—and set up a bachelor's establishment for himself. One morning the elder gentleman, who seems to have been of a peppery turn, was roused to fury by the disappearance of a magnificent brass knocker which had hitherto formed the glory of his front door. It had clearly been wrenched off in the course of the night, by way of a ' spree,' as this lively diversion afterwards came to be called. Mr. Barham *senior* raved ; Mr. Barham *junior* condoled ; both were indig-, nant. But nothing came of raving, condolence, or indignation! The offender could not be punished, for the offender could not be found, and so by degrees the offence dropped out of memory. It chanced, some time after, that on a certain day the old gentleman rode in from the country, and, not disposed to spend the evening alone in his own rather gloomy mansion, he betook him to the lodging of his son. Richard Harris was of course delighted to see his father, and taxed his resources to the uttermost in the endeavour to entertain him. Dinner was discussed, and after dinner a liberal allowance of port wine,[1] and then, according to the fashion of the age, preparations were made for winding up the feast with a bowl of punch. ' The materials' were at hand and available —all save the sugar, and the sugar was in large refractory lumps that defied ordinary manipulation. The housekeeper was accordingly summoned, and desired to reduce a sufficient quantity of the ' best loaf ' to powder. Quietly proceeding to a cupboard in the room, the woman provided herself with an implement which, if not expressly constructed for the purpose of trituration, was evidently well enough adapted to it, and commenced pounding away. The old gentleman raised his eyes at the noise, then sprang to his feet, then fired off expression after expression of a sort that no old gentleman ought to fire off. It must, however,

[1] I am not speaking at hap-hazard here. My grandfather always drank a bottle of port wine a day. The doctors interfered at last when his bulk became enormous, and limited him to a pint. 'Well,' said he, 'if I am to have only a pint, a pint it shall be ; I will not be fobbed off with one of those abominations that contain little more than a half.' And so, anticipating the Imperial measure movement, he had a number of bottles made expressly for him, holding each a legitimate pint. A few of these with his cipher stamped upon the shoulder I still possess, One pint of wine, however, he found scarcely sufficient, and so he tried two, thus, in place of reducing his former allowance by half, increasing it by about a third. They argued with him, but he persisted in his opinion that two pints were equal to one bottle, and that one bottle of port could not hurt any man. He died at forty-eight.

be admitted that the provocation was not a slight one, for there was the solution of the mystery—there in calm complacency was his son's cook hammering away at the loaf sugar with the desecrated brass knocker of which he had been so heartlessly bereaved! Mr. Barham *senior* left the house immediately, would listen to no excuses, but executed a fresh will forthwith, leaving his property to be divided between his two daughters, and refused to hold any further communication with his truly penitent son. The alienation lasted for a year or two. Then at length the remonstrances of friends prevailed, and forgiveness was extended, I am exceedingly happy to say, to my too mercurial grandfather.

Of the minor characters presented in the novel, one at least was taken from the life. There are doubtless many Oxford men yet living who can remember 'Doctor Toe,' as from a peculiarity of his gait he was nicknamed, the Dean of Brasenose, and the hero of Reginald Heber's *Whippiad.* Not only defeated in battle within his very stronghold—

> ' Where whiten'd Cain the wrath of Heaven defies,
>   And leaden slumbers close his brother's eyes,
>   Where o'er the porch in brazen splendour glows
>   The vast projection of the mystic nose,'

but—more bitter humiliation still—jilted in love, deserted by his affianced bride, who ran off with her father's footman, the unfortunate doctor formed the subject of a number of University squibs, and among them of an epigram worth repeating:—

'Twixt Footman John and Doctor Toe
　　A rivalship befell,
Which of the two should be the beau
　　To bear away the belle.

The Footman won the lady's heart,
　　And who can blame her ? No man—
The whole prevailed against a part,
　　'Twas *Foot-man versus Toe-man !*

The burlesque personification of 'Doctor Toe' is said to have been actually perpetrated by an ancestor of the present Lord Lyttelton.   And again, the denial of his father by Nicholas—an incident subsequently introduced by Mr. Boucicault in his popular comedy of *London Assurance*—is no fiction, but owes its origin to a similar prank played by the well-known humorist, Bonnell Thornton.   Of the first appearance of *My Cousin Nicholas* in public Mr. Barham thus writes :—

To Mrs. Hughes.

'St. Paul's Churchyard, March 29, 1834.

'My dear Madam,—By the time this reaches you, you will, I trust, have seen in print the reason why I have not before availed myself of the permission to address you occasionally which you were kind enough to continue to me when last I had the pleasure of seeing you in London.   Blackwood can be, whether you know it or not, a great " worry" ; and having put all he had of *My Cousin Nicholas* into type, he has ever since been

uproarious, what he calls "stirring me up," and crying
with the horse-leech's daughter "Give! Give!" though
I must in all honesty avow he is quite as ready to impart
on his side, as he is insatiable in demanding. All the
spare time therefore that I have had in this, as you well
know it to be, the busiest period of the parson's year,
has been devoted to copying and rewriting for him,
till I am really grown almost to hate the sight of a pen.
Last night I received his number for the ensuing month,
which contains *Nicholas,* or at least the first four chapters
of his memoirs, and the *Tale of the Rhine.* The latter
is a pretty literal, but of course burlesque, version of a
remarkably absurd, but showy, piece brought out at the
Adelphi, the success of which has induced half the theatres
in London—Covent Garden, which ought to scorn such
piracy, among the number—to exhibit the same thing with
little more of change than that of name. Perhaps there
is more excuse for the practice in this instance than in
many others, as there is a common source, from which all
have been pilfered, in a mediocre French opera by Auber,
whose music, flimsy as it is, the good lieges of Cockaigne
do not disdain to admire. The same parcel conveyed a
note to me from "Ebony," in which he threatens us with a
new *Noctes* next month, and asks for "some *jeux d'esprit*
if I have any by me," to help him out. But, alas, as a
drysalter of this kind of commodity I am lamentably off
for stock, and find myself obliged to confess the truth of
your old acquaintance L——'s observation when he told
Mr. Sydney Smith last Sunday, in animadversion on the
want of general co-operation in "the body" that they "had

no *jeu d'esprit* among them." His reverend host, without admitting or denying the fact, hinted that it was not their only want, and that a French dictionary, to some of them, was at least as great a desideratum.

'Poor L—— has experienced a severe loss in the sudden death of one of his children, a fine boy about a year old, who was carried off by the prevailing influenza in a few hours. This disorder seems to be precisely that which was last year so fatal to young children, whom it attacks in the chest and throat, and appears to be of the scarlatina kind, and of no common malignity. In this case the poor child was bled, a mode of practice which, both for children and grown persons, last year's experience has proved to be, in almost every case, the worst that could be adopted. Should it make its way into Berkshire, pray impress upon Mr. Hughes, and all your friends who have children, a strong caution against phlebotomy. Poor Dr. Dean, my old friend, who was head of St. Mary's Hall, Oxford, lost his life entirely by having recourse to this expedient when he had caught the complaint.

'The name of Oxford reminds me that I have to communicate, what I am sure you will sympathise with me in, my great satisfaction and delight at having got Mr. Dick fairly on the books at Oriel. This I owe solely to the goodness of the Bishop, who has on this as on every other occasion acted towards me with a degree of kindness my sense of which I really want words to express. Not content with writing to Dr. Hawkins on the subject for me, when he found that the college was so full that, in the ordinary course of rotation, so long a period must

elapse that the " exhibition " from St. Paul's School would
necessarily be forfeited, he applied a second and a third
time, till he not only got him on the Provost's private
list, but even at the top of that list, for the very first
vacancy ; and two days after a vacancy actually took
place. Within an hour after its announcement the new
candidate for " Alma Mater " and myself were on the top
of the Oxford coach, which deposited us in six hours
safe at the " Angel." The next day we dined in Hall at
Oriel with the Bishop's nephew, Mr. Edward Copleston,
who gave Dick a good rattling examination more than an
hour long, and one which would have made my hair stand
on end in my best days. He got through it however, I
am happy to say, so that after breakfasting with the
Provost the next morning, the hero of the " Long-tailed
Coat " was enabled to say in verity, " Upon my life I am
a *man* indeed, and not a schoolboy, nor Christophero Sly."
If Lavater's system be not altogether a dream—if there
be any faith at all to be placed in the expression of the
human face divine—then was the newly matriculated "*man*
of Oriel" as high in the seventh heaven as the ennobled
tinker ; and I must question whether the imposition of
a mitre ever imparted greater satisfaction to the wearer
than did that of the trencher cap (the one which of all
in the shop had the longest tassel) in this instance.
" Hostess, a cup of the smallest ale !" quoth I, as the
similarity of what the dramatic folks call " situation "
struck me most forcibly. We drank it at the " Angel "
door, while the clock of St. Mary's was striking eleven,
and at six o'clock I was seated at Vivian's, in Guildford

Street, at dinner with a party to which I had been for some time engaged. The absolute necessity of my being in London the following day indeed, and the suddenness of our call to the University, alone prevented my carrying into execution a plan I had very much at heart, viz., that of taking the liberty of calling at Kingston Lisle in my way home.

'I have little or no news to tell you, though we are not quite so dull here just at present as we, or at least I, have been. I have had two dinners lately, both of them amusing enough in their way, and the more so perhaps from the contrast they offer to each other. The one was with my Lord Mayor, whom I attended in my capacity of chaplain to the Worshipful Company of Vintners (of which he is a member) on the occasion of his presenting the livery of that company and the freedom of the City, in an *oak* box (for the precious metals are rarely now called into play on these occasions), to the redoubted Captain ——, who prosed in a style decidedly *hyperbore*-an, and who, though he has found out the magnetic pole, seems, as far as I can judge, little likely to discover the longitude. The gold plate was superb and the banquet faultless. The few speeches that were made were of the most approved fashion—" Unaccustomed as I am to speaking, I should be unworthy the name of a man and a Briton," &c. &c. And as the *Morning Post* saith, " The evening concluded with the utmost festivity."

'The other was a small quiet party at the " Garrick," where a dozen persons sat down to a " leg of mutton and trimmings," the latter end of last week.

'Hook and Mathews, who were of the party, worried
John Murray—whom the former named (from his incau-
tiously giving his opinion of a book of which, it came out,
he had only seen the back) "the Hind-Quarterly Reviewer"
—in a manner that, as "Ebony" would say, "It was just a
curiosity to see!" About the small hours Hook started off,
as he often does when in his happiest vein, in an im-
provisatory gallopade, and gave every one in the room his
extempore stanza, and every stanza, as usual, an epigram.
This is a most extraordinary proof of talent, as, from the
fact of every point he made relating to something which
had passed in the course of the evening, you saw at once
that it was impossible he could have come previously
prepared.

'And now, my dear Madam, having bestowed all my
tediousness upon you, let me take my leave while you
have any patience left. You will be glad to hear that
Mrs. Barham has wonderfully improved in her health of
late, and has so far got rid of her lameness that she
walked with me the other day to Jermyn Street and
back, without feeling the slightest inconvenience either
at the time or since. She begs to join with me in kindest
regards to you and yours. Dick is now spending his Easter
vacation with his uncle, Colonel Smart, at Dover; and,
from a letter which I received yesterday, seems to be
enjoying himself there not a little. The rest of the
family, thank God, are all in excellent health and spirits,
and we are looking forward with hope to a pleasant
summer, in spite of Joe Hume and the Trades' Unions.
Mr. Capel, who was of the party at the Mansion House,

inquired earnestly after you, and, when I told him I was about to write, begged me to add his kindest remembrances to those of, my dear Madam,

' Your ever obliged servant,

' R. H. BARHAM.'

The election of Mr. Barham to the chaplaincy of the Vintners' Company, alluded to in the foregoing letter, added not a little to his professional duties, involving as it did a weekly visit to the Company's alms-houses at Mile End, where, besides the performance of Divine Service, the little and sometimes large differences incidental to a colony of twelve elderly ladies afforded ample employment for the morning. This post enabled him to appreciate the worth and charitable feeling of bodies of men whom it is too much the fashion to hold up to ridicule, if not opprobrium. That the ' love of the turtle,' indeed, is rife in the land may be admitted, that the ' rage of the vulture' has been thereby excited is also a matter of notoriety; but to the justice and liberality with which many, at all events, of these civic charities were administered he could bear ample testimony; that, so far from appropriating to private indulgence moneys committed to their charge for especial purposes, the guardians of his day made considerable addition to these funds, and were withheld from doing more chiefly from an apprehension of having the management of their bounty transferred to other hands, and their donations applied to indifferent objects, were also facts that came under his personal observation.

'*Diary.*—*May*, 1834.—William Linley, brother to the first Mrs. Sheridan, though a man of the world, and a member of the celebrated " Beefsteak Club," the hoaxing propensities of whose members are so proverbial, was a man of great good-nature and still greater simplicity of mind. He always occupied a particular table at the " Garrick," and, though a general favourite, was somewhat too fond of reciting long speeches from various authors, generally Shakespeare. It was one day in this month that he had begun to spout from the opening scene in Macbeth, and would probably have gone through it if I had not cut him short at the third line—

" When the hurly-burly's done,"

with " What on earth are you talking about? Why, my dear Linley, it is astonishing that a man so well read in Shakespeare as yourself should adopt that nonsensical reading! What is ' *hurly-burly* ' pray? There is no such word in the language; you can't find an allusion to it in Johnson." Linley, whose veneration for Dr. Johnson was only inferior to that which he entertained for the great poet himself, said,

' " Indeed! are you sure there is not? What can be the reason of the omission? The word, you see, is used by Shakespeare."

' " No such thing," was the reply; " it appears so indeed in one or two early editions, but it is evidently mistranscribed. The second folio is the best and most authentic copy, and gives the true reading, though the old nonsense is still retained upon the stage! "

' " Indeed, and pray what do you call the true reading ? "

' " Why, of course, the same that is followed by Johnson and Steevens in the edition up-stairs :—

' When the *early purl* is done; '

that is, when we have finished our ' early purl,' i.e. directly after breakfast."

' Linley was startled, and after looking steadily at me to see if he could discover any indication of an intention to hoax him, became quite puzzled by the gravity of my countenance, and only gave vent in a hesitating tone, half-doubtful, half-indignant, to the word " Nonsense ! "

' " Nonsense ?   It is as I assure you.   We will send for the book, and see what Steevens says in his note upon the passage."

' The book was accordingly sent for, but I took good care to intercept it before it reached the hands of Linley, and taking it from the servant pretended to read from the volume—

" When the hurly-burly's done."

" Some copies have it, ' When the *early purl* is done ; ' and I am inclined to think this reading the true one, if the well-known distich be worthy of credit—

' Hops, reformation, turkeys, and beer
Came to England all in one year.'

This would seem to fix the introduction of beer, and consequently of early purl, into the country to about that period of Henry VIII.'s reign when he intermarried with

Anne Boleyn, the mother of Queen Elizabeth, Shakespeare's great friend and patroness, and to whom this
allusion may perhaps have been intended by the poet as a
delicate compliment.   Purl, it is well known, was a
favourite beverage at the English Court during the latter
part of the sixteenth century ; and from the epithet then
affixed to it ' early,' an adjunct which it still retains, was
no doubt in common use for breakfast at a time when the
China trade had not yet made our ancestors familiar with
the produce of the tea-plant.   Theobald's objection, that,
whatever may have been the propriety of its introduction
at the Court of Elizabeth, the mention made of it at that
of Macbeth would be a gross anachronism, may be at
once dismissed as futile.   Does not Shakespeare, in the
very next scene talk of

' Cannons overcharged with double cracks ' ?

and is not allusion made by him to the use of the same
beverage at the Court of Denmark, at a period coeval, or
nearly so, with that under consideration—

' Hamlet, this purl is thine ' ? "

' " But, dear me ! " broke in Linley, " that is *pearl*, not
purl.   I remember old Packer used to hold up a pearl,
and let it drop into the cup."
' " Sheer misconception on the part of a very indifferent
actor, my dear Linley, be assured."
' Here Beazley, who was present, observed, " ' Early purl '
is all very well, but my own opinion has always leaned

to Warburton's conjecture that a political allusion is intended. He suggests

'When the *Earl of Burleigh's* done ; '

that is, when we have ' done,' i.e. cheated or deceived, the Earl of Burleigh, a great statesman, you know, in Elizabeth's time, and one whom, to use a cant phrase among ourselves, ' you must get up very early in the morning to take in ! ' "

' " But what had Macbeth or the witches to do with the Earl of Burleigh ? Stuff! nonsense ! " said Linley indignantly. And though Beazley made a good fight in defence of his version, yet his opponent would not listen to it for an instant.

' " No, no," he continued, " the Earl of Burleigh is all rubbish, but there may be something in the other reading."

' And as the book was closed directly the passage had been repeated, and was replaced immediately on the shelf, the unsuspicious critic went away thoroughly mystified, especially as Tom Hill, for whose acquaintance with early English literature he had a great respect, confirmed the emendation with

' " Early purl ! " Pooh ! pooh ! to be sure it is ' early purl ; ' I've got it so in two of my old copies." '

To Mrs. Hughes.

'St. Paul's Churchyard, June 26, 1834.

' My dear Madam,—What is a man to do when he is anxious to write, and at the same time has nothing to say

—nothing, that is, which he can hope will create sufficient interest to pay for the trouble of running over a long epistle, while both habit and inclination lead him to be long-winded when once he takes pen in hand ? To prate to you of my own " whereabouts," a subject for which your undeviating kindness holds out a strong temptation, were merely to give a detail of catarrhs and colds, originating in unaired shirts, or draughts issuing from the hyperborean bank eternally established in the cupola of St. Paul's ; while to talk of " the family" were only to re- vert from Mrs. Barham's sprained ancle to the alternations of chilblains and whooping-cough among the tender juveniles of our illustrious house. In fact, time has " stood still withal " here since I last had the pleasure of addressing you, nor has anything occurred to break the monotony of our lives. We go on in the old jog-trot way, varied only by my weekly visit to Mile End, where indeed my seraglio of twelve elderly odalisques certainly does, now and then, furnish me with a job in the way of composing differences which will occasionally arise even in their well- regulated minds. All the world here is now running after the Handel Commemoration at the Abbey, and the rehearsals, I hear, have gone off with great *éclat*. We have not visited this scene of harmony yet, but intend to do so before it is all over. Packe, who was there yester- day, says that he never had any idea of what Handel was before. Our own commemorations of the Sons of the Clergy and charity children went off exceedingly well ; and the collection at the latter, including the donations given at the dinner, exceeded seven hundred pounds, a much larger sum than, your old friend Capel informed me, they have been in the habit of receiving. The Bishop of Derry and his family did us the honour to breakfast with us on that day; when, just as the episcopal party arrived, fancy my horror at hearing a concatenation of sounds unblest, in which that terrible monosyllable which the French say is the root of the English language was but too distinguishable, issuing from the kitchen stairs. A cook whom we had engaged some three weeks previously was at loggerheads with the gentle Elizabeth, who, although the damnatory clauses in the conversation were, I believe, exclusively confined to her Demosthenic opponent, expressed herself with an energy of diction which would not have disgraced her Royal namesake in the golden days. The consequence of the feud has been that Mrs. Barham has dismissed the superintendent of the sauce-pans, and Elizabeth has dismissed her mistress, after an intimate union of four years and upwards, on the ground of incompatibility of temper.

'The Dean has been in Devonshire, where he recovered his health and spirits wonderfully, but no sooner did he return to town than twenty-four hours undid all that country air and the society of his friends had effected; and when I saw him two days since he was lying on his sofa in a most deplorable state of depression. He has, of course, had little or no use of a very excellent house, which he took for three months, in Whitehall Place; nor will he now, as he talks of going into the country again immediately that his duties, to which he is altogether unequal at present, will allow. I cannot tell you how deeply I regret this, and I am sure you will feel the same.

The more I see of him the more I respect and love
him. More thorough goodness of heart and kindliness of
disposition never were in man; and though to strangers
the husk may perhaps appear a little rough at times, yet
the kernel is indeed of a first-rate quality. I wish he
had more society, especially female society; had he any
of his relations to reside with him, I cannot but think it
would be of the greatest service to him. Living all alone
in that great house would give me the blue devils in a
week, and as the Thames is so temptingly near, I have
little doubt I should be found some fine morning floating
either under Westminster Bridge or Waterloo, as the tide
might suit.

'I know your devotion to Blackwood too well to suppose
that any of his numbers escape your notice; *Nicholas's*
progress, therefore, will not be unknown to you. He
begins to embarrass me cruelly. Like *Mr. Puff* in the
Critic, I have got him on the stage, and how to get him
off again with decency Heaven knows. He cannot, any
more than Sheridan's heroes, make his "exit praying;"
and whether to break his neck out of a balloon, or blow
him up in a powder-mill at Dartford, I am really, for the
present, at a loss to determine. It must be "as Fate and
Fortune will, or as the Destinies decree," I suppose. In
the meantime I have just sent off another batch to my
worthy horseleech, whose cries of "Give! Give!" are incessant. We think of getting down to Hanwell for a week
or two shortly, and then perhaps I may be able to pick up
a little sentiment, for I really fear I must make "my
cousin" fall in love, and grow as lackadaisical as Haynes

Bayley.   Nothing on earth, by the way, is so soothing as
that gentleman's verses ; but that he would be thought a
plagiarist, I think *Nicholas* might do a little in that way,
to the tune of *O, no! we never mention him,* &c. &c.

They say that I am silent, and my silence they condemn,
For O! although they talk to me, I never talk to them!
I heed not what they think, although I know 'tis thought
    by some
That I am dumb or deaf, but O! I'm neither deaf nor
    dumb!

They say I'm looking sick and pale ; and well indeed they
    may ;
They tell me, too, that I am sad ; I'm anything but gay!
They smile—but O! the more they smile, the more, alas!
    I sigh ;
And when they strive to make me laugh, I turn me round
    and cry!

They bid me sing the song I sung, as I have sung before,
The song I sung no more I sing—my singing days are
    o'er!
They bid me play the fiddle too—my fiddle it is mute!
Nor can I, as I used to do, blow tunes upon the flute!

The feeling fain would soothe my woe, the heartless say I
    sham ;
The ribald mock my grief, and call me—Sentimental
    Sam!

They cannot guess what 'tis I want—There's few indeed
    that can :
I want—
I want—
I want to be a butterfly, and flutter round a fan !

'But I really ought to be ashamed to take up your time
with such rubbish, which I only insert for the lack of
graver matter. Hook I saw yesterday; he is in high
feather, and says the world is growing Tory again. He,
John Murray, Hill, and your friend Mr. Lockhart, dined
together the other day at a French *restaurateur's* near
Regent Street on a *roasted* turbot. As this is a piece of
epicurism which I never heard of before, I took the pains
to go and ask how they managed to dress it, as it seems
an unwieldy animal for the spit. A shilling to the *garçon*
let me into the secret. It was put into the oven and
baked! Nothing but villainy in this wicked world!

'Pray give my very best regards to Mr. Hughes, who i,
I hope, in excellent health, *cum suis.* The Dean, to whom
I mentioned my intention of writing, desired his kindest
regards both to him and yourself, and bade me say that
his delay in replying to your last letter was to be attributed only to the depressed state of his spirits; I have no
doubt you will hear from him very soon. God bless you,
my dear Madam; pray let me at your leisure have the
pleasure of hearing that you are in good health and spirits,
and believe me to remain, as ever,

' Your obliged Servant,

' R. H. BARHAM.'

During the months of June and July 1834, Mr. Barham spent his summer holidays at Strand-on-Green, where he had engaged a snug little cottage. Hanwell was his usual retreat, his duties rarely allowing him to select one beyond the reach of the great bell of Paul's; but this year he pitched upon Strand-on-Green, with some design, I believe, of 'getting a little fishing.' And for the first week or two attempts were occasionally made upon the wary gudgeons of Kew, but the expedition generally ended in some grave piscatorial disaster—the line became inextricably tangled in a worse than Gordian knot, or the hooks got foul, and had to be extracted by a surgical operation from calf or coat-tail, or the worms broke loose and buried themselves in inaccessible corners of the waistcoat pocket; and then rods and winches would be packed up, and the pleasure of the day began in earnest. At times, but not without expression of utter distrust of my competency as a waterman, he would permit me to scull him about the river, and one afternoon, on our finding ourselves opposite the house of Theodore Hook at Fulham, he determined to land and make a call on his friend. Hook was not at home; so, having no card with him, Mr. Barham asked for pen and paper, and while standing in the hall scribbled off, in as short a time as the reader would take to copy them, the following—

As Dick and I
Were a sailing by
At Fulham Bridge, I cock'd my eye,
And says I, ' Add-zooks !
There's Theodore Hook's,
Whose Sayings and Doings make such pretty books.

' I wonder,' says I,
Still keeping my eye
On the house, ' if he's in—I should like to try ;'
With his oar on his knee,
Says Dick, says he,
' Father, suppose you land and see ! '

' What ! land and *sea*,'
Says I to he ;
'Together ! why Dick, why how can that be ? '
And my comical son,
Who is fond of fun,
I thought would have split his sides at the pun.

So we rows to shore,
And knocks at the door—
When William, a man I'd seen often before,
Makes answer and says,
' Master's gone in a chaise
Call'd a homnibus, drawn by a couple of bays.'

So I says then,
' Just lend me a pen ;'
' I wull, sir,' says William—politest of men,[1]
So having no card, these poetical brayings
Are the record I leave of my doings and sayings.

'*Diary: August* 26, 1834.—Party at Williams's. Macready, Jerdan, &c. Abbot had just disappeared, an execution having been put into the Victoria Theatre by Randle Jackson. Talleyrand spoken of as "having a cold grey eye and perfect impassibility of feature." He being asked if Sebastiani was not a relative of Napoleon, answered, "Yes, while he was emperor; not now!" Meeting the Duke of Wellington on his return from his installation as Chancellor of Oxford, he (Talleyrand) told him that he was now covered with glory; adding that no doubt they would end by making him a bishop; " *Vous finissez où j'ai commencé!*"

' Williams told me the history of Counts A—— and B——, whom I had met a few days before at Strand-on-Green. The former, a Venetian Greek, had just married his second wife. His first had brought him a fortune of twenty thousand pounds, of which he sold out seven thousand for the purpose of pigeoning a young man of more money than wit, residing in this neighbourhood. His associates, however, a Pole and a Frenchman, finding that

---

[1] This proved eventually not to be a well-placed epithet ; William, who had lived many years with Hook, grew rich and saucy. The latter used to say of him, that for the first three years he was as good a servant as ever came into a house ; for the next two a kind and considerate friend ; and afterwards an abominably bad master.

he had actually got this money, thought they might make a better thing of it by turning the tables. They went therefore and let the intended victim into the secret, kept the appointment, and having won all the Count's seven thousand pounds, broke up the party. His second wife's fortune was large, but settled upon herself. He wore a profusion of diamond rings, studs, &c., and looked the very *beau ideal* of a handsome sharper. His friend too was a very handsome man. He sang beautifully, and accompanied himself with considerable skill on the guitar. He was said to be a noble Pole, exiled for political offences. He had just got into some scrape at Cheltenham, which he had been obliged to leave in consequence ; and though exceedingly gentlemanly and insinuating in his manners, was, I have no doubt from what I heard, a thorough scamp. Macready told a story of George B——— the actor, who, it seems, is not popular in the profession, being considered a sort of time-server : " There goes Georgius," said some one. " Not Georgium Sidus," replied Keeley ; " Yes," added Power, " Georgium *Any*-sidus." '

To Mrs. Hughes.

'London, November 1, 1834.

' My dear Madam,—*Fraser* having been left in London I could not before get at him, or you would have received him sooner. With him is enclosed a small pamphlet, which Mr. Capel has entrusted to me for transmission, and in which I have no doubt you will take an interest, from the subject on which it treats. How is it, my dear Madam, that, while we are familiar with what is going on at Brussels and Madrid, we know nothing of what is passing under our very noses? You will no doubt think it strange that the first intimation I have had of Mr.——'s nuptials should be from Kingston Lisle! Yet so it was; and the fact confirms me fully in Sir Walter Raleigh's opinion, that no man knows anything of what is done before his face. I assume that there must be a corresponding defect in our mental vision to that which, in our physical, precludes us from distinguishing that, when close to the eye, which we read easily at arm's length. Since you have given me a clue, however, I have followed it up, and find that a very amusing interview took place between the expectant bridegroom and Mr. (Sydney) Smith, whose consent he thought it necessary to obtain for the marriage: " Be a fool, sir, if you will be a fool!" was the gracious accordance to the enamoured swain's petition, and your vivid imagination will paint to you, in much livelier colours than I can, the mode in which Oroondates hung his ears as he walked off with this canonical authority to be frisky. Of Elinor I can learn nothing certain at present, unless I were to apply to her papa, which I have not done; all our vestry, however, agree in affirming her to have reached what Rochester considered the greatest pitch of calamity—the being " married and settled in the country." By the time I have next the pleasure of addressing you, I doubt not I shall have obtained some more definite information.

' And now let me thank you, which I do most gratefully, for your fine moral poem, which has amused my wife and myself amazingly. I have not yet read *Ayesha*, but shall do so forthwith, Inshallah! In the meanwhile, I have picked out enough of the story from the reviews to appreciate the excellence of the principles you inculcate. I have ever been the enemy of sans-culottism in all its ramifications, and am delighted with so admirable a testimonial to the value of that fine old national appendage to Toryism which, by an odd jumble of the numbers, O'Connell would call "A Breeches." It is a noble institution, which seems always to have flourished and decayed as good or evil principles have prevailed in a state; and one of the worst features in the French Revolution was its contempt of this splendid proof of the wisdom of our ancestors. The history of "A Breeches," from the fall to the 19th century, would afford grave matter for reflection to the poet, the philosopher, and the statesman, and nothing but the conviction of my being incompetent to the task of worthily handling so great a subject prevents my undertaking it. What a halo of glory John Wilson would throw around the most tattered pair of "Galligaskins" that ever affected to envelope the nether end of a lowlander!

'I turn with reluctance from so interesting a theme, but the mention of Wilson naturally carries my thoughts towards Edinburgh. I have had a very excellent letter from Robert Blackwood with the last proofs of *Nicholas*, which is now in type, and will appear in the December number. There are three chapters, which run to above a sheet and a half, and which will not well bear division. This circumstance, and the length of Wilson's article on Spenser in the present number, full two sheets, induce him to let it stand over till next month, as otherwise he must throw over the *Midge* and the *Nights at Mess*; and he is right in thinking two light articles better than one. From Cadell's people I find with pleasure that the late Baillie's old friends have rallied well round the family, and if they can but keep the Wilsonian stream within its banks, I should not be surprised if *Maga* even rises in circulation.   There will be a double number next month.

'I have just had a letter from Dick; he has now been a fortnight domiciled at Oriel, close to " Sally," an approximation which sounds rather dangerous, and at first affected his mother with a vague apprehension, not unlike that which seized upon the mamma of a Cambridge student, on being told that her son was " sticking close to Catherine Hall."   Mr. Hughes, however, will be able to inform you what sort of a belle " Sally "[1] is.   His rooms, which, however, he will only keep this term are confessedly the worst in college, but he has been, and thinks himself, much too fortunate in getting in at all, to whisper the ghost of a murmur at the temporary inconvenience.   That they are not *à la Louis Quatorze* you will conceive, when I tell you that I have just remitted nine pounds three shillings, in full payment for " all those movables whereof his predecessor stood possessed;" and as a bed, and its concomitants, form items in the inventory, I conclude that either it is not stuffed with eiderdown, or that he has got his furniture a bargain.

'I very much regret to hear what you tell me of poor Mr. Southey's situation.   A heart like his does not the less speak because a strong sense of religious duty induces

---

[1] The chapel bell was so named.

him to attempt to silence it. Let us hope he will be spared the additional affliction which you appear to anticipate.[1] I should be the most ungrateful of beings if I did not sympathise with one to whom I am indebted for more comfort and resignation under calamity than to any other source save one. Of news, public or private, I have little to tell you. You have, of course, heard of Tom Duncombe's absurd challenge to Fraser, for quizzing his liaison with Madame Vestris ; if not, the enclosed doggrel will make you *au fait* of the facts.

---

[1] The affliction alluded to was the insanity of Mrs. Southey. In a letter dated October 1834, Southey thus writes on the subject to his friend Mr. Henry Taylor :—' Mine is a strong heart. I will not say that the last week has been the most trying in my life, but I will say that the heart which could bear it could bear anything. It is remarkable, that the very last thing I wrote before this affliction burst upon me in its full force was upon Resignation, little foreseeing, God knows, how soon and how severely my own principles were to be put to the proof. The occasion was this :—Mrs. Hughes thought it would gratify me to peruse a letter which she had just received from one of her friends, a clergyman [Mr. Barham], who had recently suffered some domestic affliction. He said that his greatest consolation had been derived from a letter of mine which she had allowed him to transcribe some years ago, and which he verily believed had at that time saved his heart from bursting. The letter must have been written upon my dear Isabel's death ; I have no recollection of it, but that must have been the subject, because Mrs. Hughes and her husband had both been exceedingly struck with her, and declared, when such a declaration could without unfitness be made, that she was the most radiant creature they had ever beheld. This made me reflect upon the difference between religious resignation and that which is generally mistaken for it, and, for immediate purpose, in no slight degree supplies its place. You will see what I am thus led to write in its proper place.'—*Life and Correspondence of Robert Southey*, vol. vi. p. 246.

THE TWO M.P.'s.

(*Magazine Publisher, and Member of Parliament.*)

BEING A TRUE AND PARTICULAR ACCOUNT OF THE GRAND
MILLING MATCH THAT *DIDN'T* TAKE PLACE.

Says Tom Duncombe to Fraser
T'other morning, ' I say, sir,
You've called me a *Roué*, a Dicer, and Racer ;
Now I'd have you to know, sir,
Such names are " no go," sir ;
By Jove, sir, I never knew anything grosser.

' And then Madame Vestris
Extremely distrest is
At your calling her Lais.   She's more like Thalestris,
As you'll find, my fine joker,
If you only provoke her, .
She's a d—l if once she gets hold of a poker.

' For myself, to be candid,
And not underhanded,
I write thus to say, I'll be hang'd if I stand it.
So give up the name
Of the man or the dame
Who has made this infernal attack on my fame,
And recall what you've said of
A man you're afraid of,
Or turn out, my Trump, and let's see what you're made of.

'I have "barkers" by Nock, sir,
    With percussion locks, sir,
Will give you your gruel—hang me if I box, sir,
    And I've sent my old Pal in,
    My "noble friend Allen,"
To give you this here, and to stop your caballing!'

    Then says Fraser, says he,
    'What a spoon you must be,
Tommy Duncombe, to send such a message to me:
    Why, if I was to fight about
    What my friends write about,
My life I should be in continual fright about!

    'As to telling you who
    Wrote that thing about you,
One word's worth a thousand—Blow me if I do!
    If you *will* be so gay, sir,
    The people *will* say, sir,
That you *are* a *Roué*,—and I'm
                Yours,
                    JEMMY FRASER.'

'Hook is locking himself up and very busy about something—what I don't know. I am afraid that *l'argent comptant* induces him to fritter himself away in the magazines when he should be flying at higher game. His autobiography of *Gurney* in the *New Monthly* is in some parts very funny, and not the less so for being little more than a literal narrative of some of his own early manœuvres. Of politics I know little and care less, for in times like these one acquires a recklessness that was once most foreign to us. But they say that the grand struggle is to be between Brougham and Lambton in the next session, and that the whole of the *soi disant* liberal press is to support the latter. If so, the Chancellor's nose will acquire tenfold flexibility; nor do I envy the noble coal merchant his antagonist. The *Globe* and *Chronicle*, I think, already show symptoms of veering, and the *Times* has long been decidedly hostile to Brougham. Barnes, I hear, says that he put him on the woolsack, and will pull him off again. *Nous verrons* whether Macvey Napier and his *Edinburgh Review* can keep him on. They say that when a certain class of " reformers " fall out, honest men get their own. Let us hope it may so turn out. Pray remember me in the kindest manner to Mr. Hughes, and with the best and sincerest wishes towards yourself,

'Believe me to remain, as ever,

'Your much obliged,

'R. H. BARHAM.'

'*Diary: November* 16, 1834.—Dined with Sydney Smith. He said that his brother Robert had, in George III.'s time, translated the motto, " *Libertas sub rege pio*," The pious King has got liberty under; also, that he had originally proposed to Jeffrey, Horner, and Brougham, as a motto for the *Edinburgh Review*, " *Musam meditamur avenâ*," We cultivate literature on a little oatmeal.

' " If ever a religious war should arise again, " he said, " I should certainly take arms against the Dissenters.

Fancy me with a bayonet at the heart of an Anabaptist, with—' Your church-rate or your life!'"

' He said nothing should ever induce him to go up in a balloon, unless indeed it would benefit the Established Church. I recommended him to go at once, as there would at least be a chance of it.'

In a few days afterwards, Mr. Barham received the following invaluable recipe ; it was forwarded from Taunton by post, without signature or comment of any kind ; he, of course, had far too much respect for the modesty of the author to hazard even a conjecture as to his name. Others may be less scrupulous ; under any circumstances, it is commended to the serious consideration of all housekeepers possessed of a spark of culinary enterprise, their special regards being directed to the final monition : —

A RECEIPT FOR A WINTER SALAD.

(For five or six persons.)

LAST EDITION.

Two large potatoes, passed through kitchen sieve,
Unwonted softness to the salad give ;
Of ardent mustard add a single spoon,
Distrust the condiment which bites so soon ;
But deem it not, thou man of herbs, a fault
To add a double quantity of salt :
Three times the spoon with oil of Lucca crown,
And once with vinegar, procured from town ;
True flavour needs it, and your poet begs
The pounded yellow of two well-boiled eggs ;

Let onion atoms lurk within the bowl,
And, scarce suspected, animate the whole;
And lastly, on the flavoured compound toss
A magic tea-spoon of anchovy sauce;
Then, though green turtle fail, though venison's tough,
And ham and turkey are not boiled enough,
Serenely full, the epicure may say,—
' Fate cannot harm me,—I have dined to-day.'

N.B. As this salad is the result of great experience and reflection, it is to be hoped young salad-makers will not attempt any improvements upon it.

To Mrs. Hughes.

' December 6, 1834.

' My dear Madam,—I seize the opportunity of a frank, at a time when such articles are rare, to thank you most heartily for your last two favours. The songs are admirable, and calculated, I think, at this moment to do a vast deal of good. Alexander Blackwood has written to me, asking for something of the sort, and I had turned my thoughts that way so far as to begin a parody on the *Tight Little Island,* a lyric once popular in the good old times. The song however, if finished, would be so much behind those you have enclosed that I doubt whether I shall go on with it. To be sure, Blackwood has the alternative of throwing it into the fire, and I assure him he will not hurt my vanity by so doing, for I never could write a song in my life to please myself—*let alone* other people, as your friend Dan would say. I give you the commencement : —

' Daddy Melbourne, one day,
    Said to old Gaffer Grey,
" We must now hold a grand consultation !
    For Spencer's ' gone dead,'
    And we want a new head
To conduct the affairs of the nation ;
For, removed to a different station,
Althorpe can't hold his old situation ;
    And unless some three-decker
    Shall take the Exchequer,
All 's up with our Administration ! " ' &c.[1]

' I had thought of running through the list of candidates,
real or supposed, for the vacant Chancellorship of the
Exchequer, from Abercrombie down to Spring Rice ; but
I fear it would be flat, stale, and unprofitable. However,
I have till the 12th to think about it. I thank you
sincerely for your kindness to *Nicholas.* I was afraid you
would think I had huddled up the catastrophe too rapidly,
but I dreaded his becoming a bore, and wanted to get him
fairly off my hands. Whatever his demerits may be, they
must in fairness rest at your door, since you certainly, if
you did not absolutely call him into life, prevented his
being overlaid in his *première jeunesse.* Therefore while I
may truly say " *quod placeo, si placeo, tuum,*"—I make
no apology for quoting Horace to you,—at the same time
I must also debit you with the demerits of one who, but
for your fostering care, had expired long since of laziness

---

[1] The song was completed and sent, not to *Blackwood*, but to *John Bull*,
in whose columns it appeared, January 1835. It will be found entire in
the collection of Miscellaneous Poems at the end of the second volume.

and indigestion. I have not yet been able to see Mr. Capel, but hope to do so in a day or two; in the meantime I shall strictly observe your caution as to giving no copies.

'God bless you, my dear Madam!—the bellman, a worse nuisance by half than the poor sweeps whom the Whigs have silenced, is reminding me by repeated peals under the windows of the flight of time. Perhaps, as I turn forty-six to day, I ought not to abuse him for it, but when I am writing to you I cannot " thank him that he cuts me from my tale." I have only time to say, in the way of news, that Elinor S——, on the *latest authorities, is* married and gone to America with her husband. The Dean is returned in apparently excellent health and spirits; and the Chapter have this morning given young Beckwith St. Michael Bassishaw. Mr. (Sydney) Smith is at open feud with all the minor canons; and, if a' tales be true, scarce cater-cousin with the more exalted members of the Cathedral. As I know all connected with St. Paul's interests you, I will send you some day my version of the affair, much of which is, of course, mere conjecture. Pray give my kindest regards to Mr. and Mrs. Hughes, and thank Mr. Cooke for not having forgotten me.

'Ever your most obliged,

'R. H. BARHAM.'

CHAPTER VI.

[1835—1836.]

Story of Yates—Letters to Mrs. Hughes—The *John Bull*—St. Paul's—
East Kent Election—Politics—' Veritas'—Gossip—A Day's fishing with
Theodore Hook—Anecdotes—Lines on the Birthday of Sir Thomas White
—Letter to Mrs. Hughes—' The Sheriff's Ball'—*Fraser*—Chancery
Suit—Mr. Trelawney—Edward Walpole—Dinner with Owen Rees—Anec-
dotes—Moore and O'Brien—Letter from Sydney Smith—The Literary
Fund—Portrait of Sir John Soane—Correspondence—Sydney Smith—
Anecdote of Sir Walter Scott—St. Paul's—' The Irish Fisherman'—Din-
ner at Sydney Smith's—Anecdotes—Mr. Barham's younger Son—Poeti-
cal Epistle—His Love of Cats—' Address to Jerry'—Letter to Miss
Barham—The non-officiating Minister—' A Medley'—Negotiation with
Mr. Moore—Mrs. Ricketts' Ghost Story.

'*DIARY: January* 1, 1835.—The following story was
told me as a fact by George Raymond. Yates (the well-
known actor and manager of the Adelphi Theatre) met a
friend from Bristol, in the street, whom he well recollected
as having been particularly civil to his wife and himself
when at that town, in which the gentleman was a merchant.
Yates, who at that time lived at the Adelphi Theatre, invited his friend to dinner, and made a party, among whom
were Hook and Mathews, to meet him. On reaching
home he told his wife what he had done, describing the
gentleman, and calling to her mind how often they had
been at his house near the cathedral.

' "I remember him very well," said Mrs. Yates, " but I don't just now recollect his name—what is it ?"

' "Why, that is the very question I was going to ask you," returned Yates. "I know the man as well as I know my own father, but for the life of me I can't remember his name, and I made no attempt to ascertain it, as I made sure you would recollect it!"

'What was to be done ? all that night and the next morning they tried in vain to recover it, but the name had completely escaped them. In this dilemma Yates bethought him of giving instructions to their servant which he considered would solve the difficulty, and calling him in told him to be very careful in asking every gentleman, as he arrived, his name, and to be sure to announce it very distinctly. Six o'clock came, and with it the company in succession, Hook, Mathews; and the rest—all but the anonymous guest, whom Yates began to think, and almost to hope, would not come at all. Just, however, before the dinner was put on the table, a knock was heard, and the lad being at that moment in the kitchen, in the act of carrying up a haunch of mutton which the cook had put into his hands, a maid-servant went to the door, admitted the stranger, showed him up stairs, and opening the drawing-room door allowed him to walk in without any announcement at all. At dinner time everybody took wine with the unknown, addressing him as "Sir,"—"A glass of wine, sir?" "Shall I have the honour, sir?" &c., but nothing transpired to let out the name, though several roundabout attempts were made to get at it. The evening passed away, and the gentleman was highly delighted with the company, but about half-past ten o'clock he looked at his watch and rose abruptly, saying,—

' " Faith, I must be off or I shall get shut out, for I am going to sleep at a friend's, in the Tower, who starts for Bristol with me in the morning. They close the gates i t eleven precisely, and I sha'n't get in if I am a minute after, so good-bye at once. Be sure you come and see me whenever you visit Bristol."

' " Depend on me, my dear friend ; God bless you, if you must go ! "

' " Adieu," said the other, and Yates was congratulating himself on having got out of so awkward a scrape, when his friend popped his head back into the room, and cried hastily,—

' " Oh, by the bye, my dear Yates, I forgot to tell you that I bought a pretty French clock as I came here to-day at Hawley's, but as it needs a week's regulating, I took the liberty of giving your name, and ordering them to send it here, and said that you would forward it. It is paid for."

' The door closed, and before Yates could get it open again, the gentleman was in the hall.

' " Stop ! " screamed Yates over the balusters, " you had better write the address yourself, for fear of a mistake."

' " No, no, I can't stop, I shall be too late ;—the old house, near the cathedral ; good-bye ! "

' The street door slammed behind him, and Yates went back to the company in an agony.

' Douglas repeated a story very similar of King the

actor, who, meeting an old friend, whose name he could not recollect, took him home to dinner. By way of making the discovery, he addressed him in the evening, having previously made several ineffectual efforts :—

' " My dear sir, my friend here and myself have had a dispute as to how you spell your name ; indeed, we have laid a bottle of wine about it."

' " Oh, with two P's," was the answer, which left them just as wise as before.'

To Mrs. Hughes.

'St. Paul's Churchyard, February 14, 1835.

' My dear Madam,—The date of your last letter but one, the " penultimate," as our friend P—— would call it, absolutely frightens me. That circumstances had forced me into delinquency I knew, but till your kind missive of yesterday reached me, I was not aware of the full enormity of my offence. All I have to plead in mitigation is, one Chancery suit in full operation, another in prospect (both, thank God, arising out of my public situation as Rector of St. Mary Magdalene, and not from private litigation), all sorts of returns to ecclesiastical commissioners (bores of the first magnitude), the Kent election, with other matters " too numerous to mention in this advertisement," the whole surmounted and crowned with a most intolerable attack of tic douloureux, which quite prevents my sleeping o' night. Indeed, I never remember the time when I have been so fully occupied, and I have in consequence been obliged to break my pledged word both to Black-

wood and Mudford, in whose good graces I must, I fear,
have fallen full fifty per cent. That you have not received the *Bulls* is also my fault; I made certain that
you would see them in the good city of Bath, and therefore did not send any down. *John* would gladly forward
them from his office, but this would perhaps tell tales.
Hook, whom the world *accuses*, but whom no human being
can *convict* of having something to do with him, always,
as I know, takes him in regularly through a newsman
in the usual manner. You may depend upon it, however, there shall be no omission in future. Have you
the last? By the tenor of yours, and the enclosure of the
verse, I fear not, as unluckily the latter came too late,
the *Protestant Church* having appeared in the last *Bull,*
whence it was copied the following day in the *Standard,*
and has since been into several " provincials." *My name
is Squire Bull* follows to-morrow. *John* is of opinion, and so
are some of his council, that a fire well kept up is more
effective than a single volley, and this is the reason why
the shots have been delivered in succession, rather than
at once. *Fraser* would be too late; it would be running
to the rescue after the battle was over: besides Maginn
is such a queer body, and so given to *improve* articles
without, occasionally, having the least conception of their
spirit and tone, that his reforms, like many others, may
justly come under Mrs. Ramsbottom's definition of that
much-abused word—"making bad worse." Now it is
mighty provoking, when you mean to put in a neat little
thrust in *tierce,* or pink your adversary prettily *carte* over
arm, to have your delicate hit metamorphosed by some

" out-and-outer " into an unmannerly cross-buttock, or a clumsy poke in the eye.   Thus much for strategetics.

'And now for the news of what I know is always upper-most in your thoughts—St. Paul's.   Our anticipations with respect to the new rector of ——— were but too well founded.   I gave him, in my mind, three months to disgust all his parishioners;—he has done it in three weeks!   The day before the Dean left town, a deputation from the parish waited on him officially to represent, remonstrate, and complain, one of whom, "the *spruck.speaker*" of the party, harangued his Lordship for a long hour by the Cathedral clock; and this at a moment when every minute was precious to the object on whom they were bestowing all their tediousness.   What the precise nature of their application, or of the Dean's answer was, I cannot say; I saw his Lordship just afterwards, and he had entered upon the subject, when we were interrupted, and I saw him no more before he left Town.   You, my dear Madam, will, I am sure, be almost as much gratified as I was myself, when I tell you that, hurried as he was, he yet was kind enough to devote some portion of the time left him to a visit to Street's in Brewer Street, where he selected one of the handsomest Monkbarns arm-chairs of carved oak that I have ever seen, and one which the dealer—the first in his way—says is as fine a specimen of antique carving as ever went through his hands, for a present to my unworthy self.   I need not say how much I shall prize it; and woe betide the individual among my posterity who shall inflict so much as a scratch on the heirloom!

What they will do about —— I cannot conceive, but
am led to imagine that all they can do will amount to—
nothing! Though a perfect Trulliber in all but his pigs,
bearishness is no ecclesiastical offence ; nor does any one
of the canons prescribe *in terms* the adoption of a bow or
a smile, or repudiate a fit of the sulks. All I know is,
that the deputation went away much pleased with their
reception, delighted with the courtesy shown them by the
Dean, and resolved to do all in their power to annoy their
new incumbent. It is an ill wind that blows nobody
good : by way of commencement, they have voted their
late rector a piece of plate, in testimony of their appreciation of his "urbanity and attention to his duties ;" with
an inscription, denoting their regret at losing him. This,
as you may well suppose, knowing the man, is wormwood
to his successor. It is, after all, a great pity that he
should have been inducted to a London living, especially
in these times. Had he been presented to one in the
country, where he might have kept a curate and never
gone near it, all might have been well. I cannot but
think it was Sydney Smith's doing (who, by the way, I
hear is now playing up to the Tories), arising from his
pique towards the minor-canons, whose wishes and opinions
on the subject he said he well knew. You wish to know
the reason of that pique :—The body had repeatedly re--
ceived messages from him, some verbal, some written, the
purport of which it was not very easy to penetrate.
"Would they do so and so, in such a given case?" "Would
anyone give up his stall in the event of such a living
being offered him ?" "Would they do this or that, if,

&c. "—all tending to no specific object that could be discovered, but seeming to require pledges as to some general line of conduct to be pursued by the minor-canons under supposed circumstances, which might never occur, or if they should occur, such as would leave themselves bound, and others free. All these questions, too, were asked with a declaration, somewhat ostentatiously put forward, that it was to satisfy him alone—that he spoke quite independently of the Chapter and all its members—that all our replies were to be addressed to him, &c., tending to no conceivable object that our wits could find out or conjecture, unless it were that, for some inscrutable purpose, he was wishing to make head against the Chapter, or some individual members of it, and that by affecting to put himself at the head of our body, he might make any discontent or dissatisfaction among us an instrument to forward his own views.

'I may wrong him in putting this construction upon his interrogations, but after long consideration, neither I nor anyone else could come to any other. And at length, to one of his applications an answer was returned that gave him great offence. I need not tell you that I, for one, would never lend myself to any design which, by taking advantage of the Radical outcry against Deans and Chapters, might even have the appearance of an attack on ours. I would rather a thousand times forego insisting upon even a just right, at such a period of difficulty and danger; and I am glad to say the general feeling was the same in our body. We wanted to form no party, to fight no battle, —and the reply was to the effect, that the minor-canons begged to decline giving specific answers to hypothetical propositions. You may judge of the temper in which the communication was received, when I tell you that on poor Bennet's enquiring of him, some days after, whether there were any papers connected with his living of Barling at the Chapter House to which he might have access, he replied that " he must decline answering any question." I leave you to guess whether my lungs did not crow like Chaunticlere at this: an antagonist in a passion is half beaten.

' I told you that we had been busy with the West Kent election ; in East Kent the Tories walked over the course. Oh, had we but *known* our strength, not only would Rider have been unseated, as he was, but " Hodges' *best*" exertions would have failed to have kept him, too, in the saddle. " Backallum ! we shall see." What amused me very much was, that on landing from the steamboat at Gravesend, where my vote was to be taken, the rain was falling pretty steadily, and every one of the passengers who boasted an umbrella of course had it in play. A strong detachment of the friends of all the candidates lined the pier, to see us come on shore, and loud cheers from either party arose as anyone mounted the steps bearing their respective colours; with that modesty which is one of my distinguishing characteristics, I had endeavoured to decline the honour of a dead cat at my head, with which I was favoured on a previous occasion, by mounting no colours at all, but something *distingué* in my appearance, as self-complacency fondly whispered in my ear, made the Tory party roar out as I mounted the platform,—

' " Here comes von o' hour side ! " '

' " You be blowed ! " said a broad-faced gentleman in sky-blue ribbons, " I say he's our'n."

' " Be blowed yourself ! " quoth one of my discriminating friends opposite. " Why, don't you see the gemman 's got a *silk umbreller ? " '

' The conclusion was irresistible—Tory I must be ; and the " *I know'd it* " which responded to my " Geary for ever " was truly delicious.

' By the time you receive this the struggle about the Speakership will be approaching. The Radical party are in a high fever about it, because they feel they can strike no blow on any other point. If Sutton carries it, and the odds at Tattersall's, where they now bet on other animals than horses, are three to one in his favour, it will be decisive for the stability of Peel's ministry ; if he fails, they are but where they were, and are determined not to go out on any question but the supplies—no, not if the Address be carried against them. The Conservatives are, of course, in high spirits, especially as, notwithstanding their attempts at consolidation, there is a great division in the enemy's camp. This you will easily perceive, when you find that such men as Burdett and Cobbett vote for Sutton. What think you of a series of Parliamentry conundrums for the session, to amuse the country gentlemen during the intolerably long and vulgar harangues they will have, not to listen to, but to sit out for the next four months ? Pray ask Mr. Hughes if he can construe the one which I enclose ; and perhaps, as I know he is a capital Sphinx, he

will cut out a little work for a Radical Œdipus in the
same way, e. g. :—

    " " I can tip you my first, I can tell you my second,
      For Fire and for Physic most famous I'm reckoned,
      Of my name any more are you anxious to know?
      You will find it consists of a word and a blow." [1]

'I am afraid you will think I am leading a sad life, and
that the whole of my time is wasted in these tomfooleries.
All I can plead in extenuation is, that the intent is better
than the deed; and in the meanwhile, by way of a little
set-off, the work, of which you chalked out the design and
recommended me to attempt, has at last made its appearance under the combined auspices of Hall and myself. In
appearance and size it corresponds exactly with the *Pietas,*
and the name, *Veritas,* being as it is a short compendium
of the Evidences, harmonises, I think, very fairly with that
of its predecessor. Peacock is pleased with it, and I hope
its sale will remunerate him. How can I send you down
a copy? Lord Conyngham, whose frank would carry any
weight, is, laud we the gods, out of office, and I have no
present means of getting at Lord Maryborough. I shall,
therefore, try Mr. Twining; and at all events, will forward
one the first opportunity.

'It is very rarely that I dine from home, except at the
Residentiary's table, on a Sunday; to-morrow, however, I
must break a custom, as I am invited to meet your friend
Mrs. Kemble, with her husband, at Fladgate's, near Brompton; and I cannot resist the opportunity of making her

[1] Wakley?

acquaintance. The whole family I understand to be in very good health, and Charles himself is looking ten years younger than when he had all the weight of Covent Garden on his brow.

'Dr. Blomberg is, I hear, just returned to Cripplegate. Great rejoicings in the parish, bells ringing, and a flag hoisted on the church tower! In the meantime the money, I hear, comes in but slowly, and this is in some measure attributed to the impertinent interference of his coffee-coloured ally, who made himself very busy in " arranging" matters for his patron. Dick continues at Oriel, whence I have not only very satisfactory accounts from, but of him; and the Dean sent for me just before he left Town, to say that Mr. Copleston, his tutor, made honourable mention of him, in a letter he had just received.

'I have been a good deal grieved by the death of my Kentish neighbour, poor Lord Darnley. We have met but very little of late, but I knew him well at college, and though of different sides in political feeling, I always found him a gentlemanly and good neighbour. Handling an axe awkwardly he let it slip, and cut off two of his toes; still all might have gone on well, for the wound was well dressed by Beaumont, the Gravesend surgeon, till Brodie could arrive from Town; but he was afraid it was otherwise, got alarmed, and excessive nervous agitation brought on lock-jaw, which was fatal in an inconceivably short time. Why will noblemen meddle with edge tools? Lord Winchelsea, only about a year ago, contrived to whip a pitchfork through his own leg instead of a truss of hay, and laid himself up for half-a-year.

'All *chez moi* are, thank God, in excellent preservation. Pray thank Mr. Hughes for his kindness. May I hope to hear from him soon? I am very anxious that he and Hook should meet, and hope to accomplish this when he next visits Town. And now, my dear Madam, having exhausted my own paper, and, as I much fear, your patience, allow me to subscribe myself

'Your much obliged servant,

'R. H. BARHAM.'

To Mrs. Hughes.

'April 18, 1835.

'My dear Madam,—You have, I trust, received the *Kentish Observer* with Mr. Hughes' excellent song in it. I am not sorry to have so good an opportunity of introducing to your notice one of the best and staunchest prints of the day. It is, as I think I mentioned, conducted by Mudford, who edited *The Courier* in its bright and palmy days, before its wretched tergiversations had reduced it below contempt. I regret much that *Squire Bull* did not come out in his namesake, but John seems terribly afraid of being thought to repeat himself, and the general idea of the two songs is certainly similar, though unfortunately this is by far the better of the two. I shall endeavour to get Ryde to copy it into the *Bucks Gazette.* We are by no means out of spirit here; though Sir Robert has given in for the present, his character and that of his Ministry is so raised by his manly and able fight, in the opinion of all classes, save and except the mere Marats and Robespierres, who are happily contemptible.

in point of numbers, that it is quite clear—indeed, many of his opponents admit it—that no stable Administration can be formed without him. Even my poor friend V.—that " delicately tinted Radical," as *The Age* not unhappily calls him—admits this, sore as he is at having been just turned out of his seat, when he was settling himself quietly down and half making up his mind to turn Conservative. After all, he is a gentleman and a good-natured one, as you will admit when I tell you he did not knock me down for the following piece of impertinence. They were roasting him at the Garrick Club, just before he was unseated, and charging him with belonging to " The Tail," which he indignantly denied. " I will appeal," said he, " to the biggest Tory in the room; Barham, what say you ? Do I deserve, after the manner I have twice voted, to be called a part of the ' Tail' ? " " Certainly not," was the reply: " you are the canister ! " He did not seem so flattered by my taking his part as he ought to have been, but I escaped a broken head.

' I forgot to tell you in my last, that I had met your friend Mrs. Kemble, with her daughter Adelaide, at Mr. Fladgate's, and how much I was pleased with both of them. Mrs. Kemble is evidently a very clever woman, and her conversation much superior to what is generally met with. You were the link that bound us together; and to that circumstance alone can I attribute my being favoured with so much of her attention. I was scarcely less pleased with the young lady. She is very unaffected—a prime quality—and at present quite •unspoiled, though the attention she excites is enough to turn an older head.

'I met Hook this morning just after the formation of the new Ministry was announced. You will be glad to learn that it is quite the old Melbourne clique, without any admixture of the Radicals, properly so called. Sir Henry Parnell comes in, *vice* Ned, *alias* Bear, Ellis; and little Lord John (whom Hook has christened since his marriage " The Widow's Mite ") is to be Home Secretary; Brougham Speaker of the House of Lords, from which the Chancery business is to be separated, and the Seals put into Commission. Of course this can't stand : without a Tory coalition they must go to the dogs in a very short time, as they do not mean to dissolve, and if they did would hardly better themselves.

' I regret much that Mr. Hughes's engagements and the short time he was in town prevented my having more than a few minutes' conversation with him or telling him half what I had to say. Hook is very anxious to make his acquaintance, and I do hope that the next time he visits town he will oblige me so far as to spare me one day at least, that I may bring them together. I think that they would be mutually pleased, and *John Bull* would, I am sure, give up any engagement rather than miss the opportunity.

' God bless you, my dear madam, and give you a pleasant journey. I calculate on this reaching you just before you start for Lady Greenly's, with whom I hope you will pass your time as delightfully as ever. I should have enclosed you some lines *à la* Hemans, the production of a Nursery Muse, to read upon your journey, but find, if I attempt it, I must lose the post. But no! I have yet, I see, five

minutes good, so, if you will excuse bad and hurried hiero-
glyphics, I will try.[1]   In the meantime believe me to
remain, as ever,

' Your much obliged

' R. H. BARHAM.'

' *Diary: August* 18, 1835.—Took young Tom Haffenden over with me to Capt. Williams's at Strand-on-Green,
and went with him and Theodore Hook to Twickenham,
fishing; caught little or nothing.   Hook observed that as
we often had fish without *roe*, now we must be content
with *row* without fish.   Gave excellent imitation of the
Duke of Cumberland and Col. Quentin.

' Story of Lord Middleton, out hunting, calling to
Gunter, the confectioner, to " hold hard " and not ride
over the hounds. " My horse is so hot, my Lord, that I
don't know what to do with him." " Ice him, Gunter;
ice him."

' Dined at Williams's afterwards.   Hook in high spirits,
and full of anecdote.   Stories of Grattan, C. Fox, and
Marquis of Hertford. The latter said after all his expenses
were paid he had 95,000*l.* per annum he did not know
what to do with; yet Hook said he questioned much
whether, intimate as they were, and kind as he always was
to him, he would lend him or any other friend a thousand
pounds.   At his fêtes the dinners always ordered at two
guineas and a-half a head, exclusive of wine.   Duke of

---

[1] The lines enclosed were *Nursery Reminiscences*, published in *Blackwood*,
and afterwards in the *Ingoldsby Legends*, with illustrations from the hand, I
believe, of the lady whom Mrs. Hughes was about to visit.

Buccleugh, on the other hand, with a yearly income of
172,000*l.*, not a rich man; his property consumed by his
houses; can go to Scotland by easy stages, stopping
always to sleep at some place of his own.

'The house in which I used to visit F. Gosling, the
banker, at Twickenham, viz. that with the octagon room
once occupied by Louis Philippe, the one alluded to in
Gilbert Gurney. The wealthy citizen described as at
Hill's dinner in the same, an imaginary character; the
others, Dubois and Mathews.

'Anecdote of Phil Stone, the property-man of Drury
Lane:—"Will you be so good, sir, as to stand a little
backer?" said Phil to a gentleman behind the scenes
who had placed himself so forward as to be seen by the
audience.

'"No, my fine fellow," returned the exquisite, who
quite mistook his meaning; "but here is a pinch of snuff
at your service."'

The 'young Tom Haffenden' who accompanied Mr.
Barham in his visit to Capt. Williams was a nephew of
the former. He was at that time a bright handsome lad,
residing at Hanwell, where also his uncle was staying; he
was moreover a scholar of Merchant Taylors' School.
Just before the breaking-up for the Midsummer holidays
he had made a dutiful call upon Mr. Barham, who asked
him to dinner, and proposed to take him to the theatre in
the evening. A little difficulty, however, was found to
exist in the shape of an unfinished task, a copy of verses
on the subject of Sir Thomas White, the founder of the
school, which was required absolutely to be shown up on

the following morning. The consequences of omitting to
comply with this demand were likely to prove particularly
unpleasant. Would uncle afford a little help? In that
case the play would be the very thing. 'By all means,'
was uncle's reply; and taking up a sheet of paper he
filled it in a few minutes with the requisite, or nearly the
requisite number of—

LINES ON THE BIRTHDAY OF SIR THOMAS WHITE
(Founder of Merchant Taylors' School).

THE ANNUAL TRIBUTE TO HIS MEMORY.

Sir Thomas White
Was a noble knight,
Extremely desirous of doing what's right;
So he sat himself down one beautiful night,
When the moon shone so bright
That he asked for no light
Beyond that of her beams, and began to indite
His last will,—so remarkably good was his sight,—
And he charged and bound down his executors tight,
As soon as his soul should have taken its flight,
To erect a good school of proportionate height,
Length, and breadth—Suffolk Lane he proposed for its site,
And its order what architects term Composite—
In which all such nice little good boys who might
At the date of their entrance have not attained quite
Their tenth year, should be brought up to read and to write;
Not to give way to spite,
Nor to quarrel nor fight,

But to show themselves always well-bred and polite,
Keep hands and face clean, and be decently dight
In clothes of a grave colour rather than bright—
At least not so light as remark to excite—
And to make Greek and Latin their chiefest delight ;
To be mild in demeanour, in morals upright ;
    Not to kick, nor to bite,
    Nor to pinch, nor affright
Each other by practical jokes, as at night
By aping a goblin, humgruffin, or sprite ;
And never to wrong of so much as a mite,
Or a bat, or a ball, or a hoop, or a kite,
Any poor little schoolfellow——Oh, what a plight
I am in after all—poor unfortunate vight !
I can't make my number of verses up 'uite ;
    For my paper's expended,
    My rhymes too are ended,
And I *can* write no more, for I've no more to write ;
So if a line short, I'm in hopes Mister Bellamy
Will pity my case, and not cease to think well o' me.

What Mr. Bellamy happened to think I do not remember to have heard, nor indeed whether the *carmen encomiasticum* in question was actually submitted to him ; but Master Tom went to the play.

To Mrs. Hughes.

'St. Paul's Churchyard, December 4, 1835.

'My dear Madam,—You will, before you receive this, have seen that *Blackwood* has celebrated the No Ball of the illustrious ex-sheriff [Raphael].[1] What can have induced you to suppose that he has given one? We have heard nothing of any such event here, and the City ladies still scream when his name is mentioned. I am sorry to be obliged to agree with you about *Maga*: she is certainly not so lively as she was wont to be, though this month's number is not so prosy as some have been, but decidedly takes the lead of all the others, including *Fraser*, who is occupied with a long article that takes up half his number—savage enough to excite attention certainly, in parts, but falling into the common mistake of levelling its attacks against people whom nobody knows or cares about. It's all very well for some couple of hundred of people here in town; but who out of it knows anything about the " whereabouts " or personal habits and qualities of such folks as John Poole or Thomas Hill? Their very names are no more known fifty miles from town than my own, which, by the way, he has thought proper to introduce among those of the gentlemen summoned to his Parliament; though on what my pretensions to sit there are founded it would puzzle anybody to tell, as I never sent him anything but a single *Fragment* two or three years ago. As I do not, on recollection, think you ever had a copy of this, and as it originated, moreover, in your old and esteemed friend Jack Rice,[2] though *esprit de corps* made me transfer the scene from home to some two miles off, I enclose it.

---

[1] See ' The Sheriff's Ball,' *Ingoldsby Legends*, vol. ii. p. 428, annotated edition; also the *Fragment*, vol. ii. p. 174.

[2] One of the vergers of St. Paul's Cathedral.

'Many thanks for your admirable sketch of *Ketch*. Unluckily, a small volume entitled the *Autobiography of Jack Ketch* was published last spring. As well as I recollect, it was but a poor affair ; but I fear that, for the present at least, the name might induce a suspicion of plagiarism, though the narrative is totally dissimilar. The idea is, however, far too good to be lost sight of; and I shall forthwith lay hands upon all matrimonial advertisements I may find in the papers, for the purpose of concocting a good one out of their blended excellences, as the painter is said to have done with his *chef-d'œuvre* taken from the collective beauty of Greece. Indeed, you cannot tell how thankful I shall be for any legend or tradition—tragedy-comedy-pastoral-comical, &c.—in the whole range of Autolycus's catalogue, as I should really like to help the Blackwoods if I could. But the fact is, that though I can tell a story in my own way, such as it is, when I have got one to tell, yet I literally have no invention, and, with the single exception of the *Amours of Prince Tantadlin the Fat and the Princess Skinny-lean-a*, which my children extracted from my very bowels, on New Year's Eve, never to my knowledge wrote anything which had any pretensions to originality either in conception or execution. At present I am engaged in the delicious occupations of winding up a long executor-ship account on the one hand, and watching the progress of a Chancery suit brought against me in my capacity of Rector of St. Mary Magdalen's on the other ; and though I have no personal interest in either, yet the time and trouble consumed and occasioned by both leave little room for other and more pleasurable employment. When to this is added the fact that I can most truly say, with the Conservative knife-grinder, " Story ! God bless you, I have none to tell, sir ! " you will not wonder if the little spare time I have is consumed, like that of my brother Tory, in " drinking at the Chequers," playing bo-peep and riddle-me-ree with Mary Anne and her cat, Ned having ever since the end of term forsaken my knee for that of the illustrious Dick.   A hint for a good ghost-story now were invaluable ; for let wise people say what they will, I never knew one yet that did not read or listen to one with interest and attention, however he might affect to hold them in contempt.

' Of news I have but little to give you. Isaac Saunders— the " Beauty of Holiness," as he was called— died in his pulpit on New Year's Day, and your old acquaintance Mr. De la Chaumette on the same morning. Indeed the alternations of hot and cold here have been very trying to the constitution lately. On the other hand, our excellent Dean is in the best of health and spirits, as are all *chez moi*, not even excepting him who has great pleasure in subscribing himself, as ever,

' Your much obliged Servant,

' R. H. BARHAM.'

' *Diary :   December* 12, 1835.'—Dined at Charles Kemble's : a quiet dinner. In the evening Mr. Trelawney (Byron's Trelawney) came in : very like a goodish-looking bandit ; Radical to the extreme ; talked of having " no objection to calling a man a king, with a moderate salary, when the House of Peers should be purged," &c. ; said that women might induce him to commit murder, or, "what was *worse*, petty larceny!"

'Story of Edward Walpole, who, being told one day at the "Garrick" that the confectioners had a way of discharging the ink from old parchment by a chemical process, and then making the parchment into isinglass for their jellies, said, "Then I find a man may now eat his deeds as well as his words." This has been very unfairly, like a great many other *bons mots*, attributed to James Smith.'

'*February* 8, 1836.—Dined at the "Garrick" with Hook, Lockhart, W. Broderip, Hayward, &c. A very pleasant evening. Hook in good spirits, and Lockhart in good humour. Hook gave in an elaborate speech, "The *Blackguards* of the Press" as a toast, for which Lockhart returned thanks with equal humour.'

'*April* 18, 1836.—Dined with Owen Rees in Paternoster Row. Present, Mr. Longman, senr., Messrs. C. Longman, T. Longman, W. Longman, Tom Moore, Dr. M'Culloch, Mr. Green, the host, and myself. Dr. Hume, Sydney Smith, and Mr. Tate asked, but could not come.

'Moore gave an account of the King's (George IV.) visit to Ireland. One man, whom the King took notice of and shook hands with, cried, "There, then, the divil a drop of wather ye shall ever have to wash that shake o' the hand off of me!" and by the colour of the said hand a year after it would seem that he had religiously kept his word. Moore told this story to Scott, together with another referring to the same occasion.[1] He spoke of Jeffrey as an

---

[1] This is narrated in a letter to Mrs. Hughes. See page 287 of the present volume.

excellent judge, and remarked on the difference between his conversation and that of Scott.   Scott all anecdote, without any intermediate matter—all fact ; Jeffrey with a profusion of ideas all worked up into the highest flight of fancy, but no fact.   Moore preferred Scott's conversation to Jeffrey's : the latter he got tired of.

' Anecdote of the little Eton boy invited to dinner at Windsor Castle, and being asked by Queen Adelaide what he would like, replied, " One of those twopenny tarts, if you please, ma'am."   Lord Lansdowne's description of Sydney Smith as " a mixture of Punch and Cato."   Moore lamented that though his son had just distinguished himself by gaining an exhibition at the Charterhouse, when his historical essays had been particularly applauded, the prize would be of no use to him, barring the honour, as he is determined to enter the army.   His father consoled himself by reflecting that he had given up his original wish, which was for the navy.

' J. Longman's story of the rival convents, each possessing the same (alleged) relics of St. Francis, the one having furnished its reliquary with the beard of an old goat belonging to the establishment, the other asserting its superiority *non pour la grandeur, mais pour la fraîcheur.*

' Moore talked of O'Connell, and said that he had recently met him in a bookseller's shop ordering materials, in the shape of books, for his new Quarterly Review, and that he had inadvertently offered to lend him a small volume respecting Ireland, but added that he must manage to slip out of his promise somehow.

' Dan, he said, manœuvred evidently that they might

walk away together, but he (Moore) fought shy of the companionship and outstayed him. He spoke of O'Brien, the author of the *Round Towers*, and said that that person's hostility to him was occasioned by his declining a proposal for a sort of partnership in publication. O'Brien wrote to him when he undertook the History of Ireland, saying that he had a complete key to the origin and meaning of the Round Towers, and proposed to communicate his secret. If Moore used O'Brien's MS., the compensation was to be a hundred pounds; if he took the materials and worked them up in his own way, a hundred and fifty was to be the sum. This was refused, and O'Brien was deeply offended. He died of an epileptic fit at Hanwell in 1835, and lies buried in the extreme northwest corner of the churchyard, close to the rector's garden. I happened accidentally to be present at his funeral. Mr. Mahony, the *Father Prout* of *Fraser*, was a mourner, and, as I have heard, paid the expenses.

'Conversation respecting Hook's proposed History of Hanover—all of opinion that it would not answer. Moore said that he had met Hook twice only, once at Croker's, in Paris; that he was very silent both times, and called Croker " Sir." '

It was, I believe, on this occasion that one of the Messrs. Longman present mentioned to my father the following quaint answer returned by Sydney Smith to an invitation to dinner :—

'Dear Longman,—I can't accept your invitation, for my house is full of country cousins. I wish they were once removed. Yours,　　　　　'SYDNEY SMITH.'

Mr. Barham's connection with the Literary Fund, and the active part he took in its management, have already been mentioned. The general conduct of this association has ever been beyond suspicion, and nothing had occurred at the time of which I am writing seriously to disturb the harmony with which its affairs were carried on. It is, however, hardly possible that a board composed of mere mortal committee-men should altogether escape imposition from without, or an occasional tendency to something like partiality within. Besides, man being reasonable must dispute, and party feeling would now and then display itself here as elsewhere.

One trifling *fracas* which occurred during this year may not altogether have passed out of memory. A portrait of Sir John Soane was presented to the society by that admirable artist, Mr. Maclise ; but the original, not deeming that his fair proportions had been treated with sufficient tenderness, peremptorily demanded its surrender, promising to replace it with a much handsomer, and *ergo* much more correct, representation by Sir Thomas Lawrence. During the somewhat lengthened discussion which ensued, a certain member of the council remarkable not more for his literary talent than for his social kindness and love of peace, put an end to all contention by entering the committee-room, and cutting the caricature of Sir John (as the latter chose to term it) into pieces with his penknife. The following *Lament* appeared a few days afterwards (May 22, 1836) in the *John Bull* :—

(Dr. Taylor *loquitur.*)

Ochone ! ochone !
For the portrait of Soane,
Jerdan ! you ought to have let it alone ;
Don't you see that instead of removing the bone
Of contention, the apple of discord you've thrown ?
One general moan,
Like a tragedy groan,
Burst forth when the picture-cide deed became known.
When the story got 'blown,'
From the Thames to the Rhone,
Folks ran, calling for ether and eau de Cologne ;
All shocked at the want of discretion you've shown.
If your heart's not of stone,
You will quickly atone.
The best way to do that's to ask Mr. RONE-
Y to sew up the slits ; the committee, you'll own,
When it's once stitched together, must see that it's SOANE.[1]

To Dr. Hume.

'June 2, 1836.

'My dear Hume,—*Homo sum : humani nihil à me
alienum puto.* I got a letter from Dick this morning,
and had my pen in my hand to tell you that he has
passed his examination, when your note to the lady
arrived. It came opportunely enough. Miss Cresswell
made her appearance about ten minutes after, and knows

---

[1] Qy. *Sewn.* Print. Dev.

of a paragon, who has lived with one of her relatives, a widow, unencumbered, very trustworthy, fond of quiet and retirement, and " all that sort of thing;" *anno ætatis* 49. She is to be trotted out for inspection forthwith, and then you will have an account of her paces.

'A very full meeting at the College of Physicians on Monday. Gentleman read a paper proving that the heart is not always on the left side. *Nous avons changé tout cela.* Saw Dr.—— there; impudent Jew seated himself next to President; Paris half inclined to blow him up and kick him out, but didn't; and " evening concluded with the utmost festivity." When shall we see you? At home every day till further notice, save Wednesday.

' Thine,

' R. H. BARHAM.'

To Mrs. Hughes.

' St. Paul's Churchyard, June 7, 1836.

' My dear Madam,—At last I am enabled to take up my pen and write to you. St. Paul's stands where it did, and as yet we have felt nothing of the anticipated changes; though the unprovided juniors are looking very blank at the hint given them some time since by Mr. Smith, that they are to expect no more livings from the Chapter. Some other mode of remuneration is, I believe, to be adopted, but of what nature or from what funds I am ignorant. Mr. Smith himself is as lively as ever, though they tell me he is losing caste with his party for turning Tory! Certain it is that the language he now holds is to

the full as Conservative as anything that ever dropped
from Peel or Lyndhurst. I dined in company with Tom
Moore the other day, who talked to me a good deal about
him, and said that Lord Lansdowne, in allusion to his
severity as a man of business and levity at the dinner-
table, described him as being "an odd mixture of Punch
and Cato." He could hardly have hit him off better. I
know you are not over fond of Moore : *I* hate his politics,
but he is a very amusing companion.

'I must tell you one of his stories, because as Sir
Walter Scott is the hero of it I know it will not be un-
acceptable to you. When George IV. went to Ireland,
one of the "pisintry," delighted with his affability to the
crowd on landing, said to the toll-keeper as the King
passed through,—

' " Och, now ! and his Majesty, God bless him, never paid
the turnpike ! an' how's that ? "

' " Oh ! Kings never does : we lets 'em go free," was the
answer.

' " Then there's the dirty money for ye," says Pat. " It
shall never be said that the King came here, and found
nobody to pay the turnpike for him."

'Moore, on his visit to Abbotsford, told this story to
Sir Walter, when they were comparing notes as to the two
royal visits.

' " Now, Mr. Moore," replied Scott, " there ye have just
the advantage of us. There was no want of enthusiasm
here : the Scotch folk would have done anything in the
world for his Majesty, but—pay the turnpike." [1]

[1] Sir Walter in turn narrated another anecdote in connection with the same
event. 'The Marquis —— in passing through one of the streets of Dublin,

' Hook goes to Hanover in July, for the purpose of collecting materials for a history of that country which he is going to write at the instance of the King, and to publish by subscription. His list already contains half the names in the Peerage; and he tells me that he calculates on making four or five thousand pounds by it. At present he is hard at work on a couple of tales for Bentley, which will be out before he goes. I have seen part of the MSS., and think there will be as much fun as in anything he has yet done: the character of *Jack Brag* is capitally drawn, and a good likeness of a man very well known about town.

' I do not believe that it is at all in contemplation to do away with the services or anthems at St. Paul's; though if the number of the minor canons is to be reduced to six, the chanting the prayers must necessarily be abandoned. The Dean is fighting hard to retain eight; but even that number—allowing for absences from ill-health and other sufficient causes—would be too small to carry on the duty as at present conducted. The early prayers have, I believe, quite fallen into abeyance: a Dr. Rogers, it is true, attends every morning as usual, but he tells me he has no congregation, and Mr. Smith has expressed his wish to do away with the service altogether. This the body opposes, and the intention is, for the present at least, abandoned.

' Your friend Dudley has, I believe, gone to his ancestors; at all events it is long since he paid St. Paul's a

during the King's visit, happened accidentally to run against and overturn an old applewoman's barrow. The enraged lady called after him, ' Och, now! go your ways, ye big ugly *comb.* Sure ye're all back and teeth, anyhow!' To those acquainted with the peculiarities of the noble lord's person, the simile will not perhaps appear very inappropriate.'   *

visit, and the only hope that he is yet in the land of the living consists in the circumstance that none of the vergers have yet seen his ghost in the gloaming wandering about the north aisle. The charity children anniversary takes place on Thursday : I have just been lucky enough to secure a ticket for a friend of Mr. R. Twining, Professor Von Reaumur, who has been writing a book about us, and I suppose means to write another. His last work does not seem altogether to suit John Bull's taste, as his strictures on our manners, &c., are considered rather too Trollop-y.

' Alexander Blackwood has passed through town on his way to Cheltenham. I saw him at his relative's, Mr. Hastie, the Member, in the Regent's Park. We have, I believe, settled matters for my sending *Maga* some more " Balaam," and I have already partly concocted a story : when it will see the light Heaven knows. I shall, however, give you full intimation of that event, as you are kind enough to patronize my nonsense. He is to send me the sheets of *Nicholas* interleaved, for me to alter and amend preparatory to a separate publication. I think I shall make some additions, as well as restore a good deal of what was omitted in the original MS. as too little calculated for a magazine. I have had no heart to put pen to paper of late ; indeed, the only thing I have perpetrated since I saw you is the few lines in *John Bull*, about three weeks ago, on Jerdan's mutilation of Sir John Soane's picture, which put us all into hot water at the Literary Fund. The anniversary of that Society takes place to-morrow : I have not missed attending it for years, but must on this occasion, as I have to preach to the "Vintners" at Stepney, and say grace over their turtle afterwards. It is to be a very Conservative sort of thing, and Lord Wynford, with a choice selection of Tories true, is to be among the company.

'Things, I think, are looking up here towards the good cause. The Whigs are sadly put out about the smallness of their majority the other night, and Whittle Harvey's defalcation. They have disappointed him, and he is turning Tory, taking his seat on this occasion on the bench between Stanley and Peel. Of a verity politics, like misery, acquaint us with strange bed-fellows! In the meanwhile some sacrifice of feeling may well be submitted to for the purpose of detaching from the enemy by far the ablest of their partisans. Charles Pearson, too, falls off from them in the City; and Raphael, whose purse was an object, is extinguished. I believe I have just room for a ditty on that worthy: it may be called—

'THE IRISH FISHERMAN.

'I sat by the side of a murmuring brook,
　　As sad as sad mote be ;
　In my hand were a rod and a line and a hook,
　　And a newspaper on my knee.

'Of Carlow the sad and sorrowful tale
　　I conn'd with curious eye,
　When a sunlight beam display'd in the stream
　　A speckled trout sailing by.

' But I laid down the rod, and I said to the fish,
  " How all the world would grin
If in trying, small trout, to pull you *out*,
  You should happen to pull me *in*!"

' God bless you, my dear Madam.

               ' Your obliged

                    ' R. H. B.'

' *Diary.—June* 29, 1836.—Mr. Rae Wilson gave me some of the water which he brought from the Dead Sea in Palestine to taste. Offensive smell, very like Harrogate water, with a bitter salt taste.'

' *July* 17, 1836.—Dined at Sydney Smith's; Dr. Wainwright, from America, and Professor Senior present. Account of Archbishop Whateley's bothering a whole company at the Lord Lieutenant's with his elaborate description of the fecundity and parturition of rabbits. His abrupt exclamation as to the vocative case of the word " Cat," which was decided to be " O Puss." Dr. Wainwright observed that a Frenchman who had recently been endeavouring to make a dictionary of the Indian language had put down as an Indian word " *Poo Poush*—Cat." He had evidently mistaken it from the name originally introduced by the English, " Poor Puss."

' Smith mentioned that his brother Bobus, seeing Vansittart (Lord Bexley) come into the House of Commons with Joseph Hume, said, " Here come Penny Wise and Pound Foolish." '

In his intercourse with his children, but more particularly with his youngest son, Ned, my father was always playful and affectionate. He loved to have them about him, and would continue to read and write, keeping them up of an evening far beyond the canonical hours, wholly unmindful of the chattering that raged around. Our delight was at its height when he could be coaxed into laying aside pen and book, and induced to draw round to the fire and 'tell us a story.' He had a manner of doing this, half thrilling, half comic, leaving the audience in a pleasing state of excitement, mingled with uncertainty as to the exact amount of credit to be given to the narrative, that proved strangely fascinating to us young folks, to say nothing of our elders. The pleasure second only in degree was to receive a letter from him. This would not unfrequently be written in verse, but always with a liveliness and easy humour which, while specially adapted to the taste and capacity of the child, may be read perhaps with some degree of amusement by those of larger growth. At all events, a trait of character is exhibited in these unstudied effusions without some notice of which the present slight sketch would be yet more incomplete.

TO MASTER EDWARD BARHAM (*ætat.* 8).

'August 17, 1836.

'My dear little Ned,
    As I fear you have read
All the books that you have, from great A down to Z,
    And your aunt, too, has said
    That you're very well bred,
And don't scream and yell fit to waken the dead,

I think that instead
Of that vile gingerbread
With which little boys, I know, like to be fed
(Though, lying like lead
On the stomach, the head
Gets affected, of which most mammas have a dread),
I shall rather be led
Before you to spread
These two little volumes, one blue and one red.
As three shillings have fled
From my pocket, dear Ned,
Don't dog's-ear nor dirt them, nor read them in bed !

'Your affectionate Father,
'R. H. B.'

Next to his wife and children, I verily believe my
father loved his cats. One or two would commonly be
seen sitting on his table—sometimes on his shoulder—as
he wrote ; and these animals, constantly taught and tended
by his youngest daughter, attained a degree of docility
and intelligence that in good King James's day might
have brought their mistress into disagreeable communication with His Majesty's Witchfinder-General. The
progenitor of the race was brought home by Mr. Barham,
not without serious detriment to his broadcloth, one wet
night soon after his arrival in London. He had rescued
the poor little creature, bleeding and muddy, from a band
of juvenile street Arabs, who were engaged in studying
practically 'the art of ingeniously tormenting.' The
progeny survived, and was ever held in high esteem. One

of my father's last injunctions was, 'Take care of "Chance" (an interloper) for my sake: Jerry (the representative of the true breed) will be taken care of for his own.' On the back of an old letter there is scribbled a sort of remonstrance addressed to the latter :—

TO JERRY.

> Jerry, my cat,
> What the deuce are you at?
> What makes you so restless? You're sleek and you're fat,
> And you've everything cosy about you,—now that
> Soft rug you are lying on beats any mat;
> Your coat 's smooth as silk,
> You've plenty of milk,
> You've the fish-bones for dinner, and always o' nights
> For supper you know you've a penn'orth o' lights!
> Jerry, my cat,
> What the deuce are you at?
> What is it, my Jerry, that fidgets you so?
> What is it you're wanting?
> (Jerry) Moll roe! Moll roe!

> Oh, don't talk to me of such nonsense as that!
> You've been always a very respectable cat;
> As the Scotch would say, 'Whiles'
> You've been out on the tiles;
> But you've sown your wild oats, and you very well know
> You're no longer a kitten.
> (Jerry) Moll roe! Moll roe!

Well, Jerry, I'm really concerned for your case ;
I've been young, and can fancy myself in your place :
    Time has been I've stood
    By the edge of the wood,
And have mew'd—that is, whistled, a sound just as good ;
But we're both of us older, my cat, as you know,
And I hope are grown wiser.
              (Jerry) Moll roe ! Moll roe !

It was necessary to mention this peculiarity of taste
prevailing in the family, in order to render the frequent
allusions to the feline members of it intelligible.

To Miss Barham (ætat. 13).

'St. Paul's, August 24, 1836.

'My dear Fanny,—I have been so poorly, and so fussy,
and so busy, that though I have fixed every day this
week for answering your letter, every day being fixed
" positively for the last time of answering," as the play-
bills say, yet I really have been unable to accomplish it
till " this present writing," and even now I am obliged to
crib a few minutes while your mother, whose elaborate
epistle to your aunt is on the other side, is scrambling
into bed. I need not tell you that your letter gave me
great pleasure, and that I am delighted to find you have
been, and are, so happy. I only hope that, in return for
so much kindness on the part of Mr. and Mrs. Scoones,
you are a good girl, give little trouble, and don't *talk at all.*
   'I have just been taking places for mamma and myself

by the Norwich coach for our journey into Suffolk on Tuesday : we shall stay till towards the end of the following week; and I do hope the change of air may be of service to me ; for, though much better, I have as yet not been able to shake off the cough, and, what is still worse, the debility which this complaint, it seems, always leaves behind it.

'We heard from your uncle George this morning. Dear little Ned is in great force, and very happy, though I do not find that he gets any colour in his cheeks. If he continues so delicate, and goes into the Church, I suppose he will lose his old name of Howley,[1] and be called in future Dr. Paley. In other respects he is very well, and would eat an horseshoe for breakfast ; but they do not let him, as it is considered by Mr. Sankey to be rather hard of digestion. I understand that the bellows are also prohibited, as having a tendency to produce flatulence ; but everything else he feeds on without scruple. Mary Anne we have visited, and found her a regular Tom-boy, running about and kicking up a prodigious dust at Hanwell. She has some thoughts, I believe, of offering herself as a supernumerary barrow-woman at the railroad constructing in that parish, and I should think, from what I have observed of her prowess, is fairly worth fourpence-halfpenny a day. I rather think they split about the odd farthing, which is to her an object, but to them, I should conceive, of comparatively trifling importance. Dick has got a new pair of corduroy-shooting breeches, with pearl

---

[1] Cannon had nicknamed him 'Howley,' from some slight resemblance which he bore to the Archbishop of Canterbury.

buttons at the knees, which embarrass him sorely; and I think he would not be sorry to have you at home to assist in arming him for the slaughter, as the ladies used to do to the knights of old. Buckling on armour is, you know, grown out of fashion; but a young lady with a button-hook in her hand, and kneeling upon an ottoman, is still much appreciated when a modern chevalier is equipping himself for a day's sporting. As you have, I believe, few correspondents beside myself in London, you will naturally expect me to say something about the fashions. This is by no means my *forte*; but as Jenny will probably be equally curious with yourself upon the subject, you may tell her, and recollect yourself, that the prevailing colour in ribands seems at present to be a delicate yellow with a faint dash of green, much resembling a rainbow or a black eye. *Pompons* are much worn as head-dresses, and the bell-shaped hoop is more used at Court than the more flat and elongated circumferences which prevailed in the time of George IV. Apple-green breeches with plum-coloured coats are the last importation of the beaux from Paris; but as these relate only to gentlemen, the information is of less importance to you. Guinness's stout is much drunk on the coal-wharves in the immediate neighbourhood of Northumberland House, but in my walks to Mile End I observe "ginger-pop" in greater request with the higher orders of society: at the turnpike, indeed, they drink nothing else. The oyster season has commenced very happily: Colchester natives, as usual, bear the bell, notwithstanding the recent squabble with Mr. Whittle Harvey, late Member for that borough. If in passing through the town on our way to Suffolk I meet with any *very* fine specimens, I will save you *the shells* as the nucleus of a collection of conchology. I have little else of importance to tell you in the way of news, except that your mamma has just bought a remarkably strong Cheshire cheese, and that the cat yesterday had a dose of salad oil. He has, as you know, been poorly for some time, but I hope is now convalescent.

'My paper is full, so God bless you, my dearest girl, and believe me to be

'Your most affectionate Father,

'R. H. BARHAM.'

'*Diary.*—*September* 20, 1836.—Drove down to Harrow with the Rush's. While I was engaged in taking an impression of a brass plate in the church, I heard sounds of lamentation and woe proceeding from the church. It seemed the curate, a Mr. Bruce, had gone to London, forgetting there was a couple to be married that morning. No other clergyman could be procured; twelve o'clock was rapidly approaching; at length, much to their relief and the clerk's amazement, I volunteered to perform the ceremony. The service over, I left my card with that functionary, and also with the newly-married couple, but never heard one word from Mr. Bruce on the subject. Probably he thought I had been guilty of a great piece of intrusion. I wrote the following " occasional lines " on Byron's tomb (as it is called), in the churchyard :—

'Mr. Bruce, Mr. Bruce,
When the matrimonial noose
You ought here at Harrow to be tying,
     If you choose to ride away
     As you know you did to-day,
No wonder bride and bridegroom should be crying.
     It's a very great abuse,
     Mr. Bruce, Mr. Bruce!
And you're quite without excuse,
     And of very little use
          As a curate,
               Mr. Bruce!'

When Lord Melbourne said he was not a subscribing sort of a fellow, the expression clearly implied the existence of a class of people who *are* a sort of subscribing fellows, if not that of a class who make the getting up subscriptions the great occupation of their lives. That such a class flourishes, and that the ladies are the most adroit, persistent, and courageous members of it, need hardly be said. They will ask anybody, especially a clergyman, for anything, and they generally contrive to get it, whether it be a contribution to a fund for the erection of a cathedral at Timbuctoo, or for the procuring more becoming garments for the curate of *Fudley-cum-Pipes.* Of course Mr. Barham had to undergo his share of this persecution, and of what that share was likely to be none but a London incumbent can form a reasonable conjecture; but he was in addition subjected to solicitations of a kind yet more annoying than those for money.

People of whom he knew little were the bearers of requests from people of whom he knew nothing, for just half a dozen lines to be inserted in an album: anything would do—anything in his peculiar style— anything lively and characteristic. There were few things he disliked more than this being required to write to order. One of these few, perhaps, was a petition 'to be funny,' which I have myself heard preferred at a dinner-party. But as regards the epigram, or impromptu, or whatever it was to be, he was generally too good-natured to decline; and at times when he felt any interest in the applicant, as in the case of a young friend of Mrs. Hughes, he would set to work with a will: witness—

A MEDLEY.

(FOR A YOUNG LADY'S ALBUM.)

Here's a pretty dilemma !
The cruel Miss Emma
Insists upon verses, insists upon verses,
While Apollo refuses,
Nor one of the Muses
Assistance disburses, assistance disburses.
How can I escape
From this terrible scrape ?
What ! an album's petition, an album's petition !
No prospect I can see,
Unless Madam Fancy
Vouchsafes me a vision, a vision, a vision !

Stay, methinks I see Phœbus,
To make me a rebus,
Has laid down his fiddle, has laid down his fiddle,
When in comes Judge Park
With Sir Charles Mansfield Clark,
And runs off with the riddle, the riddle, the riddle!
Up starts Mrs. Hughes
When she hears the news,
And calling a Jarvey, and calling a Jarvey,
Drives after them straightway,
Through Lincoln's Inn gateway,
With Dan Whittle Harvey, with Dan Whittle Harvey!

The special attorney
Stops short on the journey,
Not liking the weather, the weather, the weather;
So quitting the coach
At Lord Melbourne's approach,
They both begin waltzing together, together!
While stout Mr. Bentley
Trips after them gently,
Assisted by Colburn, assisted by Colburn,
Till Prince Esterhazy
Runs off with his jasey,
And pawns it in Holborn, in Holborn, in Holborn!

Charles Kemble in vain
Tries to get it again,
And taps at the wicket, and taps at the wicket;

But little John Russell
Contrives in the bustle
To purloin the ticket, the ticket, the ticket !
    Colonel Evans comes up,
    And invites him to sup
At the ' Carlton,' with Lockhart, and Croker, and
    Croker,
    Where the ghost of Horne Tooke
    Blackballs Theodore Hook
For being a joker, a joker, a joker !

    Then in comes Earl Grey,
    In his dignified way,
Saying, ' Dress me some dumplings with dripping,
    with dripping,'
    And ends by observing
    To Washington Irving,
That Harrington's whiskers want clipping, want
    clipping.
    Unable to read, he
    Turns round to Macready,
And tells him that yawning is catching, is catching,
    While the Duke of Buccleugh
    Assures Rothschild the Jew
That Solomon's Temple wants thatching, wants
    thatching !

    So, locking his desk, he
    Roars out to Fieschi
To shoot the Lord Mayor through the body, the body

For Lord Alvanley's groom,
　With Ducrow and Joe Hume,
Are quaffing gin toddy, gin toddy, gin toddy.
　'Look here,' says Tom Moore ;
　'I've a chop on a skewer,
Which I mean to get dress'd for my dinner, my
　　dinner,
　Since Lord Holland says Rogers
　And I are queer codgers,
And calls Sydney Smith an old sinner, old sinner!'

　Then mounting his horse he
　Rides off with Count d'Orsay
To call on Beau Brummel at Calais, at Calais,
　Where Little Bob Keeley
　And young D'Israeli
Have opened a splendid gin-palace, gin-palace !
　Below stairs John Britton
　Is teaching a kitten
To lap all the cream in the dairy, the dairy,
　And tells Sir John Soane
　That her mother is grown
A profound antiquary, profound antiquary !

　But stay, Mrs. Hughes
　Will fall foul of my Muse,
And call her a gipsy, and call her a gipsy ;
　For says she 'Only look
　How you're spoiling the book !
Why, you're certainly tipsy, certainly tipsy !'

And the man in the moon,
Taking snuff with a spoon,
Cries, ' For shame! Have some conscience, some
conscience, some conscience.'
So I drop my pen gaily,
And challenge Haynes Bailey
To write in eight stanzas more nonsense, more non-
sense.

In the autumn of 1836 Mr. Barham was requested by
Mr. Bentley, the publisher, to lend his assistance in per-
suading Thomas Moore to undertake some new and
original work in prose.   The exact nature of the proposal
will be understood from the subjoined letter addressed to
Dr. Hume by Mr. Moran, the editor of the *Globe and
Traveller.*   The plan fell through, but the poet was subsequently induced to form one of the band of contributors
to the *Miscellany* which, under the auspices of Mr. Charles
Dickens, was launched the year following.

E. Moran, Esq., to Dr. Hume.

'November 16, 1836.

' My dear Sir,—I have invaded your territory so far as
to have come down to dine at the " Duke of York," in
your village of Hanwell.   This is, as you know, the only
time at which I can leave business, and business has
brought me here now.

' Mr. Bentley, the bibliopolist, is with me, and my object
is to tempt Moore again : would it be indelicate to do so

after the last slight indication of his wishes ? Barham, no doubt, has told you of Bentley's offer; it is 1,400*l*. certain for a new work of prose fiction, and two-thirds of any and all profit beyond that sum.

'Now, with your aid, as well as the promptings of the god of all poetical idolatry, Plutus, the matter might be arranged. It would amuse the poet in the intervals of that labour of love—Ireland ; and as Moore has once freed himself from the Row he should enter into the field as extensively and advantageously as possible for himself. That removal, as you know, has done away with the delicate objection he entertained as to treating with a new man.

'We are meditating a flying visit (a couple of hours some Sunday) to Sloperton ; ought we to go ? How and when ? You can sound head-quarters as to the most agreeable period for doing so, or find out whether the negotiation could be carried on otherwise. We await your answer here in hope of its being the prelude to the immortal bard's pocketing 1,400*l*. That would give you as well as me—and not more in one case, I believe, than in the other—infinite pleasure. Bentley, who is a bold campaigner, wishes to attack at once ; hence our visit to this place so suddenly.

'Yours very truly,
'ED. R. MORAN.'

The last entry in Mr. Barham's note-book for 1836 contains some extraordinary particulars relating to a 'haunted house' in Hampshire. They were furnished by

Mrs. Hughes, who heard them originally from Mrs. Gwynne, an eye-, or rather ear-witness of the strange occurrences narrated. This lady's account was subsequently confirmed by many others (the late Duchess of Buckingham, a resident in the neighbourhood, among the rest), all of whom were perfectly familiar with the details, and, I believe, impressed with their truth, many having had opportunities of examining the 'attested Diary' referred to. It is right to premise, that certain slight alterations have been made by Mr. Barham in this narrative, since Mrs. Hughes communicated it to him.

'It is evident,' he says, 'that she must have confounded Mr. Ricketts, who was a bencher of Gray's Inn, and had large estates in the Island of Jamaica, with his son, Captain William Ricketts, who took his uncle's name, Jervis, in 1801, and was the father of the present Viscount. Mary Jervis married Mr. Ricketts in 1757, and lived to the advanced age of ninety, dying in 1828.' A MS. pedigree seems to justify these amendments, which, however, in no respect affect the authenticity of the incidents themselves.

'MRS. RICKETTS' GHOST STORY.

'It was about the period when Captain Jervis, afterwards Earl St. Vincent, commanded the 'Thunderer' (Foudroyant?) in which he so much distinguished himself, that on the return of that gallant commander to England, he found his sister, Mrs. Ricketts, the wife of Mr. Ricketts, of Jamaica, a bencher of Gray's Inn, residing in a house between Alston and Alsford in Hampshire, about four or

five miles from Abingdon, the seat of the Buckingham
family. This house, then called ' New House,' was part of
the property of the noble family of Legge, and of that particular branch of it of which the Lord Stawell (a peerage
now extinct) had been the head. It had been principally
occupied during his life by a Mr. Legge, a scion of the
family, notorious for his debauched and profligate habits,
and after his decease had remained for some time unoccupied, gradually acquiring, as is the case with most
unoccupied mansions of a similar description, the reputation of being the resort of supernatural visitants.

' To this circumstance, perhaps, and the consequent
difficulty of finding a tenant, may be attributed the easy
terms on which Mr. Ricketts obtained it as a residence
for his wife and family, during his own absence on a visit
to his estates in the West Indies. This gentleman seems
to have held the stories connected with the building in
thorough contempt, a sentiment partaken of by Mrs.
Ricketts herself, who was naturally a strong-minded woman,
and whose good sense had acquired additional strength
from the advantages of an excellent education.

' To " New House " then the lady had repaired almost
immediately after her husband's departure for Jamaica,
purposing in quiet retirement to superintend there the
education of her daughter (afterwards married to the Earl
of Northesk).

' Mrs. Ricketts had not long been located in her new
domicile, before the servants began to complain of certain
unaccountable noises which were heard in the house by
day as well as by night, and the origin of which they

found it impossible to detect. The story of the house being haunted was revived with additional vigour, especially when its mistress became herself an ear-witness of those remarkable sounds, and an investigation, set on foot and carried on under her own immediate superintendence, assisted by several friends whom she called in upon the occasion, had proved as ineffectual as those previously instituted by the domestics. The noises continued, as did the alarm of the servants, which increased to an absolute panic, and the whole of them at length, with the exception of an old and attached attendant on Mrs. Ricketts' person, gave warning and left their situations in a body.

' A thorough change in the household, however, produced no other effect than that of proving beyond a doubt that the noises, from whatever cause they might proceed, were at least not produced by the instrumentality or collusion of the domestics. A second and a third set were tried, but with no better result; few could be prevailed upon to stay beyond the month.

' It was at this time that Mrs. Gwynne, from whose mouth Mrs. Hughes had this relation, came to reside a short time with her old and dear friend, and being a woman of strong nerve she remained with her longer than she had originally intended, although not a day or night passed without their being disturbed. Mrs. Gwynne described the sounds as most frequently resembling the ripping and rending of boards, apparently those of the floor above, or below (as the case might be) that in which her friend and herself were sitting; but

on more than one occasion she herself distinctly heard
the whisperings of three voices, seemingly so close to her
that, by putting out her hand, she fancied she could have
touched the persons uttering them. One of the voices
was clearly that of a female, who appeared to be earnestly
imploring some one with tears and sobbings ; a manly,
resolute voice was evidently refusing her entreaty, while
rough, harsh, and most discordant tones, as of some
hardened ruffian, were occasionally heard interfering ;
these last were succeeded by two loud and piercing
shrieks from the female ; then followed the crashing of
boards again, and all was quiet for the time.

'The visitations were so frequently repeated that, at
length, even Mrs. Gwynne's constancy began to give way,
and she prepared to leave her friend. Previously to her
departure, however, she was aroused one night by Mrs.
Ricketts' cries (who slept in the next chamber to her),
and on running to her assistance, was informed that, just
before, she, Mrs. Ricketts, had distinctly heard some
person jump from the window-sill down on the floor at the
foot of the bed, and that, as the chamber door had continued bolted, he must still be in the room. The strictest
search was made, but no one was discovered.

'Various were the causes assigned in the neighbourhood
by the peasantry for these supernatural visitations, the
history of which had now become rife all over that country
side. Among other things it was said that Mr. Legge
had alway been a notorious evil liver, that he had held in
his employ one Robin, as butler, a man with a remarkably
deep-toned, hoarse, guttural voice, who was well known

as a pander to all his master's vices and worst passions, and the unprincipled executor of all his oppressive dealings with his tenantry. That there was also a niece of Mr. Legge's resident with her uncle, and that dark rumours had been afloat of her having been at one time in the family-way, though, as they said, 'nothing ever came of it,' and no child was ever *known* to have been born ; heavy suspicions, indeed, had been entertained on that score by the village gossips, which had gone so far that nothing but the wealth and influence of the squire had stifled inquiry. What had eventually become of the young lady no one knew, but it was supposed she had gone abroad before her uncle's death.

'Mrs. Ricketts and her friends endeavoured to follow up these rumours, but the only thing they could arrive at with any degree of certainty was what they learned from an aged man, a carpenter, who declared that many years ago he had been sent for to the Hall, and had been taken by Robin up into one of the bed rooms, where, by his direction, he had cut out a portion of one of the planks, and also part of the joist below; upon which the butler had brought a box, which he said contained valuable title deeds that his master wished to have placed in security, and having put it into the cavity ordered him to nail down the plank as before. This, he said, he had done, and could easily point out the place.

'Mrs. Ricketts ordered the man to be conducted up stairs, when he at once fixed on the door of her own sleeping apartment, saying, that, though it was a good many years ago, he was certain that was the room. On being introduced, he looked about for an instant, and then pointed out a part of the floor where there was evidently a separation in the plank, and which Mrs. Ricketts declared was the precise spot, as near as she could have described it, where the supposed intruder had alighted on his jump from the window.

'The board was immediately taken up ; the joist below was found to be half sawn through, and the upper portion removed, precisely as the carpenter had described it ; the cavity, however, was empty, and the box, if box there had been, must have been removed at some previous opportunity. After this investigation which ended in nothing, the noises and the whisperings, though never distinct, continued with but little diminution in frequency, and proved sufficient to render the house exceedingly uncomfortable to its inmates.

'Matters were in this state, when Captain Jervis, on his return to England, made his appearance at New House, with his friend Colonel Luttrell, to pay a visit to his sister. He had already heard of her annoyance, by letter, and of her disinclination to take the step he recommended, of removing, from the fear of offending her husband, who was somewhat of a martinet at home, and would of course treat the whole story as a fable. Captain Jervis seemed himself very much inclined to look upon it at first in the same light, or rather to consider it as a trick—for he had no doubt of his sister's veracity—and a trick which he was determined to find out.

'With this view, the Colonel and himself, sending all the rest of the family to bed, sat up, each in a separate parlour on the ground-floor, with loaded pistols by their side, and all other appurtenances most approved, when people have the prospect before them of a long night to be spent in ghost-hunting.

'The clock had stricken "one," when the sounds already mentioned, as of persons ripping up the floor above, were simultaneously heard by both. Each rushed from the parlour he occupied, with a light in one hand and a cocked pistol in the other, and encountered his friend in the passage. At first, a slight altercation ensued between them, each accusing the other of a foolish attempt at a hoax; but the colloquy was brought to an abrupt termination by the same sounds which each had heard separately being now renewed, and to all outward seeming, immediately above their heads. The whispering, too, at this juncture became audible to both.

'The gentlemen rushed up stairs, aroused their servants, and commenced a vigorous and immediate search throughout the whole premises; nothing, however, was found more than on any former occasion of the same kind, with this exception, that in one of the rooms sounds were distinctly heard of a different character from any before noticed, and resembling, as Mrs. Gwynne averred, "the noise which would be produced by the rattling dry bones in a box." They seemed to proceed from one of two presses which filled up a portion of the apartment; the door was immediately burst open, and the piece of furniture knocked to pieces; every search was made around, and even in the wall to which it had adjoined; ut still, as heretofore, all investigation was fruitless.

Captain Jervis, however, at once took upon himself the responsibility of removing his sister and her family to a farm-house in the same parish, where they remained till Mr. Ricketts' return.

'That part of the county of Hants being much the resort of smugglers, an attempt has been made to account for these events by attributing them to their agency, aided by the collusion of the servants. The latter part of the supposition could not be true,—the whole household having been so frequently changed. Even Mrs. Ricketts' favourite maid had at last, most reluctantly, abandoned her ; besides which Mrs. R. had, throughout the whole business, kept a diary of the transaction, which she had regularly caused all the domestics, as they left her service, to sign, in attestation of its truth, as far as their own personal experience had qualified them so to do. Mrs. Gwynne herself, as well as a few other visitors, had done the same, and this diary coming into the hands of her daughter at her mother's decease has been in the same way transmitted to the grand-daughter, in whose possession it now is.

'It remains to be added, that with Lord St. Vincent the subject was a very sore one to the day of his death ; and any allusion to it always brought on a fit of ill-humour, and a rebuke to him who ventured to make it. The house has been since, I believe, pulled down, but it does not appear that anything has occurred to throw any light on the mystery, or to strengthen or refute the suspicions which the good folks in the neighbourhood entertained of the crime of Mr. Legge, and the unrest which his spirit, and those of his supposed coadjutor and victim, had experienced from the date of his delinquency.

'Mrs. Hughes expressed her doubt as to the accuracy of the name of the mansion in which all these strange occurrences took place, but of the fact she was positive. The way in which she first became acquainted with them was as follows:—Mrs. Gwynne, being a visitor at her mother's house, was about to relate the story when she was checked by the hostess, who requested her to wait till Mary Anne (Mrs. Hughes), at that time a child, was gone to bed. This so excited the girl's curiosity that she contrived to hide herself behind the curtains of the room till the "ghost story" was told.'

According to another version which was given by an elderly lady named Hoy to Lady Douglas, from whom I heard it, the scene of these strange events was Marwell Hall, a lonely mansion situated between Bishopstoke and Winchester. The house had been the residence of Jane Seymour, and preparations for her marriage with Henry are said to have been going on within its walls during the very day appointed for the execution of the hapless Anne Boleyn. Miss Hoy maintained that it was no other than the ghost of the unfeeling Queen Jane who used to disturb the inmates, and whose uncomfortable habits led eventually to the destruction of her former abode. For the old lady went on to say that Captain Jervis, having watched in the haunted room alone one night, during which he was heard to fire a couple of pistol shots, appeared next morning with a grave and troubled countenance; that he positively refused to answer any questions as to what had taken place, but at once sought an interview with the landlord, and in consequence of the communication made to him, but withheld from all others, the house was shortly after demolished, and a modern habitation erected in its place. It is obvious that these two versions may be partially reconciled on the very probable supposition that it is the present building which is known as the 'New House' and that it has been confounded by Mrs. Hughes with the original Marwell Hall. Of course considerable difference of opinion must continue to exist respecting the identity of the ghost, unless, indeed, it should be allowed that the two, like rival tragedians engaged at the same theatre, used to perform on alternate nights.

END OF THE FIRST VOLUME.

LONDON: PRINTED BY
SPOTTISWOODE AND CO., NEW-STREET SQUARE
AND PARLIAMENT STREET

www.ingramcontent.com/pod-product-compliance
Lightning Source LLC
Chambersburg PA
CBHW021213270326
41929CB00010B/1113